PRACTICE
MAKES
PERFECT®

# Latin
# Verb Tenses

**Also by Richard E. Prior:**

*Latin Verb Drills*
*Latin Demystified*

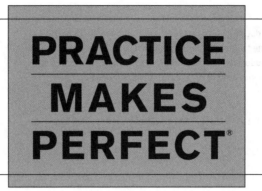

# PRACTICE MAKES PERFECT®

# Latin Verb Tenses

## SECOND EDITION

### Richard E. Prior

Mc
Graw
Hill
Education

New York  Chicago  San Francisco  Athens  London  Madrid
Mexico City  Milan  New Delhi  Singapore  Sydney  Toronto

1 2 3 4 5 6 7 8 9 10 11 12 13 14 15 16 17 18   QVS/QVS   1 0 9 8 7 6 5 4 3

ISBN   978-0-07-181783-7
MHID     0-07-181783-2

e-ISBN  978-0-07-181751-6
e-MHID     0-07-181751-4

Library of Congress Control Number 2013930335

Trademarks: McGraw-Hill Education, the McGraw-Hill Education logo, Practice Makes
Perfect, and related trade dress are trademarks or registered trademarks of McGraw-Hill
Education and/or its affiliates in the United States and other countries and may not be
used without written permission. All other trademarks are the property of their respective
owners. McGraw-Hill Education is not associated with any product or vendor mentioned in
this book.

McGraw-Hill Education products are available at special quantity discounts to use as
premiums and sales promotions or for use in corporate training programs. To contact a
representative, please visit the Contact Us pages at www.mhprofessional.com.

This book is printed on acid free paper.

# Contents

# Acknowledgments

I would like to thank my dear friend and former student Brian Lupo for his assistance and contributions to this book.

Huge thanks are also due to my partner, Scott Henderson, for his bottomless store of patience.

The publisher would like to thank Randall Childree for his assistance in preparing the second edition of this book.

# Introduction

The core of a sentence in any language is the verb. All other words in a sentence modify the verb in their own way or modify words that are modifying the verb. In Latin, the verb system is far more complex than in most modern languages, which gives it an amazing beauty all its own, but also provides a challenge to us, thousands of years later, who would like to experience that beauty on its own terms.

The greatest challenge in writing this book has been developing a format that would be the most useful to the most people studying this ancient language. There are many textbooks, offering many approaches from many different angles, and so finding a format that would be the most flexible and useful has truly been a challenge.

Another challenge has been to provide exercises beyond simple verb forms, so that verbs are used in context, but without placing unnecessary demands on the reader in nonverb areas of Latin study. To put verbs in context, however, requires nouns, which—given Latin's highly inflected nature—requires some mastery of case uses for nouns. Since this book is designed for practice with verbs, not nouns, the case uses in the exercises have been kept simple so that mastery of only the most basic ones is assumed.

Apart from certain verb forms, gender is invisible in Latin. In English, however, it is not. For the sake of simplicity and uniformity, not to mention commonality in reading Latin texts, the assumed gender in this book, unless otherwise noted, is masculine.

The reader may find discrepancies between the use of macrons in this book and that in some dictionaries. Conventions vary, but the reader should take heart in the fact that the Romans themselves didn't write macrons. In fact, they used no punctuation or any diacritics in writing, and likely did not even use spaces between words! Some vowels are long by nature and some are long by position (meaning those that are followed by two or more consonants). I have generally followed the convention of using a macron for vowels long by nature, but not for those long by position.

There are more specialized areas of verb study that are not addressed in this book, such as the ending **-ēre** instead of **-ērunt** in the third-person plural, perfect indicative active, as is often seen in epic poetry. The aim of this book is to offer mastery of fundamental Latin verb forms and applications; other details are left for advanced study.

See page 189 for a list of the abbreviations used in this book.

# Latin
# Verb Tenses

# The Latin Verb System

This chapter gives a brief overview of the Latin verb system and explains the attributes by which verbs can be described and understood. It also provides an explanation of the many grammatical terms used in this book.

## The Characteristics of Latin Verbs

In addition to meaning, a Latin verb contains five different characteristics: person, number, tense, mood, and voice. Some forms also denote gender.

### Person

*Person* refers to the relationship between the speaker and the subject of the verb.

- *First person* is the speaker himself.

- *Second person* refers to the person being spoken to.

- *Third person* is anyone or anything that is being spoken about.

### Number

*Number* quite simply refers to *singular* or *plural*. This chart illustrates the result of *person* in conjunction with grammatical *number*.

|  | Singular |  | Plural |  |
|---|---|---|---|---|
| First person | **ego** | *I* | **nōs** | *we* |
| Second person | **tū** | *you* | **vōs** | *you* |
| Third person | **is, ea, id** | *he, she, it* | **eī, eae, ea** | *they* |

PERSONAL ENDINGS. Because Latin employs personal endings on verbs to represent person and number, subject pronouns (in the nominative case) are redundant and are used to show emphasis. This is particularly true for first- and second-person singular and plural subject pronouns, since the personal endings of the verb for those persons are unique and cannot be confused with any other subject. For example, for the verb **dormiēba*m*** *I was sleeping*, the personal ending **-m** shows quite clearly that the subject is *I*. In contrast, ***ego* dormiēbam** states that *I* (as opposed to anyone else) *was sleeping*.

Personal endings are also used to signify grammatical voice (see below).

## Active Voice

|               | Singular | Plural |
| ------------- | -------- | ------ |
| First person  | -ō/-m    | -mus   |
| Second person | -s       | -tis   |
| Third person  | -t       | -nt    |

## Passive Voice

|               | Singular | Plural |
| ------------- | -------- | ------ |
| First person  | -or/-r   | -mur   |
| Second person | -ris     | -minī  |
| Third person  | -tur     | -ntur  |

There are two endings given for the first-person singular, because one or the other is used, depending on tense.

The perfect indicative active has its own special set of personal endings:

|               | Singular | Plural  |
| ------------- | -------- | ------- |
| First person  | -ī       | -imus   |
| Second person | -istī    | -istis  |
| Third person  | -it      | -ērunt  |

## Tense

*Tense* does not refer solely to the time when an action takes place. There is another dynamic involved, that of grammatical *aspect*. Aspect reflects the way a speaker views an action. There are two aspects. The *continuous aspect* (also called the *present system*) shows an action while it is happening or an action that happens repeatedly, for example, *I was running* or *I used to run*. In contrast, the *completed aspect* (also called the *perfect system*) refers to a single completed event, with the emphasis on completion rather than on process, for example, *I have run, I did run,* or *I ran.*

In Latin, there are six tenses, each representing a point of intersection between the two aspects and the three time frames of "now," "before now," and "after now."

| Time       | Aspect          |                      |
| ---------- | --------------- | -------------------- |
|            | **Continuous**  | **Completed**        |
| Now        | Present tense   | Perfect tense        |
| Before now | Imperfect tense | Pluperfect tense     |
| After now  | Future tense    | Future perfect tense |

## Mood

*Mood* reflects the way a speaker treats an action, whether as a fact, a command, or a wish or idea. There are three moods in Latin.

The *indicative mood* treats an action as a fact.

  Ībis.     *You will go.*

The *imperative mood* treats an action as a command.

  Ī!      *Go!*

The *subjunctive mood* treats an action as a wish or idea.

  Eās.     *You might go* or *I wish you would go.*

The translations in this example reflect only the spirit of the subjunctive mood. In Latin, the subjunctive mood is used in several different grammatical constructions for which English uses other verb forms, so there isn't a single way to translate the subjunctive mood out of context.

## Voice

*Voice* shows the relationship between a verb and its subject; it tells whether the subject performs or receives the action of the verb. There are three voices in Latin.

The *active voice* shows that the subject is performing the action.

  Canem lavat.  *He is washing the dog.*

The *middle voice* shows that the subject is performing an action on himself or for his own benefit or in his own interest.

  Lavātur.   *He is washing (himself).*

The *passive voice* is used when the subject receives the action.

  Lavātur.   *He is being washed.*

The middle and passive voices are identical in form. Which voice is intended must be deduced from the context in which the verb appears.

Distinctions in voice are shown by the use of specific sets of personal endings (see above). The perfect system uses an altogether different construction in the active and middle/passive voices.

## The Conjugations

Latin verbs are divided into four categories known as *conjugations*. All verbs within each conjugation are conjugated (i.e., make their various forms) in the same way. The most significant feature of each conjugation is the theme vowel it exhibits between its base and whatever ending is applied. The present tense is the only one in which each conjugation is unique.

Verbs are assigned to the four conjugations based on their present infinitive, which in dictionaries is listed as a verb's second principal part. This chart shows how a verb's conjugation can be recognized.

| First conjugation | **-āre** | **laudāre** | *to praise* |
| Second conjugation | **-ēre** | **manēre** | *to stay* |
| Third conjugation | **-ere** | **currere** | *to run* |
| Fourth conjugation | **-īre** | **audīre** | *to hear* |

There is another category of verbs referred to as third-conjugation **-iō** verbs. With few exceptions, these verbs make nearly all their forms in the same way as fourth-conjugation verbs; their present infinitive, however, ends in **-ere**, and so by the convention noted above, they are assigned to the third conjugation. They can be identified by their first principal part ending in **-iō** and second principal part ending in **-ere**.

Finally, there is a small group of verbs that have their own peculiar forms and do not fit into any conjugation. They are called *irregular* and must be learned on a case-by-case basis.

## Principal Parts

A Latin verb has four principal parts, which are found in its dictionary listing. These parts supply all the information needed to put a verb into any form, just like verb listings in English, such as *throw, threw, thrown*, where *throw* is the present-tense form, *threw* is the past-tense form, and *thrown* is the past participle. The Latin version of the principal parts follows a similar pattern. Here are the principal parts of the Latin verb that means *throw*.

**iaciō, iacere, iēcī, iactum**

Translated literally, these forms would translate as follows.

*I throw, to throw, I threw, thrown*

The first principal part is the first-person singular, present indicative active *I throw*. This form also tells whether or not the verb is an **-iō** verb. The second part in the listing is the present active infinitive *to throw*. As noted above, it tells which conjugation a verb belongs to. In the case of this verb, the ending **-ere** classes it as third conjugation. The information provided by these first two principal parts enables one to make every possible present-system form, plus a few others.

The third principal part is the first-person singular, perfect indicative active *I threw*, essentially making it the perfect-system equivalent of the first principal part. It supplies the information needed to create any form in the perfect system, but only for the active voice. To construct the perfect-system passive forms, one needs to look at the fourth principal part, which is also needed to make a few other forms.

There are two traditions regarding which form is provided as the fourth principal part of a verb. One tradition uses a verb form called the supine; it is recognized by the ending **-um**. (This book follows this tradition.) The other tradition uses the perfect passive participle ending in **-us**, or, as is the case with most intransitive verbs, the future active participle ending in **-ūrus**. For some verbs, neither participle exists. In this situation, no fourth principal part is given. Regardless of the tradition, it is the stem left when the **-um**, **-us**, or **-ūrus** is dropped that is ultimately important.

# Unit 2

# The Present Indicative Active

This unit contains a general review of the use of the present tense in Latin, followed by individual sections devoted to each conjugation. Each of these sections reviews forms and provides exercises. At the end of the unit is an exercise asking the reader to identify the conjugation of various verb forms and to translate them.

## Use

The present tense describes an action that either is in the process of happening right now (for example, *I am eating bratwurst*) or is known to happen in general (for example, *I like bratwurst*). Another way of saying the latter (*I do like bratwurst*) simply adds emphasis.

There are three ways to express the present tense in English but only one in Latin, so a verb in the present tense in Latin can be translated in three different ways.

**pōnō**     *I am putting*
             *I put*
             *I do put*

## Formation

The Latin present tense is the only tense for which each conjugation has its own method of formation. The distinctive feature in the present tense among the conjugations is the theme vowel between the base of a verb and its personal ending. Different conjugations form various tenses and moods by altering this vowel. The ending **-ēs**, for example, appears as the second-person singular form in the present subjunctive active of first-conjugation verbs, in the present indicative active of second-conjugation verbs, and in the future indicative active of third-conjugation verbs. Therefore, it is extremely important to know which conjugation a verb belongs to.

Verbs are classed into conjugations based on their present infinitive, which appears as the second principal part listed in a verb's dictionary entry. All verbs whose present infinitive ends in **-āre** are considered *first conjugation*. This chart gives the four principal parts for a representative verb in each conjugation and highlights the present infinitive ending in each.

| | | |
|---|---|---|
| First conjugation | **rogō, rogāre, rogāvī, rogātum** | *to ask* |
| Second conjugation | **teneō, tenēre, tenuī, tentum** | *to hold* |
| Third conjugation | **pōnō, pōnere, posuī, positum** | *to put* |
| Fourth conjugation | **sentiō, sentīre, sensī, sensum** | *to feel* |

Pay special attention to the infinitive endings of the second and third conjugations. The distinction is subtle—a long **ē** as opposed to a short **e**—but the way in which these two conjugations make many of their forms differs greatly.

Irregular verbs (for example, **ferō, ferre, tulī, lātum** *to carry*) do not fall into any of these conjugations. With only a few exceptions, the present tense is the only one in which irregular verbs are irregular. They must be learned individually and are treated in Unit 10.

## First Conjugation

The theme vowel of first-conjugation verbs is **ā**. It appears at the end of the base in all of the forms of all of the tenses in this conjugation, with one exception: When this **ā** is followed by **ō**, they contract into **ō** (i.e., **ā + ō → ō**).

In order to form the present indicative active of first-conjugation verbs, drop the infinitive ending **-re** from the second principal part, then add the active personal endings.

**rogō, rogāre, rogāvī, rogātum** *to ask*

| | Singular | | Plural | |
|---|---|---|---|---|
| First person | **rogō** | *I ask*<br>*I do ask*<br>*I am asking* | **rogāmus** | *we ask*<br>*we do ask*<br>*we are asking* |
| Second person | **rogās** | *you ask*<br>*you do ask*<br>*you are asking* | **rogātis** | *you ask*<br>*you do ask*<br>*you are asking* |
| Third person | **rogat** | *he/she/it asks*<br>*he/she/it does ask*<br>*he/she/it is asking* | **rogant** | *they ask*<br>*they do ask*<br>*they are asking* |

Here is a list of some common first-conjugation verbs, followed by exercises that provide practice with them in the present tense.

| | |
|---|---|
| **agitō, -āre, -āvī, -ātum** | *to agitate, think about, get (something) going* |
| **ambulō, -āre, -āvī, -ātum** | *to walk* |
| **amō, āre, -avī, -ātum** | *to like, love* |
| **appellō, -āre, -āvī, -ātum** | *to call (often by name)* |
| **armō, -āre, -āvī, -ātum** | *to equip with weapons* |
| **cantō, -āre, -avī, -ātum** | *to sing, play (an instrument)* |
| **celebrō, -āre, -āvī, -ātum** | *to visit often, make well known* |
| **certō, -āre, -āvī, -ātum** | *to struggle, decide by contest* |
| **cessō, -āre, -avī, -ātum** | *to do nothing, slack off* |
| **cōgitō, -āre, -āvī, -ātum** | *to think, ponder* |
| **comparō, -āre, -āvī, -ātum** | *to prepare, buy, furnish* |
| **constō, constāre, constitī, constātúrus** | *to stand together, stand still, stop* |
| **creō, creāre, -āvī, -ātum** | *to create, elect* |
| **cūrō, -āre, -avī, -ātum** | *to take care of* |
| **dō, dāre, dedī, datum** | *to give* |
| **dōnō, -āre, -āvī, -ātum** | *to give (as a gift)* |
| **dubitō, -āre, -avī, -ātum** | *to hesitate, doubt* |
| **errō, -āre, -āvī, -ātum** | *to wander, be wrong* |
| **existimō, -āre, -avī, -ātum** | *to think, judge, evaluate* |
| **exspectō, -āre, -avī, -ātum** | *to wait for* |
| **habitō, -āre, -āvī, -ātum** | *to live, dwell, inhabit* |
| **ignōrō, -āre, -āvī, -ātum** | *not to know* |
| **imperō, -āre, -āvī, -ātum** | *to give an order* (with dative) |
| **indicō, -āre, -āvī, -ātum** | *to make known, betray* |
| **intrō, -āre, -āvī, -ātum** | *to enter* |
| **iūrō, -āre, -āvī, -ātum** | *to swear* |
| **iuvō, iuvāre, iūvī, iūtum** | *to help, please* |
| **labōrō, -āre, -āvī, -ātum** | *to work, suffer* |
| **laudō, -āre, -āvī, -ātum** | *to praise* |
| **lavō, lavāre, lāvī, lautum/lavātum/lōtum** | *to wash* |
| **līberō, -āre, -āvī, -ātum** | *to set free* |
| **mandō, -āre, -āvī, -ātum** | *to entrust, order* |
| **memorō, -āre, -āvī, -ātum** | *to remind, mention* |
| **monstrō, -āre, -āvī, -ātum** | *to show* |
| **mūtō, -āre, -āvī, -ātum** | *to change, move* |
| **narrō, -āre, -āvī, -ātum** | *to tell (in story form)* |
| **nāvigō, -āre, -āvī, -ātum** | *to sail* |
| **necō, -āre, -āvī, -ātum** | *to kill* |
| **negō, -āre, -āvī, -ātum** | *to deny, say no* |
| **nōminō, -āre, -āvī, -ātum** | *to name, mention* |
| **nuntiō, -āre, -āvī, -ātum** | *to announce* |
| **occupō, -āre, -āvī, -ātum** | *to seize* |
| **optō, -āre, -āvī, -ātum** | *to choose* |
| **ornō, -āre, -āvī, -ātum** | *to decorate* |
| **ōrrō, -āre, -āvī, -ātum** | *to beg, ask, speak, pray* |
| **parō, -āre, -āvī, -ātum** | *to get ready, prepare; obtain* |
| **portō, -āre, -āvī, -ātum** | *to carry, bring* |
| **postulō, -āre, -āvī, -ātum** | *to demand* |
| **properō, -āre, -āvī, -ātum** | *to hurry* |
| **pugnō, -āre, -āvī, -ātum** | *to fight* |
| **putō, -āre, -āvī, -ātum** | *to think, value* |
| **regnō, -āre, -āvī, -ātum** | *to rule* |
| **revocō, -āre, -āvī, -ātum** | *to call back* |
| **rogō, -āre, -āvī, -ātum** | *to ask* |
| **simulō, -āre, -āvī, -ātum** | *to pretend* |
| **sonō, sonāre, sonuī, sonitum** | *to make a sound* |

| | |
|---|---|
| **spērō, -āre, -āvī, -ātum** | *to expect, hope* |
| **spīrō, -āre, -āvī, -ātum** | *to breathe* |
| **stō, stāre, stetī, statum** | *to stand, stay* |
| **superō, -āre, -āvī, -ātum** | *to overcome, conquer* |
| **temptō, -āre, -āvī, -ātum** | *to try, test* |
| **vetō, vetāre, vetuī, vetitum** | *to deny, say no* |
| **vigilō, -āre, -āvī, -ātum** | *to be awake, watch* |
| **vocō, -āre, -āvī, -ātum** | *to call, summon* |
| **volō, -āre, -āvī, -ātum** | *to fly* |

## exercise 2-1

*Translate these verbs into English.*

1. cōgitō _____

2. dant _____

3. lavās _____

4. narrāmus _____

5. rogātis _____

6. nōminant _____

7. stat _____

8. exspectāmus _____

9. cantō _____

10. mutās _____

11. ornās _____

12. curant _____

13. habitō _____

14. revocāmus _____

15. cessat _____

## exercise 2-2

*Translate these verbs into Latin.*

1. you (*sg.*) work _____

2. they kill _____

3. I praise _____

4. you (*pl.*) give _____

5. he is working _____

6. we work _____

7. they are singing _____

8. you (*sg.*) are decorating _____

9. I hope _____

10. he is carrying _____

11. we are hesitating _____

12. you (*pl.*) are wandering _____

13. I am making a sound _____

14. he is preparing _____

15. you (*sg.*) are calling _____

exercise    **2-3**

*Translate these sentences into English.*

1. Servus dominum suum iuvat. _____

2. Marcus amīcōs amat. _____

3. Cēnam parō. _____

4. In caelō volant avēs. _____

5. Dominus ancillam līberat. _____

exercise    **2-4**

*Write the appropriate present-tense form of the verb in parentheses, then translate the sentence.*

1. Ancilla trīclīnium _____ (purgāre). _____

2. Nōs domum _____ (ambulāre). _____

3. Tū aquam _____ (portāre). _____

4. Puerī saepe _____ (simulāre). _____

5. Māter puellam _____ (vocāre). _____

## Second Conjugation

The theme vowel of the second conjugation is $\bar{e}$. It is extremely important to note that the theme vowel shown in the infinitive is *long*. Third-conjugation verbs, which behave very differently, have a *short* e in their infinitive.

The long $\bar{e}$ of second-conjugation verbs is consistent throughout the present-system tenses. Also, unlike first-conjugation verbs, the first principal part of second-conjugation verbs shows that the theme vowel does not contract with the personal ending -$\bar{o}$. This makes conjugation of these verbs quite easy. Simply drop the -**re** from the second principal part, then add the personal endings for the active voice.

**teneō, ten*ēre*, tenuī, tentum** *to hold*

|  | **Singular** |  | **Plural** |  |
|---|---|---|---|---|
| First person | **ten*eō*** | *I hold* | **ten*ēmus*** | *we hold* |
|  |  | *I do hold* |  | *we do hold* |
|  |  | *I am holding* |  | *we are holding* |
| Second person | **ten*ēs*** | *you hold* | **ten*ētis*** | *you hold* |
|  |  | *you do hold* |  | *you do hold* |
|  |  | *you are holding* |  | *you are holding* |
| Third person | **ten*et*** | *he/she/it holds* | **ten*ent*** | *they hold* |
|  |  | *he/she/it does hold* |  | *they do hold* |
|  |  | *he/she/it is holding* |  | *they are holding* |

Here is a list of some common second-conjugation verbs, followed by exercises that provide practice with them in the present tense.

| | |
|---|---|
| **appāreō, -ēre, -uī, -itum** | *to appear* |
| **ardeō, ardēre, arsī, arsūrus** | *to burn, be on fire* |
| **audeō, audēre, ausus sum** | *to dare* |
| **augeō, augēre, auxī, auctum** | *to increase, enlarge* |
| **careō, -ēre, -uī, -itum** | *to lack, be without* (with an ablative object) |
| **caveō, cavēre, cāvī, cautum** | *to beware, be on guard* |
| **contineō, continēre, continuī, contentum** | *to hold together, contain* |
| **dēbeō, -ēre, -uī, -itum** | *to owe; should, must* |
| **dēleō, -ēre, -ēvī, -ētum** | *to destroy* |
| **doceō, docēre, docuī, doctum** | *to teach* |
| **doleō, -ēre, -uī, -itum** | *to feel pain; cause pain* |
| **exerceō, -ēre, -uī, -itum** | *to make strong, train; harass* |
| **fleō, -ēre, -ēvī, -ētum** | *to weep* |
| **habeō, -ēre, -uī, -itum** | *to have, hold; consider, regard* |
| **horreō, -ēre, -uī** | *to bristle, have one's hair stand on end* |
| **iaceō, -ēre, -uī, -itum** | *to recline, lie* |
| **impleō, -ēre, -ēvī, -ētum** | *to fill up* |
| **invideō, invidēre, invīdī, invīsum** | *to cast the evil eye; envy* (with dative) |
| **iubeō, iubēre, iussī, iussum** | *to order* |
| **lateō, -ēre, -uī** | *to lie hidden* |
| **maneō, manēre, mansī, mansum** | *to stay* |
| **mereō, -ēre, -uī, -itum** | *to deserve, earn* |
| **misceō, miscēre, miscuī, mixtum** | *to mix* |
| **moneō, -ēre, -uī, -itum** | *to warn, advise* |
| **moveō, movēre, mōvī, mōtum** | *to move* |
| **noceō, -ēre, -uī, -itum** | *to harm, be harmful* (with dative) |
| **pāreō, -ēre, -uī, -itum** | *to be obedient, obey* (with dative) |
| **pateō, -ēre, -uī** | *to lie open, exposed* |
| **persuādeō, persuādēre, persuāsī, persuāsum** | *to persuade* (with dative) |
| **placeō, -ēre, -uī, -itum** | *to please* (with dative) |
| **praebeō, -ēre, -uī, -itum** | *to offer* |
| **respondeō, respondēre, respondī, responsum** | *to answer, correspond* (usually with dative) |
| **retineō, retinēre, retinuī, retentum** | *to hold back, keep* |
| **rīdeō, rīdēre, rīsī, rīsum** | *to laugh, smile* |
| **sedeō, sedēre, sēdī, sessum** | *to sit, stay put* |

| | |
|---|---|
| studeō, -ēre, -uī | to be eager (for), be busy with (usually with dative) |
| sustineō, -ēre, -uī | to support, uphold |
| taceō, -ēre, -uī, -itum | to be quiet |
| teneō, -ēre, -uī, -tum | to hold, have |
| terreō, -ēre, -uī, -itum | to scare |
| timeō, -ēre, -uī | to be afraid of, fear |
| valeō, -ēre, -uī, -itum | to be strong |
| videō, vidēre, vīdī, vīsum | to see; (passive voice) to seem, be seen |

## exercise 2-5

*Translate these verbs into English.*

1. videō ___
2. habent ___
3. carēs ___
4. iacēmus ___
5. meret ___
6. praebētis ___
7. continent ___
8. maneō ___

9. audēmus ___
10. rīdet ___
11. delēs ___
12. movētis ___
13. dēbēmus ___
14. exercet ___
15. miscētis ___

## exercise 2-6

*Translate these verbs into Latin.*

1. you (*sg.*) are on fire ___
2. they hold ___
3. it is open ___
4. I am warning ___
5. we teach ___
6. you (*pl.*) laugh ___
7. you (*sg.*) see ___
8. they are offering ___

9. I am holding ___
10. he is ordering ___
11. we are sitting ___
12. you (*pl.*) are warning ___
13. they destroy ___
14. you (*sg.*) order ___
15. I increase ___

| exercise | 2-7 |
|---|---|

*Translate these sentences into English.*

1. Marcus mensam movet. _____

2. Saepe tacēs. _____

3. Catēnās merent. _____

4. Puerōs doceō. _____

5. Exercitum optimum habētis. _____

| exercise | 2-8 |
|---|---|

*Write the appropriate present-tense form of the verb in parentheses, then translate the sentence.*

1. Eae sub arbore _____ (sedēre). _____

2. Puer sorōrēs _____ (timēre). _____

3. Discipulī labōrī _____ (studēre). _____

4. Senātor epistulam _____ (habēre). _____

5. Ego canem iam _____ (cavēre). _____

## Third Conjugation

Unlike the first and second conjugations, where the theme vowels (**ā** and **ē**, respectively) are long and remain so throughout their conjugations in the present tense, the theme vowel of the third conjugation is short **e**, which weakens in the present tense to create an entirely new vowel pattern. This pattern is important to learn, because it also appears in other places.

**agō, ag*ere*, ēgī, actum** *to do*

|  | **Singular** |  | **Plural** |  |
|---|---|---|---|---|
| First person | **agō** | *I do* | **ag*imus*** | *we do* |
|  |  | *I do do* |  | *we do do* |
|  |  | *I am doing* |  | *we are doing* |
| Second person | **ag*is*** | *you do* | **ag*itis*** | *you do* |
|  |  | *you do do* |  | *you do do* |
|  |  | *you are doing* |  | *you are doing* |
| Third person | **ag*it*** | *he/she/it does* | **ag*unt*** | *they do* |
|  |  | *he/she/it does do* |  | *they do do* |
|  |  | *he/she/it is doing* |  | *they are doing* |

Here is a list of some common third-conjugation verbs, followed by exercises that provide practice with them in the present tense.

| | |
|---|---|
| accēdō, accēdere, accessī, accessum | to approach, go near (with **ad** or **in** and the accusative) |
| accidō, accidere, accidī | to fall down, ask for help; happen |
| addō, addere, addidī, additum | to add, give to |
| agō, agere, ēgī, actum | to do; drive, lead; be busy |
| alō, alere, aluī, altum | to cherish, nourish |
| āmittō, āmittere, āmīsī, āmissum | to send away, let go, lose |
| ascendō, ascendere, ascendī, ascensum | to climb, go up |
| bibō, bibere, bibī | to drink |
| cadō, cadere, cecidī, cāsum | to fall |
| caedō, caedere, cecīdī, caesum | to cut, kill |
| canō, canere, cecinī, cantum | to sing, play (an instrument) |
| cēdō, cēdere, cessī, cessum | to go, withdraw, yield |
| cernō, cernere, crēvī, crētum | to separate, distinguish, pick out; see |
| cingō, cingere, cinxī, cinctum | to surround, wrap |
| claudō, claudere, clausī, clausum | to close, conclude |
| cognoscō, cognoscere, cognōvī, cognitum | to learn; (in the perfect system) to know |
| cōgō, cōgere, coēgī, coactum | to compel, drive, force; gather |
| colligō, colligere, collēgī, collectum | to gather, collect |
| colō, colere, coluī, cultum | to pay attention to, nurture, tend, cultivate, grow |
| committō, committere, commīsī, commissum | to connect, combine; entrust |
| condō, condere, condidī, conditum | to found, build; put in safe keeping, hide |
| constituō, constituere, constituī, constitūtum | to stand/set (something) up; decide |
| consulō, consulere, consuluī, consultum | to consult |
| contemnō, contemnere, contempsī, contemptum | to despise |
| contendō, contendere, contendī, contentum | to strain, hurry, fight |
| crēdō, crēdere, crēdidī, crēditum | to trust, rely on, believe (usually with dative) |
| crescō, crescere, crēvī, crētum | to grow |
| currō, currere, cucurrī, cursum | to run |
| dēfendō, dēfendere, dēfendī, dēfensum | to defend, drive off |
| descendō, descendere, descendī, descensum | to climb down |
| descrībō, descrībere, descripsī, descriptum | to describe |
| dīcō, dīcere, dixī, dictum | to tell, say |
| dīligō, dīligere, dīlexī, dīlectum | to love, esteem, pick out |
| discēdō, discēdere, discessī, discessum | to leave, separate |
| discō, discere, didicī | to learn |
| dīvidō, dīvidere, dīvīsī, dīvīsum | to divide |
| dūcō, dūcere, duxī, ductum | to take (someone/some place), draw, lead |
| emō, emere, ēmī, emptum | to buy |
| exuō, exuere, exuī, exūtum | to strip |
| fallō, fallere, fefellī, falsum | to deceive |
| fīgō, fīgere, fixī, fixum | to fasten, affix |
| fingō, fingere, finxī, fictum | to shape, form |
| fluō, fluere, fluxī, fluxum | to flow |
| frangō, frangere, frēgī, fractum | to break |
| fundō, fundere, fūdī, fūsum | to pour |
| gerō, gerere, gessī, gestum | to carry, wage, accomplish; wear |
| gignō, gignere, genuī, genitum | to give birth; cause |
| impōnō, impōnere, imposuī, impositum | to put on |

| | |
|---|---|
| **induō, induere, induī, indūtum** | *to put on, dress* |
| **instituō, instituere, instituī, institūtum** | *to set up, instruct; decide* |
| **instruō, instruere, instruxī, instructum** | *to build; equip* |
| **intellegō, intellegere, intellexī, intellectum** | *to understand, be aware of, appreciate* |
| **intendō, intendere, intendī, intentum** | *to stretch; intend, aim at* |
| **iungō, iungere, iunxī, iunctum** | *to join, connect* |
| **laedō, laedere, laesī, laesum** | *to hurt, harm* |
| **legō, legere, lēgī, lectum** | *to choose, pick, gather; read* |
| **lūdō, lūdere, lūsī, lūsum** | *to play; deceive* |
| **metuō, metuere, metuī, metūtum** | *to fear, be afraid* |
| **mittō, mittere, mīsī, missum** | *to send, release, throw, to make (something) go away under its own power* |
| **neglegō, neglegere, neglexī, neglectum** | *to neglect* |
| **noscō, noscere, nōvi, nōtum** | *to learn;* (in the perfect system) *to know, recognize* |
| **occīdo, occīdere, occīdī, occīsum** | *to kill* |
| **occurro, occurrere, occurrī, occursum** | *to meet, run into* (with dative) |
| **ostendō, ostendere, ostendī, ostentum** | *to show* |
| **pandō, pandere, pandī, pansum/passum** | *to open up, stretch* |
| **parcō, parcere, peperci/parsī, parsūrus** | *to spare, be sparing* (with dative) |
| **pellō, pellere, pepulī, pulsum** | *to push, drive* |
| **pendō, pendere, pependī, pensum** | *to hang; weigh; pay* |
| **perdō, perdere, perdidī, perditum** | *to lose, squander, destroy, waste* |
| **pergō, pergere, perrexī, perrectum** | *to continue* |
| **permittō, permittere, permīsī, permissum** | *to allow, send through, throw* |
| **petō, petere, petiī/petīvī, petītum** | *to look for, ask (of someone)* (with the preposition **ā**); *head for, attack* |
| **pōnō, pōnere, posuī, positum** | *to put, lay, set down* |
| **premō, premere, pressī, pressum** | *to press, push* |
| **prōdō, prōdere, prōdidī, prōditum** | *to betray, hand over* |
| **prōmittō, prōmittere, prōmīsī, prōmissum** | *to promise; send ahead* |
| **quaerō, quaerere, quaesiī/quaesīvī, quaesītum** | *to look for, ask (of someone)* (with the preposition **ā**) |
| **quiescō, quiescere, quiēvī, quiētum** | *to rest* |
| **reddō, reddere, reddidī, redditum** | *to give back, surrender; repeat* |
| **regō, regere, rexī, rectum** | *to rule, guide* |
| **relinquō, relinquere, relīquī, relictum** | *to abandon, leave* |
| **requīrō, requīrere, requīsiī/requīsīvī, requīsītum** | *to demand, ask; miss* |
| **revertō, revertere, revertī, reversum** | *to turn back* |
| **rumpō, rumpere, rūpī, ruptum** | *to break, burst* |
| **scindō, scindere, scidī, scissum** | *to cut* |
| **scrībō, scrībere, scripsī, scriptum** | *to write, draw* |
| **sinō, sinere, sīvī, situm** | *to let, allow* |
| **solvō, solvere, solvī, solūtum** | *to loosen, untie; pay* |
| **spargō, spargere, sparsī, sparsum** | *to scatter, sprinkle* |
| **spernō, spernere, sprēvī, sprētum** | *to reject, scorn* |
| **statuō, statuere, statuī, statūtum** | *to set up; stop; decide* |
| **sternō, sternere, strāvī, strātum** | *to spread, stretch* |
| **sūmō, sūmere, sumpsī, sumptum** | *to take, assume* |
| **surgō, surgere, surrexī, surrectum** | *to rise* |
| **tangō, tangere, tetigī, tactum** | *to touch* |
| **tegō, tegere, texī, tectum** | *to cover* |
| **tendō, tendere, tetendī, tentum/tensum** | *to stretch; try* |

| | |
|---|---|
| tollō, tollere, sustulī, sublātum | *to raise; carry away; destroy* |
| trādō, trādere, trādidī, trāditum | *to hand over, surrender* |
| trahō, trahere, traxī, tractum | *to pull, drag* |
| vehō, vehere, vexī, vectum | *to carry; (in the middle voice with ablative) to ride* |
| vendō, vendere, vendidī, venditum | *to sell* |
| vertō, vertere, vertī, versum | *to turn* |
| vincō, vincere, vīcī, victum | *to conquer* |
| vīvō, vīvere, vixī, victum | *to live, be alive* |

**exercise     2-9**

*Translate these verbs into English.*

1. constituit _____

2. dīcimus _____

3. legunt _____

4. mittō _____

5. vīvis _____

6. caditis _____

7. vertunt _____

8. noscit _____

9. tollis _____

10. crescimus _____

11. dīligō _____

12. cōgunt _____

13. gignitis _____

14. curris _____

15. legō _____

**exercise     2-10**

*Translate these verbs into Latin.*

1. he is reading _____

2. I am lifting _____

3. they are saying _____

4. you (*pl.*) are sending _____

5. we are running _____

6. you (*sg.*) are writing _____

7. they are selling _____

8. I pull _____

9. he is showing _____

10. we say _____

11. you (*pl.*) allow _____

12. you (*sg.*) are cutting _____

13. they are leading _____

14. he is pushing _____

15. I loosen _____

**exercise    2-11**

*Translate these sentences into English.*

1. Puella montem ascendit. _____

2. Librum scrībō. _____

3. Puerī pilā lūdunt. _____

4. Solvō canem catēnā. _____

5. Paedagōgus puerōs cōgit. _____

**exercise    2-12**

*Write the appropriate present-tense form of the verb in parentheses, then translate the sentence.*

1. Marcus arāneās _____ (descrībere).

   _____

2. Bovēs onera ad oppidum plaustrīs _____ (vehere).

   _____

3. Māter mea mūrēs _____ (metuere).

   _____

4. Ego dē armīs virōque _____ (canere).

   _____

5. Hostēs ad urbem nōn _____ (accēdere).

   _____

## Third Conjugation -iō

Third-conjugation -**iō** verbs are classed as third-conjugation verbs, because their present infinitive (second principal part) ends in short -**ere**, just like regular third-conjugation verbs. They can be distinguished from third-conjugation verbs by their first principal part, which ends in -**iō**. In the present tense, they conjugate in the same way that regular third-conjugation verbs do, with two exceptions: the first-person singular and third-person plural forms. A good way to remember how to conjugate the two variations of third-conjugation verbs in the present tense is to insert an **i** between the base and ending of an -**iō** verb wherever the verb doesn't have an **i**.

**faciō, facere, fēcī, factum** *to make*

| | Singular | | Plural | |
|---|---|---|---|---|
| First person | **faciō** | I make<br>I do make<br>I am making | **facimus** | we make<br>we do make<br>we are making |
| Second person | **facis** | you make<br>you do make<br>you are making | **facitis** | you make<br>you do make<br>you are making |
| Third person | **facit** | he/she/it makes<br>he/she/it does make<br>he/she/it is making | **faciunt** | they make<br>they do make<br>they are making |

Here is a list of some common third-conjugation **-iō** verbs, followed by exercises that provide practice with them in the present tense.

| | |
|---|---|
| **accipiō, accipere, accēpī, acceptum** | *to receive; welcome* |
| **aspiciō, aspicere, aspexī, aspectum** | *to look at* |
| **capiō, capere, cēpī, captum** | *to take, catch* |
| **conficiō, conficere, confēcī, confectum** | *to finish* |
| **coniciō, conicere, coniēcī, coniectum** | *to hurl, throw really hard* |
| **cupiō, cupere, cupīvī, cupītum** | *to desire, long for* |
| **effugiō, effugere, effūgī** | *to escape* |
| **ēripiō, ēripere, ēripuī, ēreptum** | *to grab, take out violently* |
| **excipiō, excipere, excēpī, exceptum** | *to take out, take up, catch, receive* |
| **faciō, facere, fēcī, factum** | *to make, do* |
| **fugiō, fugere, fūgī, fugitūrus** | *to run away, flee* |
| **iaciō, iacere, iēcī, iactum** | *to throw* |
| **incipiō, incipere, incēpī, inceptum** | *to begin* |
| **interficiō, interficere, interfēcī, interfectum** | *to kill* |
| **pariō, parere, peperī, partum** | *to give birth (to); produce* |
| **percutiō, percutere, percussī, percussum** | *to hit, strike* |
| **perficiō, perficere, perfēcī, perfectum** | *to complete* |
| **rapiō, rapere, rapuī, raptum** | *to take (forcefully)* |
| **recipiō, recipere, recēpī, receptum** | *to accept, take back* |
| **respiciō, respicere, respexī, respectum** | *to look back* |
| **suscipiō, suscipere, suscēpī, susceptum** | *to undertake; accept* |

**exercise** **2-13**

*Translate these verbs into English.*

1. recipiunt _____
2. conicitis _____
3. faciō _____
4. suscipimus _____
5. aspicis _____
6. respiciō _____
7. accipit _____
8. cupiunt _____
9. percutit _____
10. paris _____

| exercise | **2-14** |

*Translate these verbs into Latin.*

1. we are completing _____

2. he is taking forcefully _____

3. I am taking out _____

4. you (*sg.*) are throwing _____

5. you (*sg.*) are running away _____

6. he is killing _____

7. they are escaping _____

8. he is grabbing _____

9. they begin _____

10. I am taking _____

| exercise | **2-15** |

*Translate these sentences into English.*

1. Dōna nostra recipimus. _____

2. Gladiātor gladium ab alterō ēripit. _____

3. Avēs ōva pariunt. _____

4. Ad iuventūtem respiciunt senēs. _____

5. In theatrō ad spectātōrēs saepe aspicimus. _____

| exercise | **2-16** |

*Write the appropriate present-tense form of the verb in parentheses, then translate the sentence.*

1. Dīves plūs pecūniae semper _____ (cupere).

_____

2. Mīlitēs multās post hōrās proelium _____ (conficere).

_____

3. Fulgor turrim _____ (percutere).

_____

4. Graecī captīvōs Trōiānōs _____ (interficere).

_____

5. Servī multa in agrīs _____ (facere).

_____

## Fourth Conjugation

The conjugation of fourth-conjugation verbs is remarkably similar to that of third-conjugation -**iō** verbs; the only differences are that the **i** in the second-person singular and first- and second-person plural forms is long rather than short. Fourth-conjugation verbs can be recognized by their present infinitive ending in -**īre**.

**ven*iō*, ven*īre*, vēnī, ventum** *to come*

|  | **Singular** |  | **Plural** |  |
|---|---|---|---|---|
| First person | **ven*iō*** | *I come* | **ven *īmus*** | *we come* |
|  |  | *I do come* |  | *we do come* |
|  |  | *I am coming* |  | *we are coming* |
| Second person | **ven*īs*** | *you come* | **ven*ītis*** | *you come* |
|  |  | *you do come* |  | *you do come* |
|  |  | *you are coming* |  | *you are coming* |
| Third person | **ven*it*** | *he/she/it comes* | **ven*iunt*** | *they come* |
|  |  | *he/she/it does come* |  | *they do come* |
|  |  | *he/she/it is coming* |  | *they are coming* |

Here is a list of some common fourth-conjugation verbs, followed by exercises that provide practice with them in the present tense.

| | |
|---|---|
| **aperiō, -īre, -uī, -tum** | *to open, uncover* |
| **audiō, -īre, -īvī/-iī, -ītum** | *to hear, listen* |
| **custōdiō, -īre, -iī/-īvī, -ītum** | *to guard* |
| **dormiō, -īre, -īvī, -ītum** | *to sleep* |
| **ēveniō, ēvenīre, ēvēnī, ēventum** | *to come out; result* |
| **fīniō, -īre, -īvī, -ītum** | *to finish* |
| **inveniō, invenīre, invēnī, inventum** | *to come upon, find* |
| **mūniō, -īre, -īvī, -ītum** | *to fortify* |
| **nesciō, -īre, -īvī, -ītum** | *not to know* |
| **perveniō, pervenīre, pervēnī, perventum** | *to arrive* |
| **reperiō, reperīre, repperī, repertum** | *to find* |
| **sciō, -īre, -īvī, -ītum** | *to know* |
| **sentiō, sentīre, sensī, sensum** | *to perceive, experience, realize* |
| **sepeliō, sepelīre, sepeliī/sepelīvī, sepultum** | *to bury* |
| **serviō, -īre, -īvī, -ītum** | *to be a slave, serve* (with dative) |
| **veniō, venīre, vēnī, ventum** | *to come* |

| exercise | 2-17 |
|---|---|

*Translate these verbs into English.*

1. aperit _____

2. scit _____

3. audītis _____

4. custōdiunt _____

5. inveniunt _____

| exercise | 2-18 |
|---|---|

*Translate these verbs into Latin.*

1. you (*sg.*) are a slave (**servīre**) _____

2. I am fortifying _____

3. you (*pl.*) are coming _____

4. you (*sg.*) don't know _____

5. she is arriving _____

6. you (*sg.*) are burying _____

7. they are finding _____

8. you (*pl.*) know _____

9. it is resulting _____

10. they serve _____

| exercise | 2-19 |
|---|---|

*Translate these sentences into English.*

1. Lūdum nostrum nunc fīnīmus. _____

2. Omnia bene ēveniunt. _____

3. Paucōs amīcōs vērōs inveniō. _____

4. In cōmissātiōnem cum turbā cōmissātōrum pervenīmus. _____

5. In Viā Appiā fratrem tuum sepelīs. _____

| exercise | 2-20 |
|---|---|

*Write the appropriate present-tense form of the verb in parentheses, then translate the sentence.*

1. Tū Messallae adhūc _____ (servīre). _____

2. Caesar castra celeriter _____ (mūnīre). _____

3. Ego dolōrem vestrum _____ (sentīre). _____

4. Nōs larvam in spēluncā _____ (reperīre). _____

5. Quī custōdēs custōdēs _____ (custōdīre)? _____

| exercise | 2-21 |
|---|---|

*This exercise contains verbs in the present tense from all the conjugations. Indicate which conjugation each verb belongs to, then translate the verb into English.*

EXAMPLE    canunt    ***third***    ***they are singing***

1. contendunt    _____    _____

2. docētis    _____    _____

3. dīligō    _____    _____

4. scindunt    _____    _____

5. vigilāmus    _____    _____

6. persuādēmus    _____    _____

7. accipiō    _____    _____

8. pugnat    _____    _____

9. pugnātis    _____    _____

10. appellant    _____    _____

11. crēdit    _____    _____

12. laudō    _____    _____

13. suscipimus    _____    _____

14. caditis    _____    _____

15. consulimus      _____      _____

16. interficiunt     _____      _____

17. constant       _____      _____

18. contemnunt    _____      _____

19. cantat        _____      _____

20. iūrō          _____      _____

# The Imperfect Indicative Active

The imperfect is one of the two most commonly found tenses in Latin literature, the other being the perfect tense, which is treated in Unit 5. It is the past tense for the continuous aspect, and as its name implies, it shows an action that is incomplete or not (*im-*) thoroughly (*-per-*) done (*-fect*).

## Use

As opposed to the perfect tense, which refers to a single completed action in past time, the imperfect emphasizes the process over the product of an action. It refers to something in the middle of its happening or to something that happened habitually or repeatedly in the past and may or may not still be going on in the present. Although the imperfect tense can sometimes suggest the beginning of an action, the important thing to remember is that as of right now in the present, the action is incomplete. This is extremely important to bear in mind when reading or translating, since English has many different ways of expressing the same concept.

currēbant
*they were running*
*they used to run*
*they kept running*
*they were in the habit of running*
*they were accustomed to run*
*they started to run*
*they began to run*

You could even translate **currēbant** *they ran*, as long as the context makes it clear that the event was not an isolated incident.

Ab hostibus semper **currēbant**.　　　*They always ran from the enemy.*

There is no single correct way to translate the imperfect tense. Let context and personal taste be your guide.

## Formation

Fortunately, not only is the imperfect tense one of the most commonly used, it is also the easiest tense to recognize. Positioned between a verb's stem and the personal ending is the tense indicator **-ba-**. This is true for verbs of all conjugations, as well as for all irregular verbs, with the sole exception of **sum** (see below). The imperfect endings are as follows.

| | |
|---|---|
| **-bam** | **-bāmus** |
| **-bās** | **-bātis** |
| **-bat** | **-bant** |

First- and second-conjugation verbs drop the **-re** from their present infinitive forms, leaving their theme vowels (as they do in the present tense), then add the tense indicator **-ba-**, and finally a personal ending. For the imperfect tense, the personal ending for the first-person singular is **-m**.

### First Conjugation

**amō, amāre, amāvī, amātum** *to love*

| | |
|---|---|
| amābam | amābāmus |
| amābās | amābātis |
| amābat | amābant |

### Second Conjugation

**moneō, monēre, monuī, monitum** *to warn*

| | |
|---|---|
| monēbam | monēbāmus |
| monēbās | monēbātis |
| monēbat | monēbant |

For third-conjugation verbs, the short **e** theme vowel does not weaken; instead, it lengthens.

### Third Conjugation

**mittō, mittere, mīsī, missum** *to send*

| | |
|---|---|
| mittēbam | mittēbāmus |
| mittēbās | mittēbātis |
| mittēbat | mittēbant |

The conjugation of third-conjugation **-iō** and fourth-conjugation verbs in the imperfect tense is identical.

## Third Conjugation -iō

**iaciō, iacere, iēcī, iactum** *to throw*

| | |
|---|---|
| **iaciēbam** | **iaciēbāmus** |
| **iaciēbās** | **iaciēbātis** |
| **iaciēbat** | **iaciēbant** |

## Fourth Conjugation

**sentiō, sentīre, sēnsī, sēnsum** *to feel*

| | |
|---|---|
| **sentiēbam** | **sentiēbāmus** |
| **sentiēbās** | **sentiēbātis** |
| **sentiēbat** | **sentiēbant** |

As noted above, the only verb irregular in the imperfect tense is **sum**. Although it lacks the **b** from the tense indicator **-ba-**, it does retain the **a**. Its forms are as follows.

**sum, esse, fuī, futūrus** *to be*

| | |
|---|---|
| **eram** | **erāmus** |
| **erās** | **erātis** |
| **erat** | **erant** |

**exercise 3-1**

*Translate these verbs into English.*

1. perficiēbās _____
2. dēbēbātis _____
3. pōnēbam _____
4. retinēbam _____
5. narrābāmus _____

6. erāmus _____
7. indicābās _____
8. iacēbant _____
9. laedēbās _____
10. errābant _____

| exercise | 3-2 |
|---|---|

*Translate these verbs into Latin.*

1. you (*pl.*) were announcing _____

2. they kept covering _____

3. we began to spare _____

4. I was denying _____

5. they were resting _____

6. you (*pl.*) were overcoming _____

7. you (*sg.*) used to take out _____

8. he was closing _____

9. she was being _____

10. we started to pull _____

11. you (*sg.*) were reading _____

12. I was changing _____

13. they used to be eager _____

14. they were living (**vīvere**) _____

15. you (*sg.*) were strong (**valēre**) _____

16. he was filling up _____

17. you (*sg.*) used to be _____

18. she was doing nothing (**cessāre**) _____

19. he was a slave (**servīre**) _____

20. I was turning back _____

| exercise | 3-3 |
|---|---|

*Translate these sentences into English.*

1. Omnia perdēbam. _____

2. Multa eī praebēbat. _____

3. Servōs līberābam. _____

4. Tōtam noctem dormiēbant. _____

5. Bellum fīniēbant. _____

| exercise | 3-4 |
|---|---|

*Write the appropriate imperfect-tense form of the verb in parentheses, then translate the sentence.*

1. Nōs in senātū _____ (sedēre). _____

2. Vōs amīcī _____ (esse). _____

3. Ego dē monte _____ (descendere). _____

4. Puerī multās fābulās _____ (audīre). _____

5. Māter līberōs suōs _____ (revocāre). _____

# The Future Indicative Active

This unit explains the use of the future tense in Latin and reviews the two ways in which it is formed, depending on a verb's conjugation. There are separate exercises for each method. In the final exercise, the reader is asked to change verb forms in mixed tenses from all the conjugations to the future tense.

## Use

The future tense refers to an action that will take place in a general sense or will be in progress at some time after the present. (A different tense, the future perfect, is used to show an action that will be *completed* at some point after the present.) Latin is quite meticulous in its use of the future tense to refer to future acts. English, on the other hand, often uses the present tense to refer to a future event. Take, for example, the following Latin sentence using the future tense and the various ways English can express the same thought.

Crās Rōmam petēmus.   *Tomorrow we will head for Rome.*
(future tense)

*Tomorrow we will be heading for Rome.*
(future tense)

*Tomorrow we head for Rome.*
(present tense)

*Tomorrow we are heading for Rome.*
(present tense)

Even though the inclusion of the adverb **crās** *tomorrow* makes the time frame for the event clear, Latin still uses the future tense.

# Formation

As is the case with the present and imperfect tenses, to indicate the future tense, Latin verbs use tense indicators between the base and personal ending—unlike English, which uses the modal (helping verb) *will.* In Latin, there are two ways to form the future tense. First- and second-conjugation verbs employ quite a different tense indicator than third- and fourth-conjugation verbs do.

## First and Second Conjugations

The tense indicator for the future tense used by first- and second-conjugation verbs is similar to that used to show the imperfect. Rather than **-bam**, **-bās**, etc., the future endings are as follows.

| | |
|---|---|
| **-bō** | **-bimus** |
| **-bis** | **-bitis** |
| **-bit** | **-bunt** |

The most noteworthy difference between the tense indicators for the imperfect and future tenses of first- and second-conjugation verbs is the vowel between the **b** and the personal ending. Rather than an **a** throughout, the future has the same **ō, i, i, i, i, u** vowel pattern seen in the present tense of third-conjugation verbs. Also noteworthy is that the personal ending for the first-person singular is **-ō** instead of **-m**.

### First Conjugation

**labōrō, labōrāre, labōrāvī, labōrātum** *to work*

| | |
|---|---|
| **labōrābō** | **labōrābimus** |
| **labōrābis** | **labōrābitis** |
| **labōrābit** | **labōrābunt** |

### Second Conjugation

**maneō, manēre, mansī, mansum** *to stay*

| | |
|---|---|
| **manēbō** | **manēbimus** |
| **manēbis** | **manēbitis** |
| **manēbit** | **manēbunt** |

The only verb irregular in its formation of the future tense is **sum**. It also shows the **ō, i, i, i, i, u** vowel pattern, and as in the imperfect tense of **sum**, the endings are actually regular except that they drop the **b**.

**sum, esse, fuī, futūrus** *to be*

| | |
|---|---|
| **erō** | **erimus** |
| **eris** | **eritis** |
| **erit** | **erunt** |

## exercise 4-1

*Translate these verbs into English.*

1. vigilābit _____
2. persuādēbō _____
3. pugnābimus _____
4. appellābitis _____
5. respondēbunt _____

6. stābit _____
7. dēbēbis _____
8. iuvābimus _____
9. vocābō _____
10. retinēbunt _____

## exercise 4-2

*Translate these verbs into Latin.*

1. we will make known _____
2. they will recline _____
3. he will announce _____
4. he will enter _____
5. you (*sg.*) will dare _____

6. I will sail _____
7. you (*sg.*) will overcome _____
8. they will change _____
9. we will be eager _____
10. I will be strong _____

## exercise 4-3

*Translate these sentences into English.*

1. Deōs laudābis. _____
2. Cīvēs magistrātūs creābunt. _____
3. Ignis omnia dēlēbit. _____
4. Fābulam dē fēminā narrābō. _____
5. In lectō iacēbitis. _____

**exercise**    **4-4**

*Write the appropriate future-tense form of the verb in parentheses, then translate the sentence.*

1. Marcus fīlium suum _____ (vocāre). _____

2. Nōs exercitum crās _____ (monēre). _____

3. Tū post bellum _____ (cessāre). _____

4. Eī sub stellīs _____ (manēre). _____

5. Ego amīcīs meīs sōlum _____ (cantāre). _____

## Third and Fourth Conjugations

Third-, third **-iō**, and fourth-conjugation verbs have a radically different way of signifying future tense. For these verbs, the first-person singular has **a** followed by the personal ending **-m**, while the rest of the forms have **e** for the stem vowel.

**petō, petere, petiī/petīvī, petītum** *to look for*

| | |
|---|---|
| **petam** | **petēmus** |
| **petēs** | **petētis** |
| **petet** | **petent** |

Third **-io** and fourth-conjugation verbs conjugate in the same way, following their practice in the present and imperfect tenses of inserting **i** before the stem vowel if the stem vowel isn't already **i**.

### Third Conjugation -iō

**faciō, facere, fēcī, factum** *to make, do*

| | |
|---|---|
| **faciam** | **faciēmus** |
| **faciēs** | **faciētis** |
| **faciet** | **facient** |

### Fourth Conjugation

**audiō, audīre, audīvī/audiī, audītum** *to hear, listen*

| | |
|---|---|
| **audiam** | **audiēmus** |
| **audiēs** | **audiētis** |
| **audiet** | **audient** |

## exercise 4-5

*Translate these verbs into English.*

1. dīligam _____
2. scindēs _____
3. cōgēmus _____
4. accipient _____
5. suscipiētis _____

6. cadēs _____
7. consulam _____
8. inveniet _____
9. pōnēmus _____
10. fīniētis _____

## exercise 4-6

*Translate these verbs into Latin.*

1. he will allow _____
2. he will hand over _____
3. they will catch (**capere**) _____
4. I will pull _____
5. you (*sg.*) will destroy (**perdere**) _____

6. you (*pl.*) will harm (**laedere**) _____
7. they will compel _____
8. he will hear _____
9. I will know _____
10. you (*sg.*) will look back (**respicere**) _____

_____      _____

## exercise 4-7

*Translate these sentences into English.*

1. Pugnā cēdēmus. _____
2. Captīvōs Rōmānīs trādētis. _____
3. Bona mea rapient. _____
4. Equitēs trans Alpēs mittēs. _____
5. Tiberius lapidēs in mare iaciet. _____

| exercise | 4-8 |
|---|---|

*Write the appropriate future-tense form of the verb in parentheses, then translate the sentence.*

1. Is _____ (fīnīre). _____

2. Eī ūvās _____ (colligere). _____

3. Nōs fīnem _____ (tangere). _____

4. Servus iānuam _____ (custōdīre). _____

5. Ego mē ad tē _____ (vertere). _____

| exercise | 4-9 |
|---|---|

*The verb forms in this exercise are drawn from all conjugations and tenses. Write the future-tense equivalent of each form, keeping the same person and number, then translate the new form into English. Just to make things interesting, some of the verb forms are already in the future tense!*

EXAMPLE    mittit    ***mittet***    ***he will send***

1. labōrās _____ _____

2. tenēbāmus _____ _____

3. iacētis _____ _____

4. laedet _____ _____

5. veniēbam _____ _____

6. studet _____ _____

7. vocāmus _____ _____

8. capiunt _____ _____

9. vidēs _____ _____

10. rogō _____ _____

11. tenet _____ _____

12. pōnent _____ _____

13. fīnīs _____ _____

14. mittēbātis _____ _____

15. timēmus _____ _____

# The Perfect Indicative Active

This unit reviews the use and formation of the perfect tense, including perfect-stem formation. Exercises provide practice with the perfect tense and identification of the ways in which Latin verbs form their perfect-system stems.

## Use

The perfect indicative is the most common verb tense in Latin literature. Unlike the imperfect tense, which describes a repeated action or an action in progress in the past, the perfect tense refers to a *single completed act*. It can denote a single completed action in a general sense (*I went to Watford*) or place emphasis on the fact that as of right now—the time of speaking—the action has been completed (*I have gone to Watford*).

In English grammar, this use is called the *present perfect—present* because it is the present tense for the completed aspect. This may be a challenging concept to comprehend. Even though an action has occurred in the past, the emphasis of the perfect tense is that at the moment of speaking, the action is completed. There are two other tenses in the completed aspect (also known as the *perfect system*), the pluperfect and the future perfect, which denote actions that have been completed as of a certain time in the past or the future, respectively. These tenses are treated further in Unit 6.

## Formation

The first two principal parts of a verb provide all the information needed to form the present-system tenses of the verb, that is, the present, imperfect, and future, in both the active and passive voices. The third principal part provides all the information needed to form the perfect-system tenses, that is, the perfect, pluperfect, and future perfect, but only in the active voice. The fourth principal part is used for the perfect-system passive tenses.

The perfect indicative active is the only tense that doesn't have the usual personal endings **-ō/-m**, **-s**, **-t**, **-mus**, **-tis**, **-nt**. Instead, there are special personal endings, as follows.

| | |
|---|---|
| -ī | -imus |
| -istī | -istis |
| -it | -ērunt |

Forming the perfect indicative active is simple, and the formation is the same for verbs of all the conjugations, as well as for irregular verbs: Drop the final **ī** of the third principal part, then add the special perfect personal endings.

### portō, portāre, portāvī, portātum *to carry*

| | | | |
|---|---|---|---|
| **portāvī** | *I carried* | **portāvimus** | *we carried* |
| **portāvistī** | *you carried* | **portāvistis** | *you carried* |
| **portāvit** | *he carried* | **portāvērunt** | *they carried* |

### timeō, timēre, timuī *to be afraid*

| | | | |
|---|---|---|---|
| **timuī** | *I was afraid* | **timuimus** | *we were afraid* |
| **timuistī** | *you were afraid* | **timuistis** | *you were afraid* |
| **timuit** | *he was afraid* | **timuērunt** | *they were afraid* |

### dīcō, dīcere, dixī, dictum *to say*

| | | | |
|---|---|---|---|
| **dixī** | *I said* | **diximus** | *we said* |
| **dixistī** | *you said* | **dixistis** | *you said* |
| **dixit** | *he said* | **dixērunt** | *they said* |

### capiō, capere, cēpī, captum *to take*

| | | | |
|---|---|---|---|
| **cēpī** | *I took* | **cēpimus** | *we took* |
| **cēpistī** | *you took* | **cēpistis** | *you took* |
| **cēpit** | *he took* | **cēpērunt** | *they took* |

### veniō, venīre, vēnī, ventum *to come*

| | | | |
|---|---|---|---|
| **vēnī** | *I came* | **vēnimus** | *we came* |
| **vēnistī** | *you came* | **vēnistis** | *you came* |
| **vēnit** | *he came* | **vēnērunt** | *they came* |

### sum, esse, fuī, futūrus *to be*

| | | | |
|---|---|---|---|
| **fuī** | *I was* | **fuimus** | *we were* |
| **fuistī** | *you were* | **fuistis** | *you were* |
| **fuit** | *he was* | **fuērunt** | *they were* |

## Perfect-Stem Formation

Several of the special perfect personal endings can be confusingly similar to present-system endings. For example, the third-person singular perfect ending **-it** is the same as the third-person singular present ending for third- and fourth-conjugation verbs.

dīcit  *he says*
dixit  *he said*

The difference lies in the stem, and so familiarity with how perfect-system stems are formed can be very useful. English also forms its past tense in various ways. The most common way is to add *-ed* (*walk/walked*), but there are others, such as changing the vowel (*say/said; drink/drank*), changing the final consonant (*send/sent*), making no change at all (*put/put*), and sometimes borrowing a form from a completely different verb (*go/went*)!

Latin has four different methods for forming perfect stems. Some verbs even employ more than one method in the same form, which certainly gets the point across. The four methods are as follows.

- **Syllabic augment:** As the name suggests, this method adds a syllable to the present stem, usually **-āv-**, **-u-**, or **-īv-**.

  - *port*ō, portāre, *portāvī*, port**ātum** *to carry*

  - *mone*ō, monēre, *monuī*, monitum *to warn*

  - *aud*iō, audīre, *audīvī*, aud**ītum** *to hear*

- **Temporal augment:** The word *temporal* is from the Latin word **tempus, temporis**, meaning *time*. This method adds time to (i.e., lengthens) the vowel of a verb's base. Sometimes, for phonetic reasons, the vowel also changes.

  - *veni*ō, venīre, *vēnī*, ventum *to come*

  - *vide*ō, vidēre, *vīdī*, vīsum *to see*

  - *vinc*ō, vincere, *vīcī*, victum *to conquer*

  - *faci*ō, facere, *fēcī*, factum *to make, do*

- **Aorist:** Here, the present stem gains an **-s-**. It must be remembered that the letter **x** is a double consonant: **c + s → x** and **g + s → x**.

  - *mane*ō, manēre, *mansī*, mansum *to stay*

  - *dīc*ō, dīcere, *dixī*, dictum *to say*

  - *reg*ō, regere, *rexī*, rectum *to rule*

- **Reduplication:** With this method, the initial consonant and vowel of a verb's present stem are more or less repeated. However, if the verb has a prefix, the prefix takes the place of the reduplication.

  - *pell*ō, pellere, *pepulī*, pulsum *to drive*

  - *curr*ō, currere, *cucurrī*, cursum *to run*

  but

  - *recurr*ō, recurrere, *recurrī*, recursum *to run back*

With some verbs, such as **dēfendō, dēfendere, dēfendī, dēfensum** *to defend*, there may be ambiguity with regard to tense: **dēfendit** could mean either *he is defending* or *he has defended*. In these situations, context is the best guide.

| exercise | 5-1 |
|---|---|

*Translate these verbs into English.*

1. amāvistī _____

2. posuit _____

3. vixērunt _____

4. cēpistī _____

5. vetuī _____

6. sēdit _____

7. dōnāvimus _____

8. petīvistī _____

9. cecinērunt _____

10. lūsit _____

11. cognōvistis _____

12. dormīvērunt _____

13. ascendit _____

14. temptāvimus _____

15. didicistis _____

| exercise | 5-2 |
|---|---|

*Translate these verbs into Latin.*

1. you (*sg.*) pushed _____

2. he rested _____

3. they chose _____

4. you (*sg.*) changed _____

5. he filled up _____

6. they destroyed (**perdere**) _____

7. you (*sg.*) offered _____

8. I did set free _____

9. you (*pl.*) carried (**vehere**) _____

10. they handed over _____

11. I obeyed _____

12. we visited often (**celebrāre**) _____

13. you (*pl.*) sat _____

14. he climbed down _____

15. we turned back _____

| exercise | 5-3 |
| --- | --- |

*Translate these sentences into English. Not all verbs are in the perfect tense, so be mindful of stems as well as endings!*

1. Ignem vīdit. _____

2. Flōrēs dēlēvistī. _____

3. Inter arborēs latuimus. _____

4. Manum meam tibi praebuī. _____

5. Hannibal Rōmānōs fefellit. _____

6. Mīles fortis ē pugnā nōn fugiet. _____

7. Lapidēs in mare iēcistis. _____

8. Heri matrem tuam terruī. _____

9. Librī mentem exercent. _____

10. Caesar bellum in plūrimōs gessit. _____

| exercise | 5-4 |
| --- | --- |

*The verb forms in this exercise are drawn from all conjugations and tenses. Write the perfect-tense equivalent of each form, keeping the same person and number, then translate the new form into English. Just to make things interesting, some of the verb forms are already in the perfect tense!*

> **EXAMPLE**    *sentiam*    <u>*sensī*</u>    <u>**I felt**</u>

1. fluit          _____    _____

2. spargam     _____    _____

3. terrēbāmus  _____    _____

4. promīsistis  _____    _____

5. movēs        _____    _____

6. addunt       _____    _____

7. recurritis    _____    _____

8. creābit       _____    _____

9. dīvidimus     _____     _____

10. tacēbant     _____     _____

11. accēditis     _____     _____

12. habitābit     _____     _____

13. ostendam     _____     _____

14. pandērunt     _____     _____

15. recipitis     _____     _____

16. occurristī     _____     _____

17. sonābimus     _____     _____

18. gignō     _____     _____

19. requīrit     _____     _____

20. ēvenient     _____     _____

## exercise     5-5

*Using a dictionary or the glossary at the end of this book, identify which of the four methods described in this unit is used by each verb to form its perfect stem.*

1. doluī _____     6. vēnī _____

2. cessī _____     7. cecidī _____

3. collēgī _____     8. aspexī _____

4. continuī _____     9. statuī _____

5. fluxī _____     10. lāvī _____

# The Pluperfect and Future Perfect Indicative Active

The pluperfect and future perfect indicative active tenses are presented together in this unit because they are so similar in usage. They both denote the completion of one action before another action. For this reason, they rely on other verbs as reference points either in the past or in the future, either expressed or implied.

## The Pluperfect Tense

### Use

The Latin name for the pluperfect tense is **plus quam perfectum**, meaning *more than thoroughly done*. In English grammar, this tense is called the *past perfect*. As the past tense of the completed aspect, it is in a sense a double past, referring to an action completed in the past before another action that occurred in the past.

Castra **posuerant** priusquam      *They **had pitched** camp before*
   sōl occidit.                      *the sun set.*

The pluperfect tense is used to sequence the two events: First they pitched camp, then the sun set.

### Formation

Since the pluperfect tense is part of the completed aspect, it uses the perfect active stem, which is obtained by dropping the final -ī from the third principal part of the verb. To this stem you attach the tense indicator **-era-**, followed by a regular active voice personal ending. English forms its past perfect with the helping verb *had* plus the past participle; this is the only way the Latin pluperfect can be translated.

**iubeō, iubēre, iussī, iussum** *to order*

| | | | |
|---|---|---|---|
| iuss**eram** | *I had ordered* | iuss**erāmus** | *we had ordered* |
| iuss**erās** | *you had ordered* | iuss**erātis** | *you had ordered* |
| iuss**erat** | *he had ordered* | iuss**erant** | *they had ordered* |

There are two other ways to remember how the pluperfect tense is formed. One of these is to think of attaching the imperfect indicative forms of **sum** to the perfect stem.

| | | | |
|---|---|---|---|
| **iuss-** | + | **eram** | **erāmus** |
| | | **erās** | **erātis** |
| | | **erat** | **erant** |

Another way is to examine the resemblance of the imperfect tense's endings and those of the pluperfect. The imperfect uses the *present* stem, then the tense indicator **-ba-**, then personal endings. The pluperfect uses the *perfect* stem, then the tense indicator **-era-**, then personal endings. Each uses the stem appropriate to its verbal aspect, each is the past tense for its respective aspect, and they share the same theme vowel for their tense indicators, not to mention the same personal endings. Apart from their stems, the only striking difference is that where the imperfect tense has **-b-**, the pluperfect has **-er-**.

| Imperfect | | Pluperfect | |
|---|---|---|---|
| iubē*bam* | iubē*bāmus* | iuss*eram* | iuss*erāmus* |
| iubē*bās* | iubē*bātis* | iuss*erās* | iuss*erātis* |
| iubē*bat* | iubē*bant* | iuss*erat* | iuss*erant* |

**exercise    6-1**

*Translate these verbs into English.*

1. exspectāverant _____

2. tetenderat _____

3. properāverās _____

4. cupīveram _____

5. tetigerat _____

6. armāverant _____

7. commīserātis _____

8. labōrāveram _____

9. nōverāmus _____

10. pepererat _____

**exercise    6-2**

*Translate these verbs into Latin.*

1. they had remained _____

2. you (*pl.*) had killed (**necāre**) _____

3. you (*sg.*) had understood _____

4. they had demanded (**postulāre**) _____

5. he had chosen (**optāre**) _____

8. we had put on (**impōnere**) _____

6. you (*pl.*) had drunk _____

9. I had wandered _____

7. you (*sg.*) had lost _____

10. you (*pl.*) had abandoned _____

**exercise    6-3**

*Translate these sentences into English.*

1. Canēs familiam monuerant priusquam hospitēs advēnērunt.

   _____

2. Corpora mortua illā nocte texeram.

   _____

3. Āram in hortō statuerās.

   _____

4. Discipulōs linguam Graecam docueram.

   _____

5. Iam vīnum hospitibus fūderāmus priusquam servī cēnam intulērunt.

   _____

**exercise    6-4**

*Write the appropriate pluperfect-tense form of the verb in parentheses, then translate the sentence.*

1. Tū bullam ā fīliō meō _____ (arripere).

   _____

2. Eī cymbala _____ (percutere).

   _____

3. Nōs hospitēs ad iānuam _____ (dūcere).

   _____

4. Caligula esse (*to be*) deus _____ (simulāre).

_____

5. Ego vultum meum ad ōrātōrem _____ (vertere).

_____

## The Future Perfect Tense

### Use

Of all the tenses in the indicative mood, the future perfect is the least common. It does for references to future events what the pluperfect tense does for the past, namely, it refers to an action that will have been completed in the future before something else will happen.

> Castra **posuerint** priusquam sōl occidet.     *They **will have pitched** camp before the sun will set.*

First they will pitch camp. After that is completed, the sun will set. The future perfect tense makes clear the order in which the events will take place.

Latin is very precise about what tenses are used in a sentence. Notice in the example above that since both are future events, both verbs have a future sense: **posuerint** *they will have pitched* is in the future perfect tense because that will have happened before the other future event of the sun setting, **occidet**, which is in the future tense.

If you read the English translation, however, you'll find that it sounds a bit stilted and awkward. A smoother rendition would be *They will pitch camp before the sun sets.* English does have a future perfect tense, which is formed by combining the future tense of the helping verb *to have* with the past participle, thus *they will have pitched* in the first version of the translation. The second version—the one that sounds more natural—uses a plain future for what will happen first, and then the *present* tense to refer to what will happen after that.

### Formation

There are also great similarities between the pluperfect and future perfect tenses in their formation. Since it is the future tense for the perfect system (the completed aspect), the future perfect tense uses the perfect active stem obtained by dropping the -ī from the third principal part, followed by its own special tense indicator and personal endings. The tense indicator for the future perfect tense is **-eri-**. It appears in every form except the first-person singular.

**iubeō, iubēre, iussī, iussum** *to order*

| | | | |
|---|---|---|---|
| **iusserō** | *I will have ordered* | **iusserimus** | *we will have ordered* |
| **iusseris** | *you will have ordered* | **iusseritis** | *you will have ordered* |
| **iusserit** | *he will have ordered* | **iusserint** | *they will have ordered* |

Just as you can add the imperfect of **sum** to the perfect stem of a verb to form the pluperfect tense, you can add the future of **sum** to form the future perfect tense—with one exception: The third person plural, **-erint**, has an **i** instead of the **u** that the future of **sum** has.

| iuss- | + | erō | erimus |
|---|---|---|---|
| | | eris | eritis |
| | | erit | ~~erunt~~ erint |

| exercise | 6-5 |
|---|---|

*Translate these verbs into English.*

1. certāveris _____

2. vēnerimus _____

3. crēdiderit _____

4. putāverimus _____

5. aspexerint _____

6. ornāveritis _____

7. cāverimus _____

8. rīseritis _____

9. perierimus _____

10. iusserō _____

| exercise | 6-6 |
|---|---|

*Translate these verbs into Latin.*

1. he will have broken _____

2. you (*sg.*) will have taken (**sūmere**) _____

3. they will have betrayed _____

4. he will have remained _____

5. you (*sg.*) will have washed _____

6. you (*pl.*) will have mixed _____

7. they will have surrounded (**cingere**) _____

8. he will have had _____

9. I will have dressed _____

10. they will have named _____

**exercise    6-7**

*Translate these sentences into English.*

1. Fābulam quandam dē Bellō Gallicō memorāveris.

2. Aedem arseritis.

3. Iūnō Manlium monuerit priusquam Gallī Rōmānōs oppugnābunt.

4. Amīcum meum reppererō priusquam urbem relinquet.

5. Princeps multa templa condiderit.

**exercise    6-8**

*Write the appropriate future perfect-tense form of the verb in parentheses, then translate the sentence.*

1. Ego piscēs in forō _____ (emere).

2. Caesar plēbem nōn _____ (neglegere).

3. Nōs nōn satis deōs _____ (laudāre).

4. Māter fīliam suam _____ (metuere).

5. Pompēius exercitum _____ (dūcere).

# The Passive Voice

The grammatical term *voice* refers to the relationship between a subject and its verb, that is to say, whether a subject performs the action (*active voice*) or receives the action (*passive voice*). This unit discusses the use of the passive voice in general and reviews the formation of the passive voice for the present-system tenses (present, imperfect, and future) in all conjugations, then for the perfect-system tenses (perfect, pluperfect, and future perfect).

## Use

Unlike the active voice, where a stated subject performs the action of the verb, in the passive voice the subject is acted on and the agent (i.e., the "doer" of the action) is unknown, or at least doesn't need to be stated.

Active voice      **The dog *is burying* the bone** *for future consumption.*

Passive voice      **The bone *is being buried*** *for future consumption.*

In the passive sentence above, the agent could be expressed by adding the phrase *by the dog*, but the placement of the phrase is important—it's easy to say something you don't mean.

*The bone is being buried **by the dog** for future consumption.*

*The bone is being buried for future consumption **by the dog**.*

These two sentences contain the same words but do not necessarily mean the same thing. Something that the two sentences *do* have in common is that they are unclear and sound awkward. Leaving the agent out, as in the original passive voice sentence, is also ambiguous. All of these considerations show why use of the passive voice in English is traditionally frowned on.

In Latin, the passive voice is used as freely as the active voice, and there is nothing seen as awkward about it. Latin recognizes and exploits the difference between grammatical *subject* and grammatical *topic*. In a Latin sentence, the *subject* is expressed in the nominative case and either performs or receives the action of the verb, depending on the voice of the verb.

45

| | |
|---|---|
| **Ego** canem in hortō spectābam. | *I was watching the dog in the garden.* |
| **Canis** in hortō ā mē spectābātur. | ***The dog** in the garden was being watched by me.* |

Even though these two sentences provide the same information, their *topics* are different. A *topic* is what is being talked about; the rest of the sentence is what is being said about it. Put another way, these sentences may provide the same information, but they answer two different questions. The first sentence answers the question "What was I doing?" The second sentence answers the question "What was happening to the dog?" Since the topic of the passive sentence is the dog, who was performing the action doesn't really matter. The addition of the agent **ā mē** is extra and essentially unasked-for information.

In order to convert a thought expressed in the active voice to the passive voice, not only does the verb need to change form, but the nouns around it do as well. Take, for example, the following simple active sentence.

| | |
|---|---|
| Puella puerum percutit. | *The girl is hitting the boy.* |

**Puella** is the nominative-case subject of **percutit**. Since the verb is in the active voice, the person receiving the action, **puerum**, is the accusative-case direct object. To say the same thing in the passive voice, the direct object of the active verb becomes the subject of the passive verb, and so its case must change from the accusative **puerum** to the nominative **puer**.

| | |
|---|---|
| Puer ā puellā percutitur. | *The boy is being hit by the girl.* |

Notice what happened to the girl. She changed from nominative **puella** to ablative **puellā** and became the object of the preposition **ā**. This is called the *ablative of agent*. It consists of the preposition **ā** followed by a noun in the ablative and is only used with "people words." If the doer in a passive sentence is a thing rather than a person, you use the ablative of means, which does *not* use a preposition.

| | |
|---|---|
| Saxum puerum percutit. | *A rock is hitting the boy.* |
| Puer saxō percutitur. | *The boy is being hit by a rock.* |

# Formation of the Present System

English forms the passive voice with the helping verb *to be* plus the past participle. For the present-system tenses, Latin uses a different set of personal endings.

| Active Voice | | Passive Voice | |
|---|---|---|---|
| -ō/-m | -mus | -or/-r | -mur |
| -s | -tis | -ris | -minī |
| -t | -nt | -tur | -ntur |

Look for the letter **r** in a personal ending as a sign of passive personal endings. All endings except the second-person plural (**-minī**) have it.

## First and Second Conjugations

Switching from active to passive voice in the present and imperfect tenses of first- and second-conjugation verbs is simply a matter of exchanging active for passive personal endings. This is also true in the future tense, with the exception of the second-person singular form, where the active-voice ending **-bis** becomes **-beris** in the passive.

## Present Passive

**amō, amāre, amāvī, amātum** *to love*

| | | | |
|---|---|---|---|
| **amor** | *I am loved* | **amāmur** | *we are loved* |
| **amāris** | *you are loved* | **amāminī** | *you are loved* |
| **amātur** | *he is loved* | **amantur** | *they are loved* |

**moneō, monēre, monuī, monitum** *to advise*

| | | | |
|---|---|---|---|
| **moneor** | *I am advised* | **monēmur** | *we are advised* |
| **monēris** | *you are advised* | **monēminī** | *you are advised* |
| **monētur** | *he is advised* | **monentur** | *they are advised* |

## Imperfect Passive

| | | | |
|---|---|---|---|
| **amābar** | *I used to be loved* | **amābāmur** | *we used to be loved* |
| **amābāris** | *you used to be loved* | **amābāminī** | *you used to be loved* |
| **amābātur** | *he used to be loved* | **amābantur** | *they used to be loved* |

| | | | |
|---|---|---|---|
| **monēbar** | *I used to be advised* | **monēbāmur** | *we used to be advised* |
| **monēbāris** | *you used to be advised* | **monēbāminī** | *you used to be advised* |
| **monēbātur** | *he used to be advised* | **monēbantur** | *they used to be advised* |

## Future Passive

| | | | |
|---|---|---|---|
| **amābor** | *I will be loved* | **amābimur** | *we will be loved* |
| **amāberis** | *you will be loved* | **amābiminī** | *you will be loved* |
| **amābitur** | *he will be loved* | **amābuntur** | *they will be loved* |

| | | | |
|---|---|---|---|
| **monēbor** | *I will be advised* | **monēbimur** | *we will be advised* |
| **monēberis** | *you will be advised* | **monēbiminī** | *you will be advised* |
| **monēbitur** | *he will be advised* | **monēbuntur** | *they will be advised* |

---

### exercise 7-1

*Translate these verbs into English.*

1. iūdicābāmur _____

2. suādēminī _____

3. portābar _____

4. dēbentur _____

5. cēlātur _____

6. movēbimur _____

7. mulceor _____

8. tenētur _____

9. rogāberis _____

10. cūrābantur _____

11. augēbātur _____

12. monēbimur _____

13. amābāris _____

14. exspectābiminī _____

15. necābor _____

| **exercise** | **7-2** |
| --- | --- |

*Translate these verbs into Latin.*

1. I will be warned _____

2. you (*sg.*) are thought _____

3. I am being ordered (**iubēre**) _____

4. they will be washed _____

5. we will be taught _____

6. it was being fought _____

7. we are praised _____

8. you (*pl.*) were prepared _____

9. I am owed _____

10. you (*sg.*) will be tested _____

11. it will be announced _____

12. they are filled _____

13. you (*sg.*) will be laughed at _____

14. we used to be supported _____

15. he used to be considered (**habēre**) _____

| **exercise** | **7-3** |
| --- | --- |

*Rewrite these sentences in the passive voice, keeping the same tense, then translate the new sentence into English.*

   EXAMPLE   Agricola agrum arat.
            *Ager ab agricolā arātur.*
            *The field is being plowed by the farmer.*

1. Frāter sorōrem vexat.

   _____

   _____

2. Mīlitēs oppidum oppugnābunt.

   _____

   _____

3. Sagitta mē vulnerābit.

   _____

   _____

4. Metus nōs numquam superābat.

_____

_____

5. Lībertātem dēsīderant servī.

_____

_____

**exercise    7-4**

_Rewrite these sentences in the active voice, keeping the same tense, then translate the new sentence into English._

EXAMPLE   Ager ab agricolā arātur.
   **_Agricola agrum arat._**
   **_The farmer is plowing the field._**

1. Caesar eō factō movēbitur.

_____

_____

2. Signum ā consule dabātur.

_____

_____

3. Omnia ā puellā narrābuntur.

_____

_____

4. Ā quō superābantur Germānī?

_____

_____

5. Aenēās longē Latiō ā Iūnōne arcēbātur.

_____

_____

**exercise    7-5**

*Write the appropriate present-tense passive form of the verb in parentheses, then translate the sentence.*

1. Tū _____ (dubitāre). _____

2. Canēs _____ (tenēre). _____

3. Ego _____ (vidēre). _____

4. Vōs _____ (spectāre). _____

5. Nōs _____ (regnāre). _____

**exercise    7-6**

*Write the appropriate imperfect-tense passive form of the verb in parentheses, then translate the sentence.*

1. Nōs _____ (dēlēre). _____

2. Mīlitēs _____ (tenēre). _____

3. Vōs _____ (laudāre). _____

4. Lūcius _____ (vītāre). _____

5. Tū _____ (monēre). _____

**exercise    7-7**

*Write the appropriate future-tense passive form of the verb in parentheses, then translate the sentence.*

1. Perīcula _____ (dēmonstrāre). _____

2. Ego _____ (docēre). _____

3. Nōs _____ (vulnerāre). _____

4. Tū _____ (habēre). _____

5. Rēgīna _____ (superāre). _____

## Third, Third *-iō*, and Fourth Conjugations

As with first- and second-conjugation verbs, third-, third **-iō**, and fourth-conjugation verbs maintain the same tense indicators and show the change from active to passive voice by way of their personal endings. There is one exception: In the second-person singular form of the present tense of third-conjugation verbs, the active ending **-is** becomes **-eris** in the passive voice. This is the same pattern shift seen in the second-person singular form of the future tense of first- and second-conjugation verbs (where **-bis** becomes **-beris**).

There are very few places where third-conjugation **-iō** verbs behave like regular third- rather than fourth-conjugation verbs, and the present tense of the passive voice is one of those places. The second-person singular ending is **-eris**, as opposed to the fourth conjugation's **-īris**.

## Present Passive

### legō, legere, lēgī, lectum *to choose*

| | | | |
|---|---|---|---|
| **legor** | *I am chosen* | **legimur** | *we are chosen* |
| **leg*eris*** | *you are chosen* | **legiminī** | *you are chosen* |
| **legitur** | *he is chosen* | **leguntur** | *they are chosen* |

### iaciō, iacere, iēcī, iactum *to throw*

| | | | |
|---|---|---|---|
| **iacior** | *I am thrown* | **iacimur** | *we are thrown* |
| **iac*eris*** | *you are thrown* | **iaciminī** | *you are thrown* |
| **iacitur** | *he is thrown* | **iaciuntur** | *they are thrown* |

### audiō, audīre, audīvī, audītum *to hear*

| | | | |
|---|---|---|---|
| **audior** | *I am heard* | **audīmur** | *we are heard* |
| **audīris** | *you are heard* | **audīminī** | *you are heard* |
| **audītur** | *he is heard* | **audiuntur** | *they are heard* |

## Imperfect Passive

| | | | |
|---|---|---|---|
| **legēbar** | *I used to be chosen* | **legēbāmur** | *we used to be chosen* |
| **legēbāris** | *you used to be chosen* | **legēbāminī** | *you used to be chosen* |
| **legēbātur** | *he used to be chosen* | **legēbantur** | *they used to be chosen* |
| **iaciēbar** | *I used to be thrown* | **iaciēbāmur** | *we used to be thrown* |
| **iaciēbāris** | *you used to be thrown* | **iaciēbāminī** | *you used to be thrown* |
| **iaciēbātur** | *he used to be thrown* | **iaciēbantur** | *they used to be thrown* |
| **audiēbar** | *I used to be heard* | **audiēbāmur** | *we used to be heard* |
| **audiēbāris** | *you used to be heard* | **audiēbāminī** | *you used to be heard* |
| **audiēbātur** | *he used to be heard* | **audiēbantur** | *they used to be heard* |

## Future Passive

| | | | |
|---|---|---|---|
| **legar** | *I will be chosen* | **legēmur** | *we will be chosen* |
| **legēris** | *you will be chosen* | **legēminī** | *you will be chosen* |
| **legētur** | *he will be chosen* | **legentur** | *they will be chosen* |
| **iaciar** | *I will be thrown* | **iaciēmur** | *we will be thrown* |
| **iaciēris** | *you will be thrown* | **iaciēminī** | *you will be thrown* |
| **iaciētur** | *he will be thrown* | **iacientur** | *they will be thrown* |
| **audiar** | *I will be heard* | **audiēmur** | *we will be heard* |
| **audiēris** | *you will be heard* | **audiēminī** | *you will be heard* |
| **audiētur** | *he will be heard* | **audientur** | *they will be heard* |

| exercise | 7-8 |
|---|---|

*Translate these verbs into English.*

1. vincitur _____
2. dīligar _____
3. consulēbāris _____
4. contemnēmur _____
5. regēbantur _____
6. raperis _____
7. agētur _____
8. inveniuntur _____

9. tegēbātur _____
10. pōnuntur _____
11. trahēminī _____
12. vehēbar _____
13. fallor _____
14. mūnientur _____
15. sciēbātur _____

| exercise | 7-9 |
|---|---|

*Translate these verbs into Latin.*

1. you (*pl.*) will be thrown _____
2. I was being elected _____
3. I was being consulted _____
4. you (*sg.*) are accepted _____
5. he is being touched _____
6. it is being struck _____
7. we will be raised _____
8. she used to be nourished (**alere**) _____

9. they used to be guarded _____
10. you (*pl.*) are joined _____
11. I will be turned _____
12. you (*sg.*) are found _____
13. it will be paid _____
14. you (*sg.*) will be abandoned _____
15. they are being looked for (**petere**) _____

| exercise | 7-10 |
|---|---|

*Rewrite these sentences in the passive voice, keeping the same tense, then translate the new sentence into English.*

    EXAMPLE  Puer pilam capit.
                 ***Pila ā puerō capitur.***
                 ***The ball is being caught by the boy.***

1. Quis exercitum ad montem dūcet?

    _____

    _____

2. Marcus omnēs terrēbat.

    _____

    _____

3. In hortō tuō multōs et pulchrōs flōrēs semper inveniō.

    _____

    _____

4. Tū sub pavīmentō pecūniam reperīs.

    _____

    _____

5. Caesar bellum in Gallōs gerēbat.

    _____

    _____

| exercise | 7-11 |
|---|---|

*Rewrite these sentences in the active voice, keeping the same tense, then translate the new sentence into English.*

    EXAMPLE  Pila ā puerō capitur.
                 ***Puer pilam capit.***
                 ***The boy is catching the ball.***

1. Crās Rōma ā nōbīs petētur.

    _____

    _____

2. Ā tē numquam trādēbar.

_____

_____

3. Equī virgā celerius aguntur.

_____

_____

4. Terra nūbibus tegēbatur.

_____

_____

5. Lupus ē fundō ā mē expellitur.

_____

_____

**exercise    7-12**

_Write the appropriate present-tense passive form of the verb in parentheses, then translate the sentence._

1. Opus _____ (perficere). _____

2. Nōs _____ (dēfendere). _____

3. Vōs _____ (mittere). _____

4. Tū _____ (capere). _____

5. Portae _____ (aperīre). _____

**exercise    7-13**

_Write the appropriate imperfect-tense passive form of the verb in parentheses, then translate the sentence._

1. Ego _____ (dīligere). _____

2. Ager _____ (colere). _____

3. Puerī _____ (pūnīre). _____

4. Sonitus _____ (audīre). _____

5. Tū _____ (āmittere). _____

## exercise 7-14

*Write the appropriate future-tense passive form of the verb in parentheses, then translate the sentence.*

1. Iānua _____ (claudere). _____

2. Saxum _____ (iacere). _____

3. Sententiae meae _____ (audīre). _____

4. Tū _____ (occīdere). _____

5. Ego _____ (dūcere). _____

## Formation of the Perfect System

As is true throughout the perfect system, all forms are constructed in the same way for all verbs, regardless of which conjugation they belong to. The passive forms for the perfect-system tenses are unique in two ways. First, rather than being stand-alone words relying on tense indicators and personal endings (as, for example, the imperfect-tense form **portābātur** *it was being carried*), perfect-system tenses use compound forms consisting of the perfect passive participle (the fourth principal part of most verbs) and a form of the verb **sum** (as, for example, the perfect-tense form **portātum est** *it was carried*). Second, since participles are verbal adjectives, issues of gender and number come into play; the participle must agree with its subject in gender and number.

| | | |
|---|---|---|
| Mīles admonit**us** est. | *The soldier was warned.* | (masculine singular) |
| Mīlitēs admonit**ī** sunt. | *The soldiers were warned.* | (masculine plural) |
| Urna fract**a** erat. | *The jug had been broken.* | (feminine singular) |
| Urnae fract**ae** erant. | *The jugs had been broken.* | (feminine plural) |
| Dōnum dat**um** erit. | *The gift will have been given.* | (neuter singular) |
| Dōna dat**a** erunt. | *The gifts will have been given.* | (neuter plural) |

### The Perfect Passive

The perfect passive tense uses the perfect passive participle with the *present* tense of **sum**. It takes a lot of practice to get used to this! Ordinarily, when you see the word **est**, you are tempted to say *is*, but in the perfect passive construction, **est** is translated *was*.

| | |
|---|---|
| Mīles fortis **est**. | *The soldier **is** brave.* |

but

| | |
|---|---|
| Mīles occīsus **est**. | *The soldier **was** killed.* |

From a linguistic standpoint, this construction makes sense if you remember that the perfect tense is the present tense of the completed aspect. The thought behind the sentence **Mīles occīsus est**, then, is actually *The soldier is, as of right now, in a present state of having been killed*, but *The soldier was killed* is a smoother translation.

**cingō, cingere, cinxī, cinctum** *to surround*

| | | | |
|---|---|---|---|
| **cinctus sum** | *I was surrounded* | **cinctī sumus** | *we were surrounded* |
| **cinctus es** | *you were surrounded* | **cinctī estis** | *you were surrounded* |
| **cinctus est** | *he was surrounded* | **cinctī sunt** | *they were surrounded* |

## The Pluperfect Passive

The pluperfect passive tense combines the perfect passive participle with the *imperfect* tense of **sum**. Since the tense indicator for both the pluperfect active and the imperfect of **sum** is **-era-**, the pluperfect passive is easy to recognize.

| | | | |
|---|---|---|---|
| **cinctus eram** | *I had been surrounded* | **cinctī erāmus** | *we had been surrounded* |
| **cinctus erās** | *you had been surrounded* | **cinctī erātis** | *you had been surrounded* |
| **cinctus erat** | *he had been surrounded* | **cinctī erant** | *they had been surrounded* |

## The Future Perfect Passive

As one would expect, the future perfect passive tense uses the perfect passive participle with the future tense of **sum**. Remember that the endings for the future perfect active look just like the future of **sum** except in the third-person plural form. In the active voice, that ending is **-erint**. The third-person plural for the future of **sum**, however, is **erunt**.

| | | | |
|---|---|---|---|
| **cinctus erō** | *I will have been surrounded* | **cinctī erimus** | *we will have been surrounded* |
| **cinctus eris** | *you will have been surrounded* | **cinctī eritis** | *you will have been surrounded* |
| **cinctus erit** | *he will have been surrounded* | **cinctī erunt** | *they will have been surrounded* |

In the following exercises, if no gender is specified, use the masculine.

**exercise    7-15**

*Translate these verbs into English.*

1. docta erat _____

2. exspectātī sunt _____

3. requīsītum erit _____

4. portātus sum _____

5. cupītae erāmus _____

6. tactus erat _____

7. armātī erunt _____

8. mandātī erant _____

9. necātus erō _____

10. intellectus es _____

11. postulātum est _____

12. optātī eritis _____

13. āmissa erant _____

14. relictī erimus _____

15. ēreptae sunt _____

16. percussī erant _____

17. monstrātus sum _____

18. sublātus es _____

19. versa erat _____

20. custōdītus sum _____

| exercise | 7-16 |
| --- | --- |

*Translate these verbs into Latin.*

1. I had been captured _____

2. she was found _____

3. they (*neut.*) were opened _____

4. he will have been doubted _____

5. it had been perceived _____

6. they were taken care of _____

7. it has been increased _____

8. we had been given back _____

9. you (*pl.*) have been watched _____

10. you (*sg.*) were pushed _____

11. I will have been armed _____

12. they (*fem.*) were abandoned _____

13. you (*sg.*) had been led _____

14. you (*pl.*) had been divided _____

15. we will have been looked back at _____

_____

| exercise | 7-17 |
| --- | --- |

*Rewrite these sentences in the passive voice, keeping the same tense, then translate the new sentence into English.*

EXAMPLE    Puer pilam cēpit.
***Pila ā puerō capta est.***
***The ball was caught by the boy.***

1. Hostēs castra nostra nōn cēpērunt.

_____

_____

2. Princeps senātōrēs convocāverat.

_____

_____

3. Servī cēnam in mensās imposuerint.

_____

_____

4. Imber ignem exstinxit.

_____

_____

5. Nuntiī epistulās Rōmam portāvērunt.

_____

_____

**exercise    7-18**

_Rewrite these sentences in the active voice, keeping the same tense, then translate the new sentence into English._

> EXAMPLE   Pila ā puerō capta est.
> **_Puer pilam cēpit._**
> **_The boy caught the ball._**

1. Mīles vulnerātus ab amīcō in campō relictus erat.

_____

_____

2. Rōma ā Rōmulō condita est.

_____

_____

3. Ōminibus monitus erō.

_____

_____

4. Puellae larvā perterritae erant.

_____

_____

5. Sociī ā nōbīs servātī sunt.

_____

_____

| exercise | 7-19 |

*Write the appropriate perfect-tense passive form of the verb in parentheses, then translate the sentence.*

1. Tū _____ (audīre). _____

2. Frūmentum _____ (emere). _____

3. Nōs _____ (sinere). _____

4. Vōs _____ (revocāre). _____

5. Ego _____ (petere). _____

| exercise | 7-20 |

*Write the appropriate pluperfect-tense passive form of the verb in parentheses, then translate the sentence.*

1. Publius _____ (consulere). _____

2. Nōs _____ (fallere). _____

3. Tū _____ (cūrāre). _____

4. Templa _____ (aedificāre). _____

5. Caecilia _____ (sepelīre). _____

| exercise | 7-21 |

*Write the appropriate future perfect-tense passive form of the verb in parentheses, then translate the sentence.*

1. Perīculum _____ (vītāre). _____

2. Nōs _____ (vincere). _____

3. Tū _____ (spernere). _____

4. Flōrēs _____ (colligere). _____

5. Omnia _____ (parāre). _____

# Unit 8 | Deponent Verbs

This unit explains deponent verbs and provides exercises to reinforce familiarity with the most common members of this unusual group.

## Use

### The Middle Voice

In addition to the active and passive voices, Latin has a third voice, known as *middle*. In the active voice, the subject performs the action of a verb; in the passive voice, the subject receives the action; in the middle voice, the subject also performs the action, but in such a way that it is personally affected or is otherwise closely involved in the action, often with a reflexive sense.

| Active voice | **mensam vertit** | *he turns the table* |
| Passive voice | **vertitur** | *he is turned* |
| Middle voice | **vertitur** | *he turns* (*himself* understood) |

There is a point of possible confusion. While the middle voice sounds active, its forms are identical to those of the passive voice. The middle voice isn't very common, but it occurs frequently enough to merit mention. When it does appear, context usually makes clear which voice is intended.

### Deponents

Latin resolves most of the potential confusion with the middle voice by maintaining a special group of verbs known as *deponents*, so called because they appear to have set (**-pōnent**) aside (**dē-**) their active forms and passive meanings. Since these verbs are restricted to passive forms with active meanings, knowledge that a verb is deponent should alleviate any confusion.

## Formation

Deponent verbs can be recognized by their principal parts, which are the passive equivalents of regular verbs. Compare the principal parts of the following two verbs, one regular, one deponent.

### scrībō, scrībere, scripsī, scriptum *to write*

| | | |
|---|---|---|
| **scrībō** | *I write* | first-person singular, present indicative *active* |
| **scrībere** | *to write* | present *active* infinitive |
| **scripsī** | *I wrote* | first-person singular, perfect indicative *active* |
| **scriptum** | *written* | supine/perfect *passive* participle |

### hortor, hortārī, hortātus sum *to urge*

| | | |
|---|---|---|
| **hortor** | *I urge* | first-person singular, present indicative *passive* |
| **hortārī** | *to urge* | present *passive* infinitive |
| **hortātus sum** | *I urged* | first-person singular, perfect indicative *passive* |

**Hortor** doesn't need a fourth principal part, because the information it would have provided, the perfect passive participle, is already included in the third principal part.

As with regular verbs, a deponent verb's conjugation is determined by its present infinitive, which appears as the second principal part. Over half of all deponents are first-conjugation verbs.

| | |
|---|---|
| First conjugation | **hortor, hortārī, hortātus sum** *to urge* |
| Second conjugation | **vereor, verērī, veritus sum** *to fear* |
| Third conjugation | **nascor, nascī, nātus sum** *to be born* |
| Third conjugation **-iō** | **patior, patī, passus sum** *to suffer* |
| Fourth conjugation | **orior, or īrī, ortus sum** *to rise* |

All forms of deponent verbs are the same passive forms that you have already learned. There are only a few exceptions to the rule that deponents have passive forms and active meanings.

1. The present and future participles of deponent verbs have active forms with active meanings.
2. The future infinitive of deponent verbs is active in both form and meaning.
3. The gerundive of deponent verbs is the only passive form that maintains a passive meaning.

The imperative of deponent verbs is also unique. In the singular, it resembles what the present active infinitive would look like if there were one (for example, **sequere!** *follow!*). The plural is the same as the second-person singular, present indicative passive (**sequiminī!**).

Here is the full conjugation of the verb **patior, patī, passus sum** *to suffer.*

### Present Indicative

| | | | |
|---|---|---|---|
| **patior** | *I am suffering* | **patimur** | *we are suffering* |
| **pateris** | *you are suffering* | **patiminī** | *you are suffering* |
| **patitur** | *he is suffering* | **patiuntur** | *they are suffering* |

## Imperfect Indicative

| | | | |
|---|---|---|---|
| **patiēbar** | *I was suffering* | **patiēbāmur** | *we were suffering* |
| **patiēbāris** | *you were suffering* | **patiēbāminī** | *you were suffering* |
| **patiēbātur** | *he was suffering* | **patiēbantur** | *they were suffering* |

## Future Indicative

| | | | |
|---|---|---|---|
| **patiar** | *I will suffer* | **patiēmur** | *we will suffer* |
| **patiēris** | *you will suffer* | **patiēminī** | *you will suffer* |
| **patiētur** | *he will suffer* | **patientur** | *they will suffer* |

## Perfect Indicative

| | | | |
|---|---|---|---|
| **passus sum** | *I suffered* | **passī sumus** | *we suffered* |
| **passus es** | *you suffered* | **passī estis** | *you suffered* |
| **passus est** | *he suffered* | **passī sunt** | *they suffered* |

## Pluperfect Indicative

| | | | |
|---|---|---|---|
| **passus eram** | *I had suffered* | **passī erāmus** | *we had suffered* |
| **passus erās** | *you had suffered* | **passī erātis** | *you had suffered* |
| **passus erat** | *he had suffered* | **passī erant** | *they had suffered* |

## Future Perfect Indicative

| | | | |
|---|---|---|---|
| **passus erō** | *I will have suffered* | **passī erimus** | *we will have suffered* |
| **passus eris** | *you will have suffered* | **passī eritis** | *you will have suffered* |
| **passus erit** | *he will have suffered* | **passī erunt** | *they will have suffered* |

## Present Subjunctive

| | |
|---|---|
| **patiar** | **patiāmur** |
| **patiāris** | **patiāminī** |
| **patiātur** | **patiantur** |

## Imperfect Subjunctive

| | |
|---|---|
| **paterer** | **paterēmur** |
| **paterēris** | **paterēminī** |
| **paterētur** | **paterentur** |

## Perfect Subjunctive

| | |
|---|---|
| **passus sim** | **passī sīmus** |
| **passus sīs** | **passī sītis** |
| **passus sit** | **passī sint** |

## Pluperfect Subjunctive

| | |
|---|---|
| **passus essem** | **passī essēmus** |
| **passus essēs** | **passī essētis** |
| **passus esset** | **passī essent** |

## Imperative

| **patere** | *suffer!* | **patiminī** | *suffer!* |
|---|---|---|---|

## Infinitives

| Present | **patī** | *to suffer* |
|---|---|---|
| Perfect | **passus esse** | *to have suffered* |
| Future | **passūrus esse** | *to be about to suffer* |

## Participles

| Present | **patiens, patientis** | *suffering* |
|---|---|---|
| Perfect | **passus** | *(having) suffered* |
| Future | **passūrus** | *about to suffer* |
| Gerundive | **patiendus** | *to be suffered* |

No English equivalent can be given for subjunctive forms that are not in the context of a sentence. For the formation of the subjunctive of regular verbs, see Unit 15. Unit 9 treats the imperative mood, Unit 11 treats participles, Unit 12 treats gerundives, and Unit 13 treats infinitives.

## Semi-Deponent Verbs

There is a small subgroup of deponents called semi-deponents. As their name suggests, they are only half deponent. In the present system, they are regular. It's only in the perfect system that they are deponent. These verbs are easy to recognize by their principal parts. There are only four.

| **audeō, audēre, ausus sum** | *to dare* |
|---|---|
| **fīdō, fīdere, fīsus sum** | *to trust (usually with dative)* |
| **gaudeō, gaudēre, gāvīsus sum** | *to rejoice, be happy* |
| **soleō, solēre, solitus sum** | *to be accustomed to, usually (do something)* |

The first two principal parts—the ones needed to form all the present-system tenses—appear as normal. The third principal part, however, is like the third principal part of deponents; it provides everything needed to make all perfect-system forms.

Here is a list of the most common deponent verbs, followed by exercises that provide practice with them. The greater your acquaintance with these verbs, the less likely you are to be thrown off by their passive-looking forms and active-sounding meanings.

| **aggredior, aggredī, aggressus sum** | *to approach, attack* |
|---|---|
| **arbitror, arbitrārī, arbitrātus sum** | *to think* |
| **audeō, audēre, ausus sum** | *to dare* |
| **complector, complectī, complexus sum** | *to hug, embrace* |
| **confiteor, confitērī, confessus sum** | *to confess, admit* |
| **cōnor, cōnārī, cōnātus sum** | *to try, attempt* |
| **consequor, consequī, consecūtus sum** | *to follow, pursue; obtain* |
| **cunctor, cunctārī, cunctātus sum** | *to hesitate, delay* |
| **ēgredior, ēgredī, ēgressus sum** | *to leave, go out* |
| **experior, experīrī, expertus sum** | *to try, test, prove* |
| **fīdō, fīdere, fīsus sum** | *to trust (usually with dative)* |
| **fruor, fruī, fructus sum** | *to enjoy (usually with ablative)* |
| **fungor, fungī, functus sum** | *to perform (usually with ablative)* |
| **gaudeō, gaudēre, gāvīsus sum** | *to rejoice, be happy* |

| | |
|---|---|
| **hortor, hortārī, hortātus sum** | *to encourage, urge* |
| **imitor, imitārī, imitātus sum** | *to copy, imitate* |
| **ingredior, ingred, ingressus sum** | *to step in, enter; begin* |
| **īrascor, īrascī, īrātus sum** | *to become angry* |
| **lābor, lābī, lapsus sum** | *to slip* |
| **loquor, loquī, locūtus sum** | *to talk, speak* |
| **mentior, mentīrī, mentītus sum** | *to lie, deceive* |
| **mīror, mīrārī, mīrātus sum** | *to marvel at, wonder, be amazed* |
| **morior, morī, mortuus sum** (*future active participle* **moritūrus**) | *to die* |
| **moror, morārī, morātus sum** | *to hesitate, delay, kill time* |
| **nascor, nascī, nātus sum** | *to be born* |
| **oblīviscor, oblīviscī, oblītus sum** | *to forget* (with genitive) |
| **orior, orīrī, ortus sum** | *to rise* |
| **patior, patī, passus sum** | *to suffer, experience, put up with* |
| **persequor, persequī, persecūtus sum** | *to chase, follow closely* |
| **polliceor, pollicērī, pollicitus sum** | *to promise* |
| **potior, potīrī, potītus sum** | *to acquire* |
| **precor, precārī, precātus sum** | *to pray* |
| **proficiscor, proficiscī, profectus sum** | *to set out, leave* |
| **queror, querī, questus sum** | *to complain (about)* |
| **reor, rērī, ratus sum** | *to think* |
| **sequor, sequī, secūtus sum** | *to follow* |
| **soleō, solēre, solitus sum** | *to be accustomed to, usually (do something)* |
| **tueor, tuērī, tūtus/tuitus sum** | *to watch, protect* |
| **ulciscor, ulciscī, ultus sum** | *to avenge* |
| **ūtor, ūtī, ūsus sum** | *to use* (with ablative)*; to benefit oneself* (with ablative of means) |
| **vereor, verērī, veritus sum** | *to be afraid* |

## exercise 8-1

*Translate these verbs into English.*

1. potītur _____
2. conābimur _____
3. ratī sunt _____
4. hortābar _____
5. solitus erās _____
6. īrascētur _____
7. ausī eritis _____
8. arbitror _____
9. experientur _____
10. mīrātī erāmus _____
11. ēgrediēris _____
12. cunctābāminī _____
13. gāvīsa est _____
14. moriēbāmur _____
15. patiar _____
16. tuēbiminī _____
17. precātī erant _____
18. sequēbātur _____
19. polliceor _____
20. verēbuntur _____

## exercise 8-2

*Translate these verbs into Latin, using deponents from the list above.*

1. he performs _____

2. they will have delayed _____

3. you (*pl.*) were accustomed to _____

4. they had lied _____

5. we avenge _____

6. he will trust _____

7. I slipped _____

8. they had attacked _____

9. you (*pl.*) will copy _____

10. he will have rejoiced _____

11. I will use _____

12. we will complain _____

13. I am marveling at _____

14. it rose _____

15. they will have embraced _____

16. I will dare _____

17. you had stepped in _____

18. we will confess _____

19. I will follow _____

20. they enjoy _____

## exercise 8-3

*Translate these sentences into English.*

1. Mihine fīsus es? _____

2. Publius multa potītus erit. _____

3. Ēgredior sine tē. _____

4. Hostēs consecūtī erāmus. _____

5. Domum vestram tuēbiminī. _____

## exercise 8-4

*Write the appropriate present-tense form of the verb in parentheses, then translate the sentence.*

1. Nōs bonī esse _____ (experīrī). _____

2. Tū fīlium meum _____ (hortārī). _____

3. Vōs deōs _____ (precārī). _____

4. Ego _____ ūvās colligere (cōnārī). _____

5. Discipulī Cicerōnem hodiē _____ (imitārī). _____

**exercise     8-5**

*Write the appropriate perfect-tense form of the verb in parentheses, then translate the sentence.*

1. Ille mē annōs trēs _____ (persequī).

   _____

2. Nōs pecūniā bene _____ (ūtī).

   _____

3. Ego tē vidēre _____ (gaudēre).

   _____

4. Cum intrāvī, tū _____ (ēgredī).

   _____

5. Ea in pavīmentum madidum _____ (lābī).

   _____

**exercise     8-6**

*Write the appropriate future-tense form of the verb in parentheses, then translate the sentence.*

1. Servus dē Marcō _____ (mentīrī).

   _____

2. Vōs sine metū _____ (loquī).

   _____

3. Tū post victōriam _____ (gaudēre).

   _____

4. Crās fortasse fīlius meus _____ (nascī).

_____

5. Canēs mē domum _____ (sequī).

_____

**exercise    8-7**

*Write the appropriate imperfect-tense form of the verb in parentheses, then translate the sentence.*

1. Marcus matrem suam _____ (complectī).

_____

2. Ego Cicerōnem _____ (imitārī).

_____

3. Cīvēs hoc numquam _____ (patī).

_____

4. Populus Rōmānus senātōribus _____ (querī).

_____

5. Vōs ē forō ēgredī _____ (morārī).

_____

# The Imperative Mood

This unit reviews how to give direct commands in Latin, with exercises after the review.

## Use

The imperative mood is used to give direct commands. The implied subject is the second-person singular or plural. The singular form is used to give a command to one person; the plural issues a command to more than one person. English does not have a separate plural form for its imperative.

If a subject is desired, it is expressed in the vocative case, which looks the same as the nominative with only two exceptions. Nouns of the second declension that end in **-us** take the ending **-e** (for example, **Marcus → Marce** and **servus → serve**), and those ending in **-ius** take the ending **-ī** (for example, **Publius → Publī** and **fīlius → fīlī**).

There are two imperative tenses in Latin, the present and the future. The future tense is archaic and quite uncommon, usually appearing only in poetry and legal writing, so it won't be included in this book.

## Formation

The formation of the imperative mood is very easy. To form the singular for most verbs, simply drop the final **-re** from the present active infinitive (the second principal part). To form the plural, drop the final **-re** from the present active infinitive, then add the ending **-te**.

|                     |         | Singular | Plural  |          |
|---------------------|---------|----------|---------|----------|
| First conjugation   | portāre | portā    | portāte | *carry!* |
| Second conjugation  | manēre  | manē     | manēte  | *stay!*  |
| Third conjugation   | mittere | mitte    | mittite | *send!*  |
| Third conjugation -iō | capere | cape    | capite  | *catch!* |
| Fourth conjugation  | audīre  | audī     | audīte  | *listen!*|

For third-conjugation verbs, the short **e** changes to **i** when the ending **-te** is applied. Third-conjugation **-iō** verbs behave the same as regular third-conjugation verbs.

Only a few verbs have irregular imperative forms.

**dīcō, dīcere, dixī, dictum** *to say*

 dīc      dīcite      *say!*

**dūcō, dūcere, duxī, ductum** *to lead*

 dūc      dūcite      *lead!*

**faciō, facere, fēcī, factum** *to do*

 fac      facite      *do!*

**ferō, ferre, tulī, lātum** *to bring*

 fer      ferte      *bring!*

**sum, esse, fuī, futūrus** *to be*

 es       este       *be!*

To give a negative command in English, you simply begin the imperative with the word *don't*. It isn't so simple in Latin. Instead, Latin uses the word **nōlī** (from the irregular verb **nōlō** *to be unwilling*), or **nōlīte** if the command is plural, plus a complementary infinitive.

**Nōlī saltāre!**     **Nōlīte saltāre!**     *Don't jump!*

Passive imperative forms are basically only found with deponent verbs. In the singular, the form is what the present active infinitive would be if the verb had one. The plural form is the second-person plural, present indicative passive. Negative commands for deponent verbs follow the formation rules for regular verbs.

|                     |         | Singular | Plural    |              |
|---------------------|---------|----------|-----------|--------------|
| First conjugation   | cōnārī  | cōnāre   | cōnāminī  | *try!*       |
| Second conjugation  | verērī  | verēre   | vereminī  | *be afraid!* |
| Third conjugation   | sequī   | sequere  | sequiminī | *follow!*    |
| Third conjugation -iō | patī  | patere   | patiminī  | *suffer!*    |
| Fourth conjugation  | orīrī   | orīre    | orīminī   | *arise!*     |

| exercise | 9-1 |
|---|---|

*Translate these verbs into English.*

1. pōne! _____
2. narrāte! _____
3. cōnāminī! _____
4. cape! _____
5. intrāte! _____

6. pellite! _____
7. nuntiā! _____
8. tege! _____
9. vetāte! _____
10. parcite! _____

| exercise | 9-2 |
|---|---|

*Translate these verbs into Latin.*

1. take out! (*sg.*) _____
2. close! (*pl.*) _____
3. lead! (*sg.*) _____
4. destroy! (*pl.*) (**perdere**) _____
5. bring! (*pl.*) _____

6. sit! (*sg.*) _____
7. pray! (*pl.*) _____
8. listen! (*pl.*) _____
9. play! (*sg.*) _____
10. sing! (*pl.*) _____

| exercise | 9-3 |
|---|---|

*Translate these sentences into English.*

1. Puer, audī matrem tuam! _____
2. Occīdite hostēs! _____
3. Serve, sepelī nunc hoc corpus! _____
4. Cape illum virum! _____
5. Timēte malum tyrannum! _____

**exercise** | **9-4**

*Translate these sentences into Latin.*

1.  Destroy (*pl.*) the ships! _____

2.  Never look back, friend! _____

3.  Throw (*sg.*) the stones into the sea! _____

4.  Students, be quiet! _____

5.  Be happy, girls! _____

# Irregular Verbs

Latin has remarkably few irregular verbs, most of which are irregular only in the present tense, indicative mood. Several are also irregular in the present tense, subjunctive mood. As with all Latin verbs, the perfect system tenses of irregular verbs are formed in the usual manner, regardless of mood.

In this unit, the verbs **sum**, **possum**, **volō**, **nōlō**, **mālō**, **eō**, **ferō**, and **fīō** are reviewed, with separate exercises for each. With a view toward keeping irregular conjugations of these verbs together, thus helping this book be useful to students of any textbook, irregular present system subjunctive mood forms are also reviewed with separate form drills, which readers may skip and return to when appropriate in their course of study.

## sum, esse, fuī, futūrus *to be, exist*

**Sum** and its compounds are extremely irregular throughout the present system, as is the verb *to be* in most languages.

### Indicative Mood

| Present | | Imperfect | | Future | |
|---|---|---|---|---|---|
| sum | sumus | eram | erāmus | erō | erimus |
| es | estis | erās | erātis | eris | eritis |
| est | sunt | erat | erant | erit | erunt |

### Subjunctive Mood

| Present | | Imperfect | | | | |
|---|---|---|---|---|---|---|
| sim | sīmus | essem | essēmus | *or* | forem | forēmus |
| sīs | sītis | essēs | essētis | | forēs | forētis |
| sit | sint | esset | essent | | foret | forent |

### Imperative Mood

| | |
|---|---|
| es | este |

### Infinitives

| | |
|---|---|
| Present | **esse** |
| Perfect | **fuisse** |
| Future | **futūrus esse** *or* **fore** |

### Participle

| | |
|---|---|
| Future | **futūrus, -a, -um** |

Note that the alternate future active infinitive **fore** can take personal endings to form an alternate conjugation for the imperfect subjunctive.

The verb **sum** is sometimes found with a prefix, which can make it difficult to recognize at times. Here is a list of the most common of these compounds. For example, **foem**, **for essem**, and so on.

| | |
|---|---|
| **absum, abesse, āfuī, āfutūrus** | *to be away, be absent* |
| **adsum, adesse, adfuī, adfutūrus** | *to be present* |
| **praesum, praeesse, praefuī, praefutūrus** | *to be in charge, be in front* |
| **prōsum, prōdesse, prōfuī, prōfutūrus** | *to profit, be useful* |
| **subsum, subesse** | *to be under, be nearby* |
| **supersum, superesse, superfuī, superfutūrus** | *to survive, be left over* |

### exercise 10-1

*Translate these verbs into English.*

1. erāmus _____
2. sunt _____
3. praeerō _____
4. fuerit _____
5. es _____

6. absum _____
7. adfuimus _____
8. este _____
9. erit _____
10. fuerant _____

### exercise 10-2

*Translate these verbs into English. Since there is no way to translate Latin subjunctive mood forms out of context, for the purpose of this exercise, translate them as if they were in the indicative mood.*

1. sim _____
2. forēs _____
3. esset _____
4. sit _____
5. prōsint _____

6. supersim _____
7. essēs _____
8. praeessēmus _____
9. forem _____
10. absint _____

**exercise    10-3**

*Translate these verbs into Latin, using the indicative or imperative mood.*

1. you (*pl.*) are _____

2. we used to be _____

3. he had been _____

4. be! (*sg.*) _____

5. they are _____

6. I am profiting _____

7. I was present _____

8. you (*pl.*) will be _____

9. you (*pl.*) used to be under _____

10. he will be _____

**exercise    10-4**

*Translate these verbs into Latin, using the subjunctive mood.*

1. he is _____

2. I used to be _____

3. you (*pl.*) were surviving _____

4. he used to be _____

5. you (*sg.*) are present _____

6. he was profiting _____

7. they used to be _____

8. they are in charge _____

9. you (*pl.*) are _____

10. we were under _____

**exercise    10-5**

*Translate these sentences into English.*

1. Marcus stultus est. _____

2. Dum adsum, omnēs attentī stant. _____

3. Fīliī tuī domī sunt. _____

4. Cum ibi aderātis, ego aberam. _____

5. Mīlitēs fēlīcēs supererunt. _____

6. Hic pānis optimus est. _____

7. Nōtī ōlim erimus. _____

8. Terrae multae erant incognitae. _____

9. Semper hīc tibi erō. _____

10. Iam Caesar Rōmā abest. _____

**exercise  10-6**

*Write the appropriate form of **sum** in the tense indicated in parentheses, then translate the sentence into English.*

1. Ego vir bonus _____ . (*present*) _____

2. Eī in Cūriā _____ . (*future*) _____

3. Hīc _____ Augustus. (*perfect*) _____

4. Ista puella mala _____ . (*present*) _____

5. Nōs in perīculō _____ . (*imperfect*) _____

6. Vōs stultī _____ . (*pluperfect*) _____

7. Scīpiō dux magnus _____ . (*perfect*) _____

8. Tū mihi tam pulcher _____ . (*present*) _____

9. Saepe amīcus meus sub arbore illā _____ . (*imperfect*, subesse)

_____

10. Nōs domī _____ . (*future*, adesse) _____

## possum, posse, potuī *to be able, can*

By far the most common compound of the verb **sum** is **possum**. It is actually a contraction of the words **potis** *able* and **sum** *to be*, and so it is irregular everywhere that **sum** is, with very few exceptions.

An easy way to form and recognize this verb is to think of **pot-** as a prefix attached to the present-system forms of **sum**, and for any form of **sum** that begins with *s*, the *t* of **pot-** changes to *s*, so **pot- + est → potest**, but **pot- + sunt → possunt**.

## Indicative Mood

| Present | | Imperfect | | Future | |
|---|---|---|---|---|---|
| possum | possumus | poteram | poterāmus | poterō | poterimus |
| potes | potestis | poterās | poterātis | poteris | poteritis |
| potest | possunt | poterat | poterant | poterit | poterunt |

## Subjunctive Mood

| Present | | Imperfect | |
|---|---|---|---|
| possim | possīmus | possem | possēmus |
| possīs | possītis | possēs | possētis |
| possit | possint | posset | possent |

## Infinitives

Present    **posse**
Perfect    **potuisse**

## Participle

Present    **potens, potentis**

The main differences between **possum** and **sum** are that **possum** has no future participle or future infinitive, and it has no imperative forms.

| exercise | 10-7 |

*Translate these verbs into English.*

1. possumus _____

2. poterat _____

3. potuērunt _____

4. poteris _____

5. potuerimus _____

6. poterō _____

7. poterunt _____

8. poterās _____

9. potuī _____

10. potest _____

**exercise  10-8**

*Translate these verbs into English. Since there is no way to translate Latin subjunctive mood forms out of context, for the purpose of this exercise, translate them as if they were in the indicative mood.*

1. possīmus _____
2. possēs _____
3. potuisset _____
4. possem _____
5. possētis _____

6. possent _____
7. possīs _____
8. potuissēmus _____
9. possint _____
10. potuerītis _____

**exercise  10-9**

*Translate these verbs into Latin, using the indicative mood.*

1. he will be able _____
2. you (*sg.*) are able _____
3. you (*pl.*) used to be able _____
4. he was able _____
5. we are able _____

6. they will be able _____
7. we will have been able _____
8. he used to be able _____
9. I will have been able _____
10. they are able _____

**exercise  10-10**

*Translate these verbs into Latin, using the subjunctive mood.*

1. I had been able _____
2. he is able _____
3. you (*pl.*) are able _____
4. they have been able _____
5. I am able _____

6. they are able _____
7. you (*sg.*) used to be able _____
8. we are able _____
9. you (*sg.*) are able _____
10. you (*pl.*) had been able _____

**exercise    10-11**

*Translate these sentences into English.*

1. Hostēs nostrī urbem perdere poterunt. _____

2. Bene semper cogitāre potes. _____

3. Fīlius meus vidēre nōn potest. _____

4. Vōs, mīlitēs, malōs caedere poteritis. _____

5. In hortīs hodiē ambulāre nōn poterat. _____

**exercise    10-12**

*Write the appropriate form of **possum** in the tense indicated in parentheses, then translate the sentence into English.*

1. Tū in rēgiam īre _____ . (*future*) _____

2. Vespāsiānus multa aedificia perficere _____ . (*imperfect*) _____

3. Nōs labōrem suscipere _____ . (*present*) _____

4. Is librum mihi dōnāre _____ . (*perfect*) _____

5. Captīvī ē vinculīs effugere nōn _____ . (*present*) _____

## volō, velle, voluī *to be willing, want*

The forms of the verb **volō** and its compounds are irregular in the present indicative and present subjunctive tenses. All the other tenses follow the formation rules for regular third-conjugation verbs, including all perfect-system tenses.

### Indicative Mood

| Present | | Imperfect | | Future | |
|---------|---------|-----------|-----------|--------|---------|
| volō    | volumus | volēbam   | volēbāmus | volam  | volēmus |
| vīs     | vultis  | volēbās   | volēbātis | volēs  | volētis |
| vult    | volunt  | volēbat   | volēbant  | volet  | volent  |

## Subjunctive Mood

| Present | | Imperfect | |
|---------|--------|-----------|----------|
| velim | velīmus | vellem | vellēmus |
| velīs | velītis | vellēs | vellētis |
| velit | velint | vellet | vellent |

### Infinitives

| Present | velle |
|---------|-------|
| Perfect | voluisse |

### Participle

| Present | volens, volentis |
|---------|------------------|

**Volō** has no perfect participle, no future participle or future infinitive, and no imperative forms.

### exercise   10-13

*Translate these verbs into English.*

1. volumus _____

2. volēs _____

3. voluī _____

4. volēbant _____

5. volētis _____

6. volueris _____

7. voluimus _____

8. volunt _____

9. vultis _____

10. volueram _____

### exercise   10-14

*Translate these verbs into English. Since there is no way to translate Latin subjunctive mood forms out of context, for the purpose of this exercise, translate them as if they were in the indicative mood.*

1. velit _____

2. vellem _____

3. vellētis _____

4. velīmus _____

5. velīs _____

6. velītis _____

7. vellent _____

8. vellēs _____

9. vellet _____

10. velim _____

**exercise     10-15**

*Translate these verbs into Latin, using the indicative mood.*

1. they want _____

2. he had been willing _____

3. I will want _____

4. we were willing _____

5. you (*pl.*) will want _____

6. you (*sg.*) wanted _____

7. they will want _____

8. you (*sg.*) are willing _____

9. I want _____

10. we wanted _____

**exercise     10-16**

*Translate these verbs into Latin, using the subjunctive mood.*

1. I am willing _____

2. they were wanting _____

3. you (*sg.*) want _____

4. you (*pl.*) were willing _____

5. we want _____

6. he wants _____

7. they want _____

8. you (*sg.*) were willing _____

9. he was willing _____

10. I was wanting _____

**exercise     10-17**

*Translate these sentences into English.*

1. Dux iam nāvigāre vult. _____

2. Flōrēs meōs colere volam. _____

3. Tum domum meam vendere voluī. _____

4. Hospitēs cēnam nunc parārī volunt. _____

5. Iānitor iānuam claudere volēbat. _____

**exercise** 10-18

*Write the appropriate form of* **volō** *in the tense indicated in parentheses, then translate the sentence into English.*

1. Ego ea dē familiā nostrā narrāre _____ . (*imperfect*)

   _____

2. Omnēs diutius vīvere _____ . (*present*)

   _____

3. Puer puellaque sub arbore sedēre _____ . (*future*)

   _____

4. Caesar mīlitibus imperāre _____ . (*perfect*)

   _____

5. Dominus servōs suōs līberāre _____ . (*present*)

   _____

## nōlō, nolle, nōluī *not to want, be unwilling*

The verb **nōlō** is a compound of **nōn** *not* and **volō** *to want, be willing*. The contraction occurs in the forms of **volō** that begin **vo-**. In these instances, the **v** changes to **n** and the **o** lengthens. The second- and third-person singular and the second-person plural forms in the present indicative don't contract at all. The infinitive is **nolle**.

### Indicative Mood

| Present | | Imperfect | | Future | |
|---------|---------|-----------|-----------|---------|---------|
| nōlō | nōlumus | nōlēbam | nōlēbāmus | [nōlam] | nōlēmus |
| nōn vīs | nōn vultis | nōlēbās | nōlēbātis | nōlēs | [nōlētis] |
| nōn vult | nōlunt | nōlēbat | nōlēbant | nōlet | nōlent |

Note: The forms in square brackets do not appear in classical literature. They are provided to fill out the chart.

### Subjunctive Mood

| Present | | Imperfect | |
|---------|---------|-----------|-----------|
| nōlim | nōlīmus | nollem | nollēmus |
| nōlīs | nōlītis | nollēs | nollētis |
| nōlit | nōlint | nollet | nollent |

### Imperative Mood

| nōlī | nōlīte |
|------|--------|

### Infinitives

| Present | **nolle** |
|---------|-----------|
| Perfect | **nōluisse** |

### Participle

| Present | **nōlens, nōlentis** |
|---------|----------------------|

**Nōlō** has no perfect participle and no future participle or infinitive. Its imperative is used with an infinitive to express a negative command (see Unit 9).

### exercise    10-19

*Translate these verbs into English.*

1. nōn vult _____

2. nōlent _____

3. nōluerit _____

4. nōn vīs _____

5. nōlēbam _____

6. nōluimus _____

7. nōlēs _____

8. nōlō _____

9. nōn vultis _____

10. nōluerant _____

### exercise    10-20

*Translate these verbs into English. Since there is no way to translate Latin subjunctive mood forms out of context, for the purpose of this exercise, translate them as if they were in the indicative mood.*

1. nōlītis _____

2. nollem _____

3. nōlīs _____

4. nollent _____

5. nōlīmus _____

6. nōluissent _____

7. nōlim _____

8. nollēmus _____

9. nollēs _____

10. nollētis _____

*Translate these verbs into Latin, using the indicative mood.*

1. he will not want _____
2. you (*sg.*) are not willing _____
3. we were not willing _____
4. you (*pl.*) had not been willing _____
5. they do not want _____

6. we will not have wanted _____
7. he is not willing _____
8. they will not want _____
9. you (*pl.*) are not willing _____
10. you (*pl.*) will not want _____

*Translate these verbs into Latin, using the subjunctive mood.*

1. you (*sg.*) do not want _____
2. they were not willing _____
3. we do not want _____
4. you (*sg.*) have not wanted _____
5. he is not willing _____

6. we were not wanting _____
7. I am not willing _____
8. he didn't used to want _____
9. you (*pl.*) were not willing _____
10. I had not wanted _____

*Translate these sentences into English.*

1. Marcus dormīre nōn vult. _____
2. Ego ōrātōrī audīre nōluī. _____
3. Exercitus montem ascendere nōlet. _____
4. Tūne epistulam legere nōn vīs? _____
5. Puerī pilā lūdere nōlunt. _____

| exercise | 10-24 |
|---|---|

*Write the appropriate form of **nōlō** in the tense indicated in parentheses, then translate the sentence into English.*

1. Ego tē occīdī _____ . (*present*) _____

2. Is corpus sepelīre _____ . (*perfect*) _____

3. Vōsne Rōmam quam prīmum īre _____ ? (*future*) _____

4. Ea tē canēs timēre _____ . (*present*) _____

5. Nautae fortēs ē proeliō effugere _____ . (*present*) _____

## mālō, malle, māluī *to want more, prefer*

**Mālō** is a contraction of the adverb **magis** *more* and the verb **volō** *to want, be willing.* In all forms of **volō** that begin **vo-**, the **vo-** changes to **mā-**. Unlike the compound **nōlō**, in the second- and third-person singular and the second-person plural forms in the present indicative of **mālō**, **mā-** serves as the prefix.

Since this verb involves a comparative form, it often appears with an ablative of comparison or a **quam** construction.

Haec illīs mālō.  or  Haec quam illa mālō.   *I want these more than those.*  or  *I prefer these over/to those.*

### Indicative Mood

| Present | | Imperfect | | Future | |
|---|---|---|---|---|---|
| mālō | mālumus | mālēbam | mālēbāmus | [mālam] | mālēmus |
| māvīs | māvultis | mālēbās | mālēbātis | [māles] | mālētis |
| māvult | mālunt | mālēbat | mālēbant | mālet | mālent |

Note: The forms in square brackets do not appear in classical literature. They are provided to fill out the chart.

### Subjunctive Mood

| Present | | Imperfect | |
|---|---|---|---|
| mālim | mālīmus | mallem | mallēmus |
| mālīs | mālītis | mallēs | mallētis |
| mālit | mālint | mallet | mallent |

### Infinitives

Present **malle**
Perfect **māluisse**

**Mālō** has no participles, no future infinitive, and no imperative forms.

exercise **10-25**

*Translate these verbs into English.*

1. māvultis _____
2. mālet _____
3. mālēbāmus _____
4. mālunt _____
5. malēs _____

6. māluit _____
7. mālent _____
8. mālam _____
9. mālumus _____
10. māluerās _____

exercise **10-26**

*Translate these verbs into English. Since there is no way to translate Latin subjunctive mood forms out of context, for the purpose of this exercise, translate them as if they were in the indicative mood.*

1. mālītis _____
2. mallent _____
3. mālim _____
4. mallēmus _____
5. mallet _____

6. mālīs _____
7. māluerīs _____
8. mālint _____
9. mālit _____
10. māluissēmus _____

exercise **10-27**

*Translate these verbs into Latin, using the indicative mood.*

1. they will prefer _____
2. I will prefer _____
3. he prefers _____
4. I prefer _____
5. we preferred (*perfect*) _____

6. you (*sg.*) will prefer _____
7. I have preferred _____
8. they used to prefer _____
9. he will prefer _____
10. we had preferred _____

**exercise    10-28**

*Translate these verbs into Latin, using the subjunctive mood.*

1. you (*sg.*) prefer _____

2. I prefer _____

3. he used to prefer _____

4. they prefer _____

5. you (*pl.*) used to prefer _____

6. he prefers _____

7. they had preferred _____

8. we prefer _____

9. they have preferred _____

10. you (*sg.*) used to prefer _____

**exercise    10-29**

*Translate these sentences into English.*

1. Mālō illud legere. _____

2. Cornēlia virō bonō nūbere mālet. _____

3. Trimalchiō hoc vīnum quam illud māvult. _____

4. Vōsne dē amīcīs vestrīs nescīre māluistis? _____

5. Eī labōrāre quam cessāre mālēbant. _____

**exercise    10-30**

*Write the appropriate form of* **mālō** *in the tense indicated in parentheses, then translate the sentence into English.*

1. Ego manēre quam exīre _____ . (*future*)

   _____

2. Aenēās in Ītaliam nāvigāre _____ . (*perfect*)

   _____

3. Mālī ōdisse quam amāre _____ . (*present*)

   _____

4. Is domī manēre _____ . (*imperfect*)

_____

5. Cūr tū meī oblīviscī _____ . (*perfect*)

_____

# eō, īre, iī/īvī, itum *to go*

The verb **eō** *to go* is so tiny that it resembles an ending without a stem. Perhaps for this reason, it is usually found with a prefix. Here is a list of the most common compounds of **eō**.

| | |
|---|---|
| **abeō, abīre, abiī/abīvī, abitum** | *to go away* |
| **adeō, adīre, adiī, aditum** | *to go to, approach* |
| **exeō, exīre, exiī/exīvī, exitum** | *to go out, end* |
| **obeō, obīre, obiī/obīvī, obitum** | *to meet; die* |
| **pereō, perīre, periī/perīvī, peritum** | *to die; go through; be lost* |
| **redeō, redīre, rediī, reditum** | *to go back, return* |

The first/second-conjugation future forms are peculiar, given how the present infinitive **īre** appears to belong to the fourth conjugation.

## Indicative Mood

| Present | | Imperfect | | Future | |
|---|---|---|---|---|---|
| eō | īmus | ībam | ībāmus | ībō | ībimus |
| īs | ītis | ībās | ībātis | ībis | ībitis |
| it | eunt | ībat | ībant | ībit | ībunt |

## Subjunctive Mood

| Present | | Imperfect | |
|---|---|---|---|
| eam | eāmus | īrem | īrēmus |
| eās | eātis | īrēs | īrētis |
| eat | eant | īret | īrent |

## Imperative Mood

| | |
|---|---|
| ī | īte |

## Infinitives

| | |
|---|---|
| Present | **īre** |
| Perfect | **isse** |
| Future | **itūrus esse** |

## Participles

| | |
|---|---|
| Present | **iens, euntis** |
| Future | **itūrus** |
| Gerund | **eundī, eundō**, etc. |
| Gerundive | **eundus, -a, -um** |

There are also third-person singular passive forms for all the tenses (for example, **ītur** and **ībātur**); these forms are used in an impersonal sense.

---

**exercise    10-31**

*Translate these verbs into English.*

1. eunt _____

2. ībīs _____

3. ītis _____

4. abībātis _____

5. īmus _____

6. redit _____

7. exībō _____

8. ībāmus _____

9. adistis _____

10. īvērunt _____

11. perībant _____

12. īverāmus _____

13. eō _____

14. adieritis _____

15. it _____

---

**exercise    10-32**

*Translate these verbs into English. Since there is no way to translate Latin subjunctive mood forms out of context, for the purpose of this exercise, translate them as if they were in the indicative mood.*

1. eātis _____

2. exeam _____

3. īrēs _____

4. redeat _____

5. obeāmus _____

6. īrem _____

7. abeās _____

8. pereant _____

9. īrēmus _____

10. adīrem _____

11. eant _____

12. redīret _____

13. peream _____

14. abeant _____

15. īrētis _____

## exercise 10-33

*Translate these verbs into Latin, using the indicative mood.*

1. he was going _____

2. I was returning _____

3. they are going _____

4. you (*pl.*) are approaching _____

5. you (*sg.*) are going _____

6. he died _____

7. we are going away _____

8. they will go _____

9. I will meet _____

10. we will have approached _____

## exercise 10-34

*Translate these verbs into Latin, using the subjunctive mood.*

1. he is going _____

2. I was going _____

3. you (*pl.*) are going out _____

4. you (*sg.*) were going _____

5. we are returning _____

6. I am going away _____

7. they are going _____

8. we were dying (**perīre**) _____

9. you (*pl.*) are going _____

10. I am meeting _____

## exercise 10-35

*Translate these sentences into English.*

1. Nunc mīlitēs Rōmam redeunt. _____

2. Caesar in Galliam iit. _____

3. Ego tēcum in proelium eō! _____

4. Perī! _____

5. Ab urbe abībant. _____

**exercise    10-36**

*Write the appropriate form of the verb in parentheses, using the tense indicated, then translate the sentence into English.*

1. Mūs sub mensam _____ . (īre, *present*)

   _____

2. Senēs ad forum mēcum crās _____ . (adīre, *future*)

   _____

3. Vōsne ad castra nōbiscum _____ ? (redīre, *imperfect*)

   _____

4. Ubi tū domum _____ ? (redīre, *perfect*)

   _____

5. Agricola in agrum cum servīs _____ . (īre, *present*)

   _____

## ferō, ferre, tulī, lātum *to bring, carry, bear*

**Ferō** shows its irregularity by lacking a theme vowel in a few forms in the present indicative active and passive, in the present infinitive, and in the imperative. Otherwise, **ferō** conjugates like a regular third-conjugation verb. All perfect-system tenses conjugate normally.

### Indicative Mood Active

| Present | | Imperfect | | Future | |
| --- | --- | --- | --- | --- | --- |
| ferō | ferimus | ferēbam | ferēbāmus | feram | ferēmus |
| fers | fertis | ferēbās | ferēbātis | ferēs | ferētis |
| fert | ferunt | ferēbat | ferēbant | feret | ferent |

### Indicative Mood Passive

| Present | | Imperfect | | Future | |
| --- | --- | --- | --- | --- | --- |
| feror | ferimur | ferēbar | ferēbāmur | ferar | ferēmur |
| ferris | feriminī | ferēbāris | ferēbāminī | ferēris | ferēminī |
| fertur | feruntur | ferēbātur | ferēbantur | ferētur | ferentur |

## Subjunctive Mood Active

| Present | | Imperfect | |
|---|---|---|---|
| feram | ferāmus | ferrem | ferrēmus |
| ferās | ferātis | ferrēs | ferrētis |
| ferat | ferant | ferret | ferrent |

## Subjunctive Mood Passive

| Present | | Imperfect | |
|---|---|---|---|
| ferar | ferāmur | ferrer | ferrēmur |
| ferāris | ferāminī | ferrēris | ferrēminī |
| ferātur | ferantur | ferrētur | ferrentur |

## Imperative

fer    ferte

## Infinitives

| | Active | Passive |
|---|---|---|
| Present | ferre | ferrī |
| Perfect | tulisse | lātus esse |
| Future | lātūrus esse | lātum īrī |

## Participles

| | |
|---|---|
| Present | ferens, ferentis |
| Perfect | lātus, -a, -um |
| Future | lātūrus, -a, -um |
| Gerund | ferendī, ferendō, *etc.* |
| Gerundive | ferendus, -a, -um |

## exercise 10-37

*Translate these verbs into English.*

1. ferunt _____
2. fertur _____
3. feram _____
4. ferēbātis _____
5. ferēbāminī _____
6. ferar _____
7. ferre _____
8. ferent _____
9. fertis _____
10. ferēbar _____

| exercise | 10-38 |

*Translate these verbs into English. Since there is no way to translate Latin subjunctive mood forms out of context, for the purpose of this exercise, translate them as if they were in the indicative mood.*

1. ferās _____

2. ferrent _____

3. ferar _____

4. ferātis _____

5. ferret _____

6. ferāminī _____

7. ferrem _____

8. ferat _____

9. ferrēminī _____

10. ferāris _____

| exercise | 10-39 |

*Translate these verbs into Latin, using the indicative mood.*

1. he is bringing _____

2. you (*pl.*) will carry _____

3. you (*pl.*) brought _____

4. he will be carried _____

5. I am being carried _____

6. they will be carried _____

7. to be brought _____

8. you (*pl.*) are carrying _____

9. we will be carried _____

10. they are being carried _____

| exercise | 10-40 |

*Translate these verbs into Latin, using the subjunctive mood.*

1. you (*sg.*) are being carried _____

2. they were bringing _____

3. we are carrying _____

4. you (*pl.*) were carrying _____

5. you (*sg.*) are bringing _____

6. he was being carried _____

7. you (*pl.*) are being carried _____

8. I was being carried _____

9. he was carrying _____

10. we were bringing _____

## exercise 10-41

*Translate these sentences into English.*

1. Agricola māla fert. _____

2. Nōs librōs tuōs domum ferēmus. _____

3. Mīlitēs nāvibus feruntur. _____

4. Haec puella flōrem ferēbat. _____

5. Cibus ā mē ferētur. _____

## exercise 10-42

*Write the appropriate form of **ferō** in the tense indicated in parentheses, then translate the sentence into English.*

1. Nōs ossa eius _____ . (*imperfect active*) _____

2. Ego lapidēs ex agrō _____ . (*present active*) _____

3. Mensa ā nōbīs _____ . (*future passive*) _____

4. Exercitus arma optima _____ . (*perfect active*) _____

5. Aqua ad urbem aquaeductibus _____ . (*perfect passive*) _____

## fīō, fierī, factus sum *to be, be made, be done, become; happen*

**Fīō** is easily the strangest, most confused verb in the Latin language. In the present system, it conjugates like a third-conjugation **-iō** verb and takes only active endings. The present infinitive, however, looks like a second-conjugation passive infinitive. In the perfect system, there are only passive forms, almost as if it were a semi-deponent. In addition to these form peculiarities, any of its forms can have an active meaning (for example, *to be, become,* or *happen*) or passive meaning (for example, *to be made, be done*). In fact, **fīō** serves as the passive voice for the verb **faciō** *to make, do.* The best way to treat this odd verb is to accept its forms as they are and think of its core meaning as *to come into being.* That is the central idea behind all the possible ways to translate it.

### Indicative Mood

| Present | | Imperfect | | Future | |
|---|---|---|---|---|---|
| fīō | [fīmus] | fīēbam | fīēbāmus | fīam | fīēmus |
| fīs | [fītis] | fīēbās | fīēbātis | fīēs | fīētis |
| fit | fīunt | fīēbat | fīēbant | fīet | fīent |

Note: The forms in square brackets do not appear in classical literature. They are provided to fill out the chart.

## Subjunctive Mood

| Present | | Imperfect | |
|---------|---------|---------|---------|
| fīam | fīāmus | fierem | fierēmus |
| fīās | fīātis | fierēs | fierētis |
| fīat | fīant | fieret | fierent |

### Infinitives

| Present | fierī |
|---------|-------|
| Perfect | factus esse |

### Participles

| Perfect | factus, -a, -um |
|---------|-----------------|
| Gerundive | faciendus, -a, -um |

---

**exercise 10-43**

*Translate these verbs into English.*

1. fit _____

2. fīēmus _____

3. fītis _____

4. fīam _____

5. fīēbant _____

---

**exercise 10-44**

*Translate these verbs into English. Since there is no way to translate Latin subjunctive mood forms out of context, for the purpose of this exercise, translate them as if they were in the indicative mood.*

1. fīāmus _____

2. fierem _____

3. fīat _____

4. fierent _____

5. fīās _____

| exercise | 10-45 |
|---|---|

*Translate these verbs into Latin, using the indicative mood.*

1.  it is made _____

2.  it will happen _____

3.  they were becoming _____

4.  you (*sg.*) were becoming _____

5.  I am being made _____

| exercise | 10-46 |
|---|---|

*Translate these verbs into Latin, using the subjunctive mood.*

1.  I was being made _____

2.  it is becoming _____

3.  we have become _____

4.  they are happening _____

5.  it was being made _____

| exercise | 10-47 |
|---|---|

*Translate these sentences into English.*

1.  Hoc ab illō fit. _____

2.  Puer ā cane fēlix fīet. _____

3.  Caecusne fīs? _____

4.  Stultī sāniōrēs fīent. _____

5.  Porcus obēsus fīēbat. _____

**exercise    10-48**

*Write the appropriate form of **fīō** in the tense indicated in parentheses, then translate the sentence into English.*

1. Caesar dictātor _____ . (*perfect*) _____

2. Hodiē fīlius meus vir _____ . (*present*) _____

3. Omnia haec mox _____ meliōra. (*future*) _____

4. Ego tristis _____ . (*imperfect*) _____

5. Mōs maiōrum mōs noster _____ . (*pluperfect*) _____

# Unit 11 | Participles

This unit reviews the present active, perfect passive, and future active participles, and offers suggestions for ways to translate participial phrases, including ablative absolute constructions. Exercises follow the reviews.

Participles are verbal adjectives. As verbs, active forms can take objects and passive forms can take an ablative of agent or means. As adjectives, they must agree with their reference noun in gender, case, and number. Latin has four participles: the present active, perfect passive, future active, and future passive. The future passive participle is most commonly known as the *gerundive* and will be treated in Unit 12.

Participles can also be used substantively. That is to say, any participle can appear without a noun, and the participle's gender and number agree with the implied noun. For example, **captī**, the perfect passive participle of **capiō** *to catch, take,* can mean *prisoners,* and the noun **hominēs** *people* may be understood since the form is masculine plural.

The names of the tenses of participles can be misleading, because the names are based on their formation, not their use. The tense of a main verb depends on the time of speaking. If I'm doing something right now as I am telling you about it, I use the present tense. If I've already done it, I use the perfect tense, and so on. But the tense value of participles (and of infinitives) is *relative* to the tense of the main verb. Participles refer to something that happens at the same time as, before, or after the action of the main verb. For example, a future participle with a main verb in the perfect could refer to something that happened after the main verb, even though the participle still refers to a past action.

Latin, being the economical language that it is, uses participles far more than English does.

## The Present Active Participle

### Use

The present participle denotes an action that is occurring at the same time as the main verb.

| | |
|---|---|
| Iūlia dormiens nihil audīvit. | *Julia, sleeping, heard nothing.* |

Julia was sleeping. At the same time that she was sleeping, she didn't hear anything. The sleeping occurred in the past, and so the present participle is considered to have occurred in the past too. These two facts imply several relationships between the two activities. These relationships pertain to all participial phrases and will be discussed later in this chapter.

The present participle is frequently used as a noun; as such, it represents a person who performs the action of the participle. For example, **interficiens** can mean *a killer*, and **monens** *an advisor*.

| | |
|---|---|
| Amans amantī verba amōris per rīmam in pariete dīcēbat. | *The lover used to express his words of love to his lover through a chink in the wall.* |

### Formation

The present participle is formed from the stem of the first principal part of a verb.

| | | |
|---|---|---|
| First conjugation | **amans** | *loving* |
| Second conjugation | **monens** | *warning* |
| Third conjugation | **dīcens** | *saying* |
| Third conjugation **-iō** | **rapiens** | *grabbing* |
| Fourth conjugation | **sentiens** | *feeling* |

It is declined like a third-declension adjective of one termination, with one exception: When it is being used as a noun, the regular noun ending **-e**, rather than **-ī**, appears in the ablative singular.

**videō, vidēre, vīdī, vīsum** *to see*

| | Masculine/Feminine | Neuter |
|---|---|---|
| **Singular** | | |
| Nominative | **videns** | **videns** |
| Genitive | **videntis** | **videntis** |
| Dative | **videntī** | **videntī** |
| Accusative | **videntem** | **videns** |
| Ablative | **videntī (vidente)** | **videntī (vidente)** |
| **Plural** | | |
| Nominative | **videntēs** | **videntia** |
| Genitive | **videntium** | **videntium** |
| Dative | **videntibus** | **videntibus** |
| Accusative | **videntēs** | **videntia** |
| Ablative | **videntibus** | **videntibus** |

## exercise  11-1

*Write the present participles for these verbs in the gender, case, and number specified, then translate them into English.*

EXAMPLE    ferō (*masc. acc. sg.*)    **_ferentem_**    **_bringing_**

1. augeō (*masc. nom. pl.*)  _____  _____

2. lābor (*neut. nom. pl.*)  _____  _____

3. habitō (*fem. acc. sg.*)  _____  _____

4. iaciō (*fem. abl. sg.*)  _____  _____

5. exuō (*fem. nom. pl.*)  _____  _____

6. nōlō (*masc. dat. sg.*)  _____  _____

7. perveniō (*neut. acc. sg.*)  _____  _____

8. ulciscor (*masc. acc. pl.*)  _____  _____

9. moveō (*masc. gen. pl.*)  _____  _____

10. taceō (*fem. abl. pl.*)  _____  _____

## exercise  11-2

*Identify all possible forms of these participles by gender, case, and number, then translate them into English.*

EXAMPLE    ferentem    _masc./fem. acc. sg._    **_bringing_**

1. currentibus  _____  _____

2. sequens  _____  _____

3. creantī  _____  _____

4. alentibus  _____  _____

5. conicientēs  _____  _____

6. confitens  _____  _____

7. sentientia  _____  _____

8. nascentis  _____  _____

9. nōlentium  _____  _____

10. rīdentem  _____  _____

# The Perfect Passive Participle

The perfect passive participle is the one most often seen, largely because it is used in all forms of the perfect passive tenses. It also occurs in participial phrases more than any other, especially in the ablative absolute construction.

## Use

Being *perfect*, the perfect participle denotes an action that is completed—that happened *before* the main verb.

> Servus captus verberātus est.          *The captured slave was beaten.*

First the slave was captured, then he was beaten.

## Formation

There are two traditions for listing the principal parts of a verb. One tradition lists the perfect passive participle as the fourth principal part; it can be recognized by its ending in **-us**. The other tradition—the one this book follows—uses the supine, which ends in **-um**.

**videō, vidēre, vīdī, vīs*us* to see**
**videō, vidēre, vīdī, vīs*um***

Whichever tradition is followed, the important thing is the stem to which the **-us** or **-um** is attached.

The perfect passive participle declines like a regular first/second-declension adjective.

**videō, vidēre, vīdī, vīsum *to see***

|  | Masculine | Feminine | Neuter |
| --- | --- | --- | --- |
| **Singular** | | | |
| Nominative | vīsus | vīsa | vīsum |
| Genitive | vīsī | vīsae | vīsī |
| Dative | vīsō | vīsae | vīsō |
| Accusative | vīsum | vīsam | vīsum |
| Ablative | vīsō | vīsā | vīsō |
| **Plural** | | | |
| Nominative | vīsī | vīsae | vīsa |
| Genitive | vīsōrum | vīsārum | vīsōrum |
| Dative | vīsīs | vīsīs | vīsīs |
| Accusative | vīsōs | vīsās | vīsa |
| Ablative | vīsīs | vīsīs | vīsīs |

| exercise | **11-3** |
|---|---|

*Write the perfect participles for these verbs in the gender, case, and number specified, then translate them into English.*

EXAMPLE   sentiō (*neut. nom. pl.*)   <u>**sensa**</u>   <u>*(having been) felt*</u>

1. cōgō (*neut. nom. sg.*)   _____   _____

2. doceō (*masc. abl. pl.*)   _____   _____

3. dīligō (*fem. gen. pl.*)   _____   _____

4. iubeō (*neut. acc. pl.*)   _____   _____

5. persuādeō (*masc. dat. pl.*)   _____   _____

6. crēdō (*neut. acc. sg.*)   _____   _____

7. laudō (*masc. acc. sg.*)   _____   _____

8. scindō (*fem. dat. sg.*)   _____   _____

9. incipiō (*fem. gen. sg.*)   _____   _____

10. iuvō (*neut. nom. pl.*)   _____   _____

| exercise | **11-4** |
|---|---|

*Identify all possible forms of these participles by gender, case, and number, then translate them into English.*

EXAMPLE   sensa   <u>*fem. nom. sg. / neut. nom./acc. pl.*</u>   <u>*(having been) felt*</u>

1. actīs   _____   _____

2. secūtus   _____   _____

3. creātum   _____   _____

4. recta   _____   _____

5. datō   _____   _____

6. dēbitus   _____   _____

7. positae   _____   _____

8. tectīs   _____   _____

9. tractōrum   _____   _____

10. clausam   _____   _____

## The Future Active Participle

In addition to a present participle (for example, **scrībens** *writing*) and a perfect participle (for example, **scriptus** *written*) like English has, Latin has a future participle (for example, **scriptūrus**), which has no English counterpart.

### Use

The future active participle denotes an action that occurs *after* the action of the main verb. Since English has no equivalent participle, it must be translated with a phrase such as *about to*, *going to*, or even *intending to*.

> Nōs moritūrī tē salūtāmus.        *We who are about to die salute you.*

When accompanied by the verb **sum**, the future participle can take the place of the future tense. This construction is called the active periphrastic.

> Rōmam sine tē itūrī sumus.        *We are going to go to Rome without you.*

### Formation

The future active participle is formed by adding **-ūrus** to the stem of the perfect passive participle.

script**us**     *written*
script**ūrus**     *about to write*

Like the perfect passive participle, the future active participle declines like a first/second-declension adjective.

## exercise    11-5

*Write the future participles for these verbs in the gender, case, and number specified, then translate them into English.*

EXAMPLE    sentiō (*fem. dat. sg.*)    <u>*sensūrae*</u>    <u>*about to feel*</u>

1. legō (*masc. nom. pl.*)    _____    _____

2. ūtor (*fem. nom. pl.*)    _____    _____

3. habitō (*fem. acc. sg.*)    _____    _____

4. iaciō (*masc. abl. sg.*)    _____    _____

5. claudō (*masc. nom. pl.*)    _____    _____

6. vetō (*neut. dat. sg.*)    _____    _____

7. mīror (*fem. acc. sg.*)    _____    _____

8. parcō (*masc. acc. pl.*) _____  _____

9. moveō (*masc. gen. pl.*) _____  _____

10. emō (*masc. abl. pl.*) _____  _____

| exercise | 11-6 |
| --- | --- |

*Identify all possible forms of these participles by gender, case, and number, then translate them into English.*

     EXAMPLE    sensūrae    *__fem. gen./dat. sg. / fem. nom. pl.__*    *__about to feel__*

1. inventūrīs _____  _____

2. volātūrum _____  _____

3. creātūra _____  _____

4. petītūrārum _____  _____

5. datūrus _____  _____

6. positūram _____  _____

7. audītūrō _____  _____

8. clausūrae _____  _____

9. hortātūrōrum _____  _____

10. factūrā _____  _____

## Participial Phrases

Latin makes far greater use of participial phrases than English does, which can make them rather challenging to translate. The best way to treat a participial phrase is to recognize it as a grammatical unit. The unit begins with a head noun and ends with a participle, which must agree with the noun in gender, case, and number.

    [Mūs perterritus] per culīnam cucurrit.    *The frightened mouse ran through the kitchen.*

If there is more information pertinent to the phrase, the head noun and participle bracket it like a sandwich.

    [Mūs ā fēle perterritus] per        *The mouse frightened by the cat ran through the*
    culīnam cucurrit.                       *kitchen.*

or as the Latin reads,

    [*The frightened by the cat mouse*] *ran through the kitchen.*

In this example, the head noun **mūs** is nominative singular, as is the participle **perterritus**, which agrees with it. They and what is sandwiched between them form a unit that acts as the subject of the entire sentence.

A participial phrase can be in any case and, as a unit, function as any simple noun might.

| | |
|---|---|
| Fēlēs fēlix [mūrem modo perterritum] comēdit. | *The lucky cat ate [the mouse just frightened].* |

In this example, the participial phrase unit functions as the direct object of **comēdit**, and so it is in the accusative case. You will notice, however, that the translation is a little awkward. The implied relationships between the participial phrase and its sentence offer different ways to translate it. These alternatives may involve extracting the phrase from the sentence, replacing it with a pronoun in the main clause or in a new clause, expanding the entire phrase into a clause, or linking it back to the main clause with a conjunction.

Fēlēs fēlix [mūrem modo perterritum] comēdit.

| | |
|---|---|
| Simple adjective | *The lucky cat ate [the mouse just frightened].* |
| Relative clause | *The lucky cat ate [the mouse **that** was just frightened].* |
| Causal clause | *The lucky cat ate [the mouse **because** it was just frightened].* |
| Temporal clause | *The lucky cat ate [the mouse **after** it had just been frightened].* |
| Coordinate clause | *[The mouse had just been frightened], **and** the lucky cat ate it.* |
| Concessive clause | *[**Although** the mouse had just been frightened], the lucky cat ate it.*   or |
| | *[The mouse had just been frightened], **but** the lucky cat ate it.* |

Three points need to be made about translating participial phrases. First, for any given sentence, not all of these approaches produce a clear English translation. The best translation depends on the translator's interpretation of the context of the passage. To an ancient Latin speaker, these were all possible interpretations.

Second, when translating a participial phrase as a temporal clause, one must remember the relative tense value of the participle. A present participle denotes an action happening *at the same time as* that of the main verb, a perfect participle *before*, and a future participle *after*, and one should translate accordingly.

Finally, when the *concessive* approach is used, the word **tamen** *nevertheless* often appears in the main clause.

| | |
|---|---|
| Fēlēs fēlix [mūrem modo perterritum] **tamen** comēdit. | *[The mouse had been frightened], **but** the lucky cat ate it **anyway**.* |

## exercise    11-7

*Bracket the participial phrases in these sentences, then translate the sentences, rendering the phrases by the simple adjective approach.*

1. Hostēs fugientēs persecūtī sunt. _____

_____

2. Rēgīna moriens deōs precāta est. _____

_____

3. Omnēs dūcem interfectum plōrāvērunt. _____

_____

4. Dē pecūniā āmissā nihil dīximus. _____

_____

5. Convīvae cēnam bene parātam laudābant. _____

_____

---

**exercise    11-8**

*Bracket the participial phrases in these sentences, then translate the sentences, rendering the phrases as relative clauses.*

1. Rēgīna moritūra deōs precāta est. _____

_____

2. Omnēs dūcem interfectum plōrāvērunt. _____

_____

3. Dē pecūniā āmissā nihil dīximus. _____

_____

4. Convīvae cēnam bene parātam laudābant. _____

_____

5. Ex aedificiō ardentī vix effūgī. _____

_____

---

**exercise    11-9**

*Bracket the participial phrases in these sentences, then translate the sentences, rendering the phrases as causal clauses.*

1. Rēgīna moritūra deōs precāta est. _____

_____

2. Omnēs dūcem interfectum plōrāvērunt. _____

_____

3.  Dē pecūniā āmissā nihil dīximus. _____

_____

4.  Convīvae cēnam bene parātam laudābant. _____

_____

5.  Ex aedificiō ardentī vix effūgī. _____

_____

| exercise | 11-10 |
| --- | --- |

*Bracket the participial phrases in these sentences, then translate the sentences, rendering the phrases as temporal clauses. Be mindful of the tense of the participle!*

1.  Hostēs fugientēs persecūtī sunt. _____

_____

2.  Omnēs dūcem moritūrum plōrāvērunt. _____

_____

3.  Dē pecūniā āmissā nihil dīximus. _____

_____

4.  Convīvae cēnam bene parātam laudābant. _____

_____

5.  Ex aedificiō ardentī vix effūgī. _____

_____

| exercise | 11-11 |
| --- | --- |

*Bracket the participial phrases in these sentences, then translate the sentences, rendering the phrases as coordinate clauses.*

1.  Dē pecūniā āmissā nihil dīximus. _____

_____

2.  Omnēs dūcem interfectum plōrāvērunt. _____

_____

3. Ex aedificiō ardentī vix effūgī. _____

_____

4. Convīvae cēnam bene parātam laudābant. _____

_____

5. Comitem tuum moritūrum in campō relīquistī. _____

_____

**exercise    11-12**

*Bracket the participial phrases in these sentences, then translate the sentences, rendering the phrases as concessive clauses.*

1. Mīles mortem metuens in proelium tamen festīnāvit. _____

_____

2. Dē pecūniā inventā nihil diximus. _____

_____

3. Convīvae cēnam male parātam tamen laudābant. _____

_____

4. In aedificium ardens celeriter cucurrī. _____

_____

5. Comitem tuum moritūrum in campō relīquistī. _____

_____

## The Ablative Absolute

The ablative absolute construction is a staple of the Latin language. It is a type of participial phrase consisting of a noun plus a participle—though a noun plus a noun or a noun plus an adjective will do—in the ablative, that is totally grammatically divorced from the main clause. Most participial phrases have specific functions in a sentence, such as subject, direct object, or any other element whose function a noun can perform.

The ablative absolute construction is unique. It presents background information in a telegraphic, almost newspaper-headline style. Unlike other participial phrases, it isn't grammatically part of a sentence, hence the name **ab-** (*from*) **-solute** (*released*).

**Gallīs victīs,** Caesar Rōmam profectus est.    *Gauls conquered, Caesar set out for Rome.*

A less awkward translation might be *Since the Gauls had been conquered, Caesar set out for Rome.*

Most of the strategies for translating participial phrases apply here as well, but since an ablative absolute construction is grammatically independent of the main clause, the relative-clause approach doesn't work. If you'd like to avoid a stilted, 19th-century Victorian rendition of an ablative absolute (as it is traditionally taught—for example, *With the Gauls having been conquered . . .*), avoid the *simple adjective* approach.

[Gallīs victīs], Caesar Rōmam profectus est.

| | |
|---|---|
| Simple adjective | [*The Gauls having been conquered*], *Caesar set out for Rome.* |
| Causal clause | [***Since** the Gauls had been conquered*], *Caesar set out for Rome.* |
| Temporal clause | [***After** the Gauls had been conquered*], *Caesar set out for Rome.* |
| Coordinate clause | [*The Gauls were conquered*], ***and** Caesar set out for Rome.* |
| Concessive clause | [***Although** the Gauls had been conquered*], *Caesar set out for Rome.* |

**exercise    11-13**

*Translate these sentences, rendering the ablative absolute phrases as causal clauses.*

1. Trōiā dēlētā, Graecī discessērunt. _____

_____

2. Principe senātōrēs in Cūriam revocantī, Marcus et Publius togās induērunt. _____

_____

3. Aeneā dē Trōiā narrātūrō, omnēs conticuērunt. _____

_____

4. Consiliō captō, gladiātor in arēnam ingressus est. _____

_____

5. Signō datō, turba clāmābit. _____

_____

## exercise 11-14

*Translate these sentences, rendering the ablative absolute phrases as temporal clauses. Be mindful of the tense of the participle!*

1. Trōiā dēlētā, Graecī discessērunt. _____

   _____

2. Principe senātōrēs in Cūriam revocantī, Marcus et Publius togās induērunt. _____

   _____

3. Aenēā dē Trōiā narrātūrō, omnēs conticuērunt. _____

   _____

4. Consiliō captō, gladiātor in arēnam ingressus est. _____

   _____

5. Signō datō, turba clāmābit. _____

   _____

## exercise 11-15

*Translate these sentences, rendering the ablative absolute phrases as coordinate clauses.*

1. Trōiā dēlētā, Graecī discessērunt. _____

   _____

2. Principe senātōrēs in Cūriam revocantī, Marcus et Publius togās induērunt. _____

   _____

3. Aenēā dē Trōiā narrātūrō, omnēs conticuērunt.

   _____

4. Consiliō captō, gladiātor in arēnam ingressus est.

   _____

5. Signō datō, turba clāmābit.

   _____

**exercise    11-16**

*Translate these sentences, rendering the ablative absolute phrases as concessive clauses.*

1. Diē nefastō, in forum tamen prōgrediēmur.

   _____

2. Trōiā dēlētā, Graecī manēbant.

   _____

3. Aenēā dē Trōiā narrātūrō, omnēs tamen cubitum iērunt.

   _____

4. Consiliō nullō captō, gladiātor tamen in arēnam ingressus est.

   _____

5. Signō datō, nēmō clāmābit.

   _____

# Unit 12

# Gerunds, Gerundives, and Supines

This unit reviews the use and formation of Latin's verbal nouns, the gerund (including the gerundive) and the supine, and provides exercises for each.

## Gerunds

The gerund is a verbal noun. In English, it ends in *-ing* and looks just like the present participle. Latin's gerund slightly resembles the present participle, but there are enough differences in use and formation that they can easily be distinguished.

### Use

As a noun, the gerund can be used in the same way as any other noun, except that—because there is no nominative form—it cannot serve as a subject. For that function in Latin, an infinitive is used. A gerund may be used to express purpose in two ways: (1) in the genitive with **grātiā** or **causā** (for example, **legendī causā** *in order to read*) or (2) in the accusative with the preposition **ad** (for example, **ad legendum** *in order to read*).

| | | |
|---|---|---|
| Nominative | — | — |
| Genitive | Cupidī **discendī** sumus. | *We are desirous of learning.* |
| Dative | Hoc idōneum **bibendō** nōn est. | *This is not suitable for drinking.* |
| Accusative | In silvam **ad vēnandum** vēnit. | *He came to the forest to go hunting.* |
| Ablative | Aegra est nimis **edendō**. | *She's ill from eating too much.* |

## Formation

The gerund is a second-declension neuter noun formed from the present stem of a verb. It appears only in the singular and has no nominative form.

|  | First | Second | Third | Third -iō | Fourth |
|---|---|---|---|---|---|
| Nominative | — | — | — | — | — |
| Genitive | amandī | monendī | discendī | capiendī | audiendī |
| Dative | amandō | monendō | discendō | capiendō | audiendō |
| Accusative | amandum | monendum | discendum | capiendum | audiendum |
| Ablative | amandō | monendō | discendō | capiendō | audiendō |

### exercise 12-1

*Translate the following gerunds and gerund phrases into English.*

1. pōnendī _____

2. narrandō (*dat.*) _____

3. ad vendendum _____

4. nāvigandī _____

5. audiendō (*abl.*) _____

6. ad quiescendum _____

7. inveniendō (*dat.*) _____

8. ad superandum _____

9. legendō (*dat.*) _____

10. mūtandī _____

### exercise 12-2

*Translate the following phrases into Latin gerunds, using the genitive case.*

1. of hanging _____

2. of growing _____

3. of pushing _____

4. of finding _____

5. of doing nothing _____

6. of destroying _____

7. of offering _____

8. of setting free _____

9. of sleeping _____

10. of finishing _____

### exercise 12-3

*Translate the following sentences into English.*

1. In cubiculum ad dormiendum it. _____

2. Hodiē ad pugnandum venit. _____

3. Ille rex aptus regnandō nōn erat. _____

4. Mīlitēs cupidī moriendī nōn sunt. _____

5. Rōmam ad habitandum redeō. _____

6. Cicerō perītus loquendō erat. _____

7. Dē labōrandō narrāre prōmittō. _____

8. Hūc ad audiendum vēnimus. _____

9. Docendō docēre discimus. _____

10. Ientāculum sine vīnō idōneum comedendō nōn est.

_____

## Gerundives

### Use

The Latin gerundive is actually the future passive participle, but it more commonly goes by the name *gerundive*. As a participle, it is a verbal adjective. It has two principal uses. One is a special relationship with gerunds, the other is in a construction known as the passive periphrastic.

### Formation

The gerundive declines like a first/second-declension adjective and is formed by adding **-ndus** to the present stem of a verb.

| | |
|---|---|
| First conjugation | **amandus, amanda, amandum** |
| Second conjugation | **monendus, monenda, monendum** |
| Third conjugation | **discendus, discenda, discendum** |
| Third conjugation **-iō** | **capiendus, capienda, capiendum** |
| Fourth conjugation | **audiendus, audienda, audiendum** |

### Gerundives and Gerunds Compared

Gerunds are verbal nouns and, as nouns, perform nearly every function that regular nouns do. As *verbal* nouns, however, they can also perform many verbal functions, such as taking objects. When this occurs, the gerundive comes into play to create a new construction.

A gerund takes the case appropriate to its use in a sentence.

In silvam **ad vēnandum** vēnit.          *He came to the forest **to go hunting**.*

Here, the gerund is neuter singular, because that's what all gerunds are. It's accusative, because the preposition **ad** takes the accusative. If an object is added, such as **aprōs** *boars*, the object keeps its number but takes the case required by the gerund's function, and the gerund changes to a gerundive to agree with whatever the object has become.

In silvam **ad aprōs vēnandōs** vēnit.          *He came to the forest **to go hunting boars**.*

Here, **aprōs** is masculine plural, because that's what boars are in Latin. It's accusative, because **ad** takes the accusative. The gerund **vēnandum** changes to the gerundive **vēnandōs**, masculine accusative plural, to agree in gender, case, and number with **aprōs**—which is what adjectives do.

Another way to look at this construction is that in Latin you don't go hunting boars, you go boar hunting, and you don't get your news by reading the paper, you get your news by paper reading.

| exercise | 12-4 |
|---|---|

*Translate the following sentences into English.*

1. In forum ad magistrātūs creandōs pervēnerant.

_____

2. Exeō ad hominēs terrendōs.

_____

3. Publius ad pecūniam habendam labōrābit.

_____

4. Hīc ad hostēs necandōs manēmus.

_____

5. Aprum ad eum occidendum percussit.

_____

6. Vōsne ad togās vestrās induendās properātis?

_____

7. Caesar nōmina mīlitum ad eōs laudandōs nuntiāvit.

_____

8. Ad illōs dē ōminibus monendōs properāvī.

_____

9. Ad hominēs lūdendōs stultus esse simulat.

_____

10. Servī ad librōs transcrībendōs vocābuntur.

_____

## The Passive Periphrastic

The gerundive may also carry a connotation of necessity or obligation. Several Latin gerundives with this connotation have come into English as words in general use. The word **memorandum**, for example, is *a thing that must be remembered*, from the Latin verb **memorō** *to call to mind*. Another common gerundive is **agenda** *things that must be done*, from **agō** *to do*.

When used with a form of the verb **sum**, the gerundive creates a construction called the passive periphrastic. The word *periphrastic* is from Greek, meaning *around-talking*, or in other words, beating around the bush. Rather than directly saying *You must eat your asparagus*, Latin takes the long way around.

    Asparagus tibi edendus est.                *The asparagus must be eaten by you.*

Also of note in this construction is the use of the dative to show the agent of the action.

---

### exercise    12-5

*Translate these sentences into English.*

1. Plaustra māne oneranda erunt. _____

2. Amīcī impiī tibi āmittendī sunt. _____

3. Salūs nōbīs omnibus quaerenda est. _____

4. Infantēs alendī sunt. _____

5. Castra nōbīs dēfendenda erant. _____

---

## The Supine

The supine is another type of verbal noun, but with very limited uses. In one tradition for listing the principal parts of a verb, such as the one used in this book, it appears as the fourth principal part. The other tradition uses the perfect passive participle. Either way, the verb stem is the same.

The supine is a fourth-declension noun with only two forms, accusative and ablative singular, each of which has only one use.

The accusative is used with verbs of motion to express purpose.

    In silvam aprōs **vēnātum** vēnit.          *He came to the forest **to hunt** boars.*

The ablative is restricted to the ablative of respect.

    mirābile **dictū**                          *amazing **to tell** or (literally) amazing **with**
                                                **respect to the telling***

**exercise     12-6**

*Translate these sentences into English.*

1. In turbam sē cēlātum effūgit. _____

2. Omnia in pompā mīrābilia spectātū fuerant. _____

3. Ille cognitū hilaris erat. _____

4. Quis hūc quaesītum veniēt? _____

5. In bibliothēcam lectum iī. _____

# Infinitives

This unit reviews the formation of all infinitives and three of the four uses they have in Latin. The fourth use, indirect statement, is treated in Unit 14. Exercises offer opportunities to practice formation and translation, as well as recognition, of complementary, subjective, and objective infinitive constructions.

## Formation

In Latin, infinitives have three tenses (present, perfect, and future) and two voices (active and passive), and they are formed in rather predictable ways.

The *present active infinitive* serves as the second principal part of a verb's dictionary listing. It is the criterion by which verbs are classed in conjugations. To form the *present passive infinitive*, the final short **e** of the present active infinitive changes to a long **ī**. In the case of third-conjugation verbs, the whole ending (essentially a short **e**) changes to a long **ī**.

|  | Active |  | Passive |  |
|---|---|---|---|---|
| First conjugation | **amāre** | *to love* | **amārī** | *to be loved* |
| Second conjugation | **monēre** | *to warn* | **monērī** | *to be warned* |
| Third conjugation | **dīcere** | *to say* | **dīcī** | *to be said* |
| Third conjugation **-iō** | **capere** | *to take* | **capī** | *to be taken* |
| Fourth conjugation | **audīre** | *to hear* | **audīrī** | *to be heard* |

Perfect infinitives are formed in the same way for all conjugations, as well as for irregular verbs. The *perfect active infinitive* form uses the perfect active stem (the third principal part minus the **-ī** ending) and adds the ending **-isse**.

**necō, necāre, necāvī, necātum** *to kill*
**necāv**isse                                          *to have killed*

All perfect passive tenses are formed with the perfect passive participle plus a form of **sum**, and so it makes sense that the *perfect passive infinitive* uses the perfect passive participle with the infinitive of **sum**.

**necātus** *esse*                                     *to have been killed*

It must be remembered that the participle in this construction is still a participle and must agree in gender, case, and number with the noun it is referring to. For example, if the subject of the infinitive above were a feminine accusative plural noun, the infinitive would be **necātās esse**.

The *future active infinitive* is also created by using **esse** with a participle, in this case, the future active participle.

**necātūrus** *esse*                                   *to be about to kill*

Note the following points:

- The future active infinitive is often seen without **esse**, so **necātūrus esse** and **necātūrus** can mean the same thing. You can tell whether the participle or the infinitive is intended by the construction.

- The future active infinitive of **sum**, **futūrus esse**, is often seen in the contracted form **fore**. This unusual infinitive can be used with a personal ending to form the imperfect subjunctive of **sum**, so **forem** is the same as **essem**, and so on, with no difference in use or meaning.

- As with the perfect participle in the perfect passive infinitive, the future active participle must agree with the noun it refers to.

The *future passive infinitive* is quite uncommon. It is formed by pairing the supine in **-um** with the word **īrī**, which is the present passive infinitive of the irregular verb **eō**.

**necātum īrī**                                        *to be about to be killed*

---

**exercise    13-1**

*Translate these infinitives into English.*

1. implērī _____
2. contulisse _____
3. revocātūrus esse _____
4. pollicitus esse _____
5. sinere _____
6. pāruisse _____
7. fīnīrī _____
8. servīre _____
9. reversus esse _____
10. instructum īrī _____

**exercise     13-2**

*Translate these infinitives into Latin.*

1. to be set free _____

2. to deserve _____

3. to have lost _____

4. to prefer _____

5. to be about to be opened _____

6. to be handed over _____

7. to encourage _____

8. to embrace _____

9. to have been heard _____

10. to be about to attack (**aggredī**) _____

## Use

Infinitives are verb forms that convey the basic meaning of a verb. In English, they are usually preceded by the word *to*, as in *to walk, to find, to cook*. The word *infinitive* itself comes from the Latin **in-** (*not*) and **fīnis** (*limit*), because they are not limited by person or number. They do, however, have tense and voice.

The voices, as may be expected, are active and passive. For Latin infinitives, there are three tenses—present, perfect, and future—just as for participles. Also like participles, the tense value of an infinitive is relative to the main verb. A present infinitive denotes an action happening at the same time as that of the main verb, the perfect infinitive denotes an action already completed before that of the main verb, and the future infinitive denotes an action after that of the main verb.

Latin infinitives have four uses: complementary, subjective, objective, and indirect statement. (Indirect statement is the topic of Unit 14.)

### The Complementary Infinitive

Some verbs, such as **possum** and **volō**, depending on how they are being used, need an infinitive to complete the thought being expressed. This usage is called complementary because it *completes* the thought of the main verb.

| | |
|---|---|
| **Nāre** nōn possum. | *I am not able **to swim**.* or *I can't **swim**.* |
| Vīsne mēcum Capuam **īre**? | *Do you want **to go** to Capua with me?* |

Notice in these examples how the infinitive and main verb work together to express a single thought. Also notice how in each sentence both verbs refer to the same subject. In the first sentence, both ability and swimming pertain to the subject *I*. In the second sentence, desire and going both refer to the subject *you*. This feature is the key to recognizing a complementary infinitive.

| exercise | 13-3 |
|----------|------|

*Translate these sentences into English.*

1. Eō diē domī remanēre constituistis. _____

2. Hodiē proficiscī in animō habuimus. _____

3. Iūlia Rōmam regredī nōn vult. _____

4. Illā nocte mīlia stellārum vidēre poteram. _____

5. Discēdere dum possumus dēbēmus. _____

## The Subjective Infinitive

As the name implies, an infinitive used as the subject of a sentence is called a *subjective* infinitive. Subject is the only "noun" role an infinitive can play. All other noun roles are played by the gerund, which has no nominative. The following example is a famous use of a subjective infinitive. Notice how, for agreement purposes, infinitives are considered neuter.

> **Errāre** est hūmānum.                **To err** is human.

Subjective infinitives are most commonly found with impersonal verbs, that is, verbs that occur only in the third-person singular and have no real subject (for example, *it's raining* in English). Some impersonal verbs use infinitives as subjects. Here is a list of such verbs in Latin that are often found with infinitives.

> **decet (with an accusative object)** *it is proper, it suits*
> Tē mēcum manēre decet.        *It is proper for you to stay with me.* or *Staying with me is the right thing to do.*

> **iuvat (with an accusative object)** *it is pleasing*
> Ōlim et haec meminisse iuvābit.        *Someday even this will be pleasing to remember.* or *And you think* this *is bad?!*

> **libet (with a dative object)** *it is pleasing*
> Cēnāre apud tē mihi libet.        *It is pleasing to me to dine at your house.* (i.e., *I enjoy dining at your house.*)

> **licet (with a dative object)** *it is allowed*
> Mihi in Cūriam intrāre licet.        *It is allowed for me to enter the Senate House.* (i.e., *They let me in the Senate House.*)

> **necesse est (with a dative object)** *it is necessary*
> Tibi mē adiuvāre necesse fuit.        *It was necessary for you to help me.* (i.e., *You had to help me.*)

> **oportet (with an accusative object)** *one should*
> Tē mēcum venîre oportet.        *You should come with me.*

**opus est (with a dative object)** *there is need*

Tibi mē adiuvāre opus est.

*There is need for you to help me.* (i.e., *I need you to help me.*)

**placet (with a dative object)** *it is pleasing*

Cēnāre apud tē mihi placet.

*It is pleasing to me to dine at your house.* (i.e., *I enjoy dining at your house.*)

**exercise    13-4**

*Translate these sentences into English.*

1. Magnam classem construere opus fuit.

_____

2. Tē sīc ineptīre nōn decet.

_____

3. Apud mē pernoctāre tē oportēbit.

_____

4. Urbem relinquere aestāte illīs placēbat.

_____

5. Oppidum mūnīre statim necesse erit.

_____

**The Objective Infinitive**

The objective infinitive is used much like the complementary infinitive, except that only the main verb in a sentence refers to the subject; the infinitive refers to the direct object of the main verb.

Māter fīliam suam **legere** docuit.

*The mother taught her daughter **to read**.*

Here, **māter** *the mother* (subject) **docuit** *taught* (main verb) **fīliam suam** *her daughter* (direct object), and it's her daughter who was then able **legere** *to read* (infinitive). In other words, the mother did the teaching and the daughter did the reading. The two verbs refer to two different people. Since the infinitive refers to the object, this use is called *objective*.

**exercise    13-5**

*Identify the type of infinitive used in each sentence, then translate the sentence into English.*

> EXAMPLE    Tēcum Capuam īre volō.    *__complementary__*
> *__I want to go to Capua with you.__*

1. Mihi licet rogāre? _____

   _____

2. Mox mihi dormīre libēbit. _____

   _____

3. Pater vōs in illam silvam ingredī vetuit. _____

   _____

4. Decimā hōrā castra pōnere cōnstituērunt. _____

   _____

5. Advenīre ante secundam hōram nōn poterant. _____

   _____

6. Nec sine tē vīvere possum nec tēcum. _____

   _____

7. Tēcum vītam meam agere mālō. _____

   _____

8. Dux equitēs equōs tenēre iussit. _____

   _____

9. Tum lūna clārius lūcēre vidēbātur. _____

   _____

10. Istī scelestō crēdere dubitō. _____

   _____

# Unit 14

# Indirect Statement

If Mark *directly* tells you, "The dog is in the garden," then you report what Mark said to Paul, "Mark says that the dog is in the garden," Paul will have learned what Mark said *indirectly*. This is indirect statement. In English, the construction is straightforward: Two clauses are joined by the conjunction *that*.

Direct statement       *The dog is in the garden.*

Indirect statement     *Mark says **that** the dog is in the garden.*

In Latin, the construction is very different. Instead of simply linking the main clause to a repetition of what was said, Latin converts what was said to an infinitive phrase.

Direct statement       Canis in hortō est.

Indirect statement     Marcus **canem in hortō esse** dīcit.

Notice how the main verb of the original quotation, **est**, changes to the infinitive **esse**. Since subjects of infinitives are always in the accusative case, there is also a case change: The nominative **canis** in the original changes to the accusative **canem**. It might make more sense if you think of the resulting infinitive phrase functioning essentially as a long direct object.

| **Marcus** | **[canem in hortō esse]** | **dīcit.** |
|---|---|---|
| Subject | Object | Main verb |

All forms of indirect discourse, including indirect questions and indirect commands, are introduced by a verb of saying, thinking, knowing, or perceiving. Here is a list of the most common ones.

| Saying | Thinking | Knowing | Perceiving |
|---|---|---|---|
| **dīcō** *to say* | **crēdō** *to believe* | **intellegō** *to understand* | **audiō** *to hear* |
| **doceō** *to teach* | **existimō** *to think* | **nesciō** *not to know* | **sentiō** *to feel* |
| **narrō** *to tell* | **putō** *to think* | **noscō** *to learn* | **videō** *to see* |
| **negō** *to deny* | **spērō** *to hope* | **sciō** *to know* | |
| **nuntiō** *to announce* | | | |
| **scrībō** *to write* | | | |

None of these verbs necessarily introduces an indirect statement; consider, for instance, the complete sentence **Videō canem.** *I see a dog.* When they do introduce an indirect statement, however, the object will be an infinitive phrase, as in the earlier example.

Here is a formula for an indirect statement construction.

Main verb of    saying    +    accusative subject    +    other information    +    infinitive

thinking

knowing

perceiving

**Sciō canem in hortō esse.**                *I know that the dog is in the garden.*

Reflexive pronouns have an important role in the construction of an indirect statement. In the English sentence *Marcus says that he loves you,* who is *he*? Marcus or someone else? Latin makes this distinction clear. When the subject of the indirect statement is the same as the subject of the main verb, the reflexive pronoun is used.

Marcus **sē** tē amāre dīcit.          *Marcus says that **he** (Marcus) loves you.*
Marcus **eum** tē amāre dīcit.          *Marcus says that **he** (some other male) loves you.*

The same rule applies to the use of reflexive possessive adjectives.

Gāius sē canem **suum** amāre dīcit.          *Gaius says that he (Gaius) loves **his** (own) dog.*
· Gāius sē canem **eius** amāre dīcit.          *Gaius says that he (Gaius) loves **his** (someone else's) dog.*

## exercise 14-1

*Translate these sentences into English.*

1. Spērō ancillās trīclīnium dīligenter purgāre.

   _____

2. Negat Marcum Rōmam iter facere.

   _____

3. Quis tē linguam Latīnam legere docet?

   _____

4. Vidēs comitem meum in hortō sedēre.

   _____

5. Scīsne fīliam ā matre domum vocārī?

   _____

6. Audiunt illum in urbe nōn iam esse.

   _____

7. Sciō tē saepe tacēre et nihil dīcere.

   _____

8. Existimāmus consulem errāre.

   _____

9. Crēdō flōrēs mihi legī.

   _____

10. Negat sē canēs timēre.

    _____

The tense value of infinitives is relative. A present infinitive refers to an action happening *at the same time as* that of the main verb, whatever the tense of the main verb may be.

| | |
|---|---|
| **Sciō** canem in hortō **esse.** | *I know* that the dog **is** in the garden. |
| **Sciēbam** canem in hortō **esse.** | *I knew* that the dog **was** in the garden. |
| **Sciam** canem in hortō **esse.** | *I will know* that the dog **will be** in the garden. |

## exercise    14-2

*Translate these sentences into English.*

1. Eum adiuvārī putābam.

   _____

2. Cūr nōs amīcōs nōn iam esse nuntiāvistī?

   _____

3. Servōs villam cūrāre mihi scripsit.

   _____

4. Senātōrēs sē errāre negābunt.

   _____

5. Perīculum haud procul cēlārī senserat.

   _____

6. Hostēs ad urbem accēdere nōn posse spērāmus.

   _____

7. Mē stultum esse existimābant.

   _____

8. Nōs omnēs hīc manēre intellegit.

   _____

9. Duo canēs in lectō sēcum dormīre dīcēbat.

   _____

10. Matrem tuam mūrēs metuere audīvimus.

   _____

Likewise, a perfect infinitive denotes an action that had happened *before* the action of the main verb.

| | |
|---|---|
| **Sciō** canem in hortō **fuisse.** | *I know* that the dog **was** *in the garden.* |
| **Sciēbam** canem in hortō **fuisse.** | *I knew* that the dog **had been** *in the garden.* |
| **Sciam** canem in hortō **fuisse.** | *I will know* that the dog **has been** *in the garden.* |

| exercise | 14-3 |
|----------|------|

*Translate these sentences into English.*

1. Eōs dōna nostra recēpisse nescīs.

   _____

2. Gladiātōrem gladium in mediā pugnā āmīsisse narrābant.

   _____

3. Iūliam fīliōs geminōs peperisse nōvī.

   _____

4. Illum bene vixisse dīcētur.

   _____

5. Rem constitūtam nōn esse intelleximus.

   _____

6. Publium amīcōs suōs ad theatrum secūtum esse crēdunt.

   _____

7. Mīlitēs duābus modo hōrīs illud proelium confēcisse scripsit.

   _____

8. Sē satis pecūniae vix habuisse dīcent.

   _____

9. Turrim fulgōre percussam esse vīdistis.

   _____

10. Mē nōn intellectum esse sentiō.

    _____

A future infinitive denotes an action happening *after* that of the main verb; this can be tricky to translate.

**Sciō** canem in hortō **futūrum esse**.    *I know* that the dog *will be* in the garden.
**Sciēbam** canem in hortō **futūrum esse**.    *I knew* that the dog *would be* in the garden.
**Sciam** canem in hortō **futūrum esse**.    *I will know* that the dog *will be* in the garden.

<table>
<tr><td>**exercise**</td><td>**14-4**</td></tr>
</table>

*Translate these sentences into English.*

1. Vōs hīc fore nesciēbant.

_____

2. Omnēs servōs in agrīs tōtam noctem labōrātūrōs esse vidēbitis.

_____

3. Nōs lūdum nostrum fīnītūrōs spērō.

_____

4. Tē fratrem tuum in Viā Appiā sepultūrum esse putāvimus.

_____

5. Caesarem castra celerrimē positūrum spērāvērunt.

_____

<table>
<tr><td>**exercise**</td><td>**14-5**</td></tr>
</table>

*Translate these sentences into English.*

1. Mē paucōs amīcōs vērōs habēre intellexī.

_____

2. Eum Messallae iamdūdum servītūrum scīvistī.

_____

3. Sē dolōrem nostrum sentīre scripsit.

_____

4. Custōdēs ā nullō custōdītōs esse audīmus.

_____

5. Nōs domum ambulāre vīderātis.

_____

6. Eōs iam profectōs esse nesciēs.

   _____

7. Rēgem morī negābat iterum iterumque Tanaquil.

   _____

8. Patrem puerōs propter pecūniam perditam pūnītūrum putāvī.

   _____

9. Narrā id quod tibi iuvenī accidisse.

   _____

10. Eum avēs volāre nōn nāre solēre docuit.

   _____

# The Subjunctive Mood

This unit reviews all subjunctive forms and provides exercises for practice with them. The various uses of the subjunctive are treated in the units that follow.

In grammar, the term *mood* refers to the way a speaker treats an action. A verb in the *indicative* mood expresses an action as a fact, while one in the *imperative* mood expresses an action as a command. The *subjunctive* mood expresses an action as an idea or wish.

The subjunctive mood exists in English, but in only a few, very restricted ways. For example, in the sentence *I demand that you be here by noon*, the subjunctive *be* replaces the indicative *are* because the action is being treated as a wish, not a fact. To say you *are* is to say that you in fact are, but that's not the case here—it's just a wish on my part as the speaker. Likewise, English uses the expression *If I were you . . .*, not *I was* or *I am*. Since I'm not you, the English past subjunctive form *were* is used.

The Latin subjunctive is used in an amazing number of ways for which English uses completely different grammatical constructions. In fact, given any random page of Latin literature, as many subjunctive forms might appear as indicative ones, and in ways that express nuance that can't help but be lost in translation. For this reason, Latin subjunctive forms are extremely important to know!

## The Present Subjunctive, Active and Passive

Like present indicative forms, the forms of the present subjunctive vary across the conjugations, but thankfully not so radically. If you are familiar with the conjugation to which a verb belongs, the easiest way to recognize the present subjunctive is by the appearance of an unexpected vowel. For a first-conjugation verb, whose theme vowel is **a**, there suddenly appears an **e**. For second-, third-, and fourth-conjugation verbs, an unexpected **a** appears. Personal endings remain understandable and predictable. An easy way to remember how to form the present subjunctive is to change the **ō** of the first principal part to **e** for first-conjugation verbs; for other verbs, change the **ō** to **a**. The verbs **sum** and **volō**, and their compounds, are irregular. They can be easily recognized by the vowel **i**, for example, **sim**, **velim**, **nōlim**, and so on.

**First Conjugation**

**spectō, spectāre, spectāvī, spectātum** *to watch*

| Active | | Passive | |
|---|---|---|---|
| spectem | spectēmus | specter | spectēmur |
| spectēs | spectētis | spectēris | spectēminī |
| spectet | spectent | spectētur | spectentur |

**exercise 15-1**

*Translate these verbs into English. Since there is no way to translate Latin subjunctive mood forms out of context, for the purpose of this exercise, translate them as if they were in the indicative mood.*

EXAMPLE    spectēris    *you are being watched*

1. labōrēs _____
2. ōrent _____
3. vocer _____
4. mūtētur _____
5. sonet _____

6. creēmur _____
7. monstrētis _____
8. dōnent _____
9. cessem _____
10. nōminentur _____

**exercise 15-2**

*Translate these verbs into Latin, using the subjunctive mood.*

EXAMPLE    you are being watched    *spectēris*

1. you (*pl.*) deny _____
2. they doubt _____
3. I am being helped _____
4. you (*sg.*) think (**putāre**) _____
5. we are pretending _____

6. they are being set free _____
7. he orders (**imperāre**) _____
8. you (*sg.*) visit often _____
9. you (*pl.*) pray (**precārī**) _____
10. they are being called back _____

## Second Conjugation

**moneō, monēre, monuī, monitum** *to warn*

| Active | | Passive | |
|---|---|---|---|
| moneam | moneāmus | monear | moneāmur |
| moneās | moneātis | moneāris | moneāminī |
| moneat | moneant | moneātur | moneantur |

**exercise    15-3**

*Translate these verbs into English. Since there is no way to translate Latin subjunctive mood forms out of context, for the purpose of this exercise, translate them as if they were in the indicative mood.*

EXAMPLE    moneāmus    *we are warning*

1. moneāminī _____

2. liceat _____

3. impleāntur _____

4. studeāmus _____

5. tenear _____

6. maneātis _____

7. mereat _____

8. habeās _____

9. dēbeātur _____

10. audeam _____

**exercise    15-4**

*Translate these verbs into Latin, using the subjunctive mood.*

EXAMPLE    we are warning    *moneāmus*

1. we are considered _____

2. I am eager _____

3. you (*sg.*) are strong _____

4. she is being persuaded _____

5. they are increasing _____

6. you (*pl.*) are supported _____

7. you (*pl.*) support _____

8. they bristle _____

9. we answer _____

10. I am being taught _____

## Third Conjugation

### agō, agere, ēgī, actum *to do*

| Active | | Passive | |
|--------|--------|---------|--------|
| agam | agāmus | agar | agāmur |
| agās | agātis | agāris | agāminī |
| agat | agant | agātur | agantur |

### exercise 15-5

*Translate these verbs into English. Since there is no way to translate Latin subjunctive mood forms out of context, for the purpose of this exercise, translate them as if they were in the indicative mood.*

EXAMPLE    agāmus    *we are doing*

1. neglegam _____

2. instituat _____

3. alāris _____

4. discēdāmus _____

5. fungātur _____

6. rumpantur _____

7. prōdat _____

8. cingātis _____

9. induāmus _____

10. iungar _____

### exercise 15-6

*Translate these verbs into Latin, using the subjunctive mood.*

EXAMPLE    we are doing    *agāmus*

1. I am dragged _____

2. they fear (**metuere**) _____

3. it is being hung _____

4. we are setting out _____

5. you (*sg.*) are shaping _____

6. he allows (**sinere**) _____

7. they are stretching _____

8. you (*pl.*) are growing _____

9. I love (**dīligere**) _____

10. we are being led _____

## Third Conjugation -*iō*

**capiō, capere, cēpī, captum** *to take*

| Active | | Passive | |
|---|---|---|---|
| capiam | capiāmus | capiar | capiāmur |
| capiās | capiātis | capiāris | capiāminī |
| capiat | capiant | capiātur | capiantur |

**exercise** **15-7**

*Translate these verbs into English. Since there is no way to translate Latin subjunctive mood forms out of context, for the purpose of this exercise, translate them as if they were in the indicative mood.*

EXAMPLE    capiantur    *they are being taken*

1. moriar _____

2. ēgrediātur _____

3. respiciāmus _____

4. rapiātis _____

5. cupiant _____

**exercise** **15-8**

*Translate these verbs into Latin, using the subjunctive mood.*

EXAMPLE    they are being taken    *capiantur*

1. I am being thrown _____

2. you (*sg.*) are escaping _____

3. they take back _____

4. he is being killed (**interficere**) _____

5. we are suffering (**patī**) _____

## Fourth Conjugation

### sentiō, sentīre, sensī, sensum *to feel*

| Active | | Passive | |
|---|---|---|---|
| sentiam | sentiāmus | sentiar | sentiāmur |
| sentiās | sentiātis | sentiāris | sentiāminī |
| sentiat | sentiant | sentiātur | sentiantur |

**exercise 15-9**

*Translate these verbs into English. Since there is no way to translate Latin subjunctive mood forms out of context, for the purpose of this exercise, translate them as if they were in the indicative mood.*

EXAMPLE    sentiat    *he is feeling*

1. fīniāmus _____

2. veniās _____

3. oriātur _____

4. ēveniat _____

5. potiar _____

**exercise 15-10**

*Translate these verbs into Latin, using the subjunctive mood.*

EXAMPLE    he is feeling    *sentiat*

1. we are guarded _____

2. you (*pl.*) are felt _____

3. they are burying _____

4. it is being opened _____

5. I am found (**reperīre**) _____

# The Imperfect Subjunctive, Active and Passive

The imperfect subjunctive is both the most commonly seen and the easiest to form and recognize. It is formed by simply adding regular personal endings to the present active infinitive (the second principal part). This is true for verbs of all conjugations, as well as for irregular verbs.

## capiō, capere, cēpī, captum *to take*

| Active | | Passive | |
|--------|--------|---------|---------|
| caperem | caperēmus | caperer | caperēmur |
| caperēs | caperētis | caperēris | caperēminī |
| caperet | caperent | caperētur | caperentur |

## ferō, ferre, tulī, lātum *to carry*

| Active | | Passive | |
|--------|--------|---------|---------|
| ferrem | ferrēmus | ferrer | ferrēmur |
| ferrēs | ferrētis | ferrēris | ferrēminī |
| ferret | ferrent | ferrētur | ferrentur |

Note that the future infinitive of **sum**, **fore**, can be used in place of the present infinitive **esse** to form the imperfect subjunctive (**forem** = **essem**, and so on).

For deponent verbs, which do not have present active infinitives, the stem is what the present active infinitive would be if the verb had one, based on its conjugation.

| hortor, hortārī, hortātus sum *to urge* | | sequor, sequī, secūtus sum *to follow* | |
|--------|--------|---------|---------|
| hortārer | hortārēmur | sequerer | sequerēmur |
| hortārēris | hortārēminī | sequerēris | sequerēminī |
| hortārētur | hortārentur | sequerētur | sequerentur |

### exercise  15-11

*Translate these verbs into English. Since there is no way to translate Latin subjunctive mood forms out of context, for the purpose of this exercise, translate them as if they were in the indicative mood.*

EXAMPLE     agerent     *they were doing*

1. ederem _____

2. flērēmus _____

3. occurrerētis _____

4. acciperēminī _____

5. cingerer _____

6. forēs _____

7. ambulāret _____

8. conicerētur _____

9. intenderent _____

10. respicerentur _____

## exercise  15-12

*Translate these verbs into Latin, using the subjunctive mood.*

EXAMPLE     they were doing     ___agerent___

1.  you (*sg.*) were standing _____

2.  I was being looked for _____

3.  they used to be owed _____

4.  you (*pl.*) were grabbing _____

5.  you (*pl.*) used to be present _____

6. she was forced _____

7. they were escaping _____

8. we were fortifying _____

9. it was being carried away _____

10. I used to be strong _____

## The Perfect Subjunctive Active

The perfect subjunctive active is identical to the future perfect indicative active, except that the first-person singular ends in **-erim** rather than **-erō**, and the second-person singular and plural and first-person plural forms have a long **ī** in the ending. The perfect subjunctive active is formed with the perfect active stem (the third principal part minus the final **-ī**), plus the tense indicator **-eri-**, followed by a regular active personal ending. As is true of all perfect-system forms, the perfect subjunctive active is formed in the same way for all verbs, regardless of conjugation.

**scrībō, scrībere, scrīpsī, scrīptum** *to write*

| | |
|---|---|
| scripserim | scripserīmus |
| scripserīs | scripserītis |
| scripserit | scripserint |

## exercise  15-13

*Translate these verbs into English. Since there is no way to translate Latin subjunctive mood forms out of context, for the purpose of this exercise, translate them as if they were in the indicative mood.*

EXAMPLE     scripserīmus     ___we have written___

1. attulerīs _____

2. cēperim _____

3. condiderit _____

4. induerint _____

5. labōrāverītis _____

| exercise | 15-14 |

*Translate these verbs into Latin, using the subjunctive mood.*

> EXAMPLE    we have written    *scripserīmus*

1. I have moved _____

2. you (*sg.*) begged (**ōrāre**) _____

3. you (*pl.*) have called _____

4. we lay hidden _____

5. it has changed _____

## The Perfect Subjunctive Passive

The formation of the perfect subjunctive passive is very logical and predictable. The perfect *indicative* passive uses the perfect passive participle with the present *indicative* of **sum**, for example, **missī sunt** *they were sent*; the perfect *subjunctive* passive uses the perfect passive participle with the present *subjunctive* of **sum**, for example, **missī sint**.

**mittō, mittere, mīsī, missum** *to send*

| | |
|---|---|
| **missus sim** | **missī sīmus** |
| **missus sīs** | **missī sītis** |
| **missus sit** | **missī sint** |

Remember that the participle in the perfect subjunctive passive has to agree with the subject in gender, case, and number.

| exercise | 15-15 |

*Translate these verbs into English. Since there is no way to translate Latin subjunctive mood forms out of context, for the purpose of this exercise, translate them as if they were in the indicative mood.*

> EXAMPLE    missum sit    *it was sent*

1. creātī sint _____

2. monitus sim _____

3. ūsa sit _____

4. consecūtī sīmus _____

5. mūtāta sint _____

**exercise  15-16**

*Translate these verbs into Latin, using the subjunctive mood.*

    EXAMPLE     it was sent     *missum sit*

1. it has been closed _____

2. he was shown _____

3. I have feared (**verērī**) _____

4. they (*neut.*) were given _____

5. you (*sg.*) were thrown _____

## The Pluperfect Subjunctive Active

There are two ways to consider how to form the pluperfect subjunctive active. One is simply that it consists of the perfect active infinitive plus a personal ending, for example, **mīsisse** + **-m, -s, -t,** and so on. The other is to think of the perfect active stem (the third principal part without the **-ī** ending), plus the tense indicator **-isse-**, followed by a personal ending, for example, **mīs-** + **-isse-** + **-m, -s, -t,** and so on.

**mittō, mittere, mīsī, missum** *to send*

| | |
|---|---|
| mīsissem | mīsissēmus |
| mīsissēs | mīsissētis |
| mīsisset | mīsissent |

**exercise  15-17**

*Translate these verbs into English. Since there is no way to translate Latin subjunctive mood forms out of context, for the purpose of this exercise, translate them as if they were in the indicative mood.*

    EXAMPLE     mīsissem     *I had sent*

1. voluissent _____

2. invēnisset _____

3. timuissem _____

4. cessāvissent _____

5. dēlēvissēs _____

**exercise    15-18**

*Translate these verbs into Latin, using the subjunctive mood.*

EXAMPLE    I had sent    *mīsissem*

1. I had named _____

2. we had finished _____

3. you (*pl.*) had arrived _____

4. they had known _____

5. he had taken (**sūmere**) _____

## The Pluperfect Subjunctive Passive

The pluperfect subjunctive passive is formed by the same logical method as the perfect subjunctive passive. Rather than combine the imperfect indicative of **sum** with the perfect passive participle, the pluperfect subjunctive passive uses the imperfect subjunctive of **sum**.

**mittō, mittere, mīsī, missum** *to send*

| | |
|---|---|
| **missus essem** | **missī essēmus** |
| **missus essēs** | **missī essētis** |
| **missus esset** | **missī essent** |

There are two points to keep in mind. First, the participle in this construction must agree in gender, case, and number with the subject. Second, **essem, essēs**, etc., can be replaced by **forem, forēs**, etc.

**exercise    15-19**

*Translate these verbs into English. Since there is no way to translate Latin subjunctive mood forms out of context, for the purpose of this exercise, translate them as if they were in the indicative mood.*

EXAMPLE    missa esset    *she had been sent*

1. revocātus essēs _____

2. doctus forem _____

3. dubitātae essent _____

4. īrātī essēmus _____

5. percussus foret _____

## exercise    15-20

*Translate these verbs into Latin, using the subjunctive mood.*

      EXAMPLE     she had been sent    *__missa esset__*

1. I had been cut _____

2. they had died _____

3. it had been filled up _____

4. you (*sg.*) had been lost _____

5. we had followed _____

# Independent Subjunctive Uses

This unit reviews and provides exercises for the main uses of the subjunctive that are not introduced by a subordinating conjunction. Included here are the hortatory, jussive, optative, potential, and deliberative subjunctives, as well as subjunctives in clauses after verbs of fearing.

## The Hortatory and Jussive Subjunctives

The imperative mood treats an action as a command given directly to another person, for example, **venī!** *come!* A verb in the present subjunctive can be used as a sort of first-person command: **Veniam!** *Let me come!* It's more of an urging than a command, which is why it is called *hortatory*, from the past participle of the verb **hortor** *to encourage*. (The same use in the third person is often called *jussive*, from the past participle of the verb **iubeō** *to order*: **Veniant!** *Let them come!*) When the encouragement is negative, the word **nē** is used: **Nē veniat!** *Don't let him come!*

The imperfect tense can be used in a hortatory construction to show that something should have happened in the past but didn't: **Nē venīret.** *He shouldn't have come.* A pluperfect can also be used to emphasize the reference as being in the past: **Nē vēnisset.** *He shouldn't have come.*

## exercise  16-1

*Translate these sentences into English.*

1. Nē iste servus umquam emptus esset.

   _____

2. Mihi cōram dīcat.

   _____

3. Portīs claudentibus, contenderēmus.

   _____

4. Tē dē avibus apibusque doceam.

   _____

5. Nē canēs forīs diutius maneant.

   _____

6. Pecūniam capiāmus et currāmus.

   _____

7. Hīc iam adesset.

   _____

8. Nē iterum tē cum istō conspiciam.

   _____

9. Nē tibi umquam crēdidissēmus.

   _____

10. Prīmā lūce proficiscātur.

    _____

## The Optative Subjunctive

The Latin subjunctive represents the merger of two originally distinct moods. One, the subjunctive, expressed an action as an idea. The other, the optative, expressed an action as a wish on the part of the speaker. The optative subjunctive is an independent subjunctive use that features the original optative mood.

Tense is an important consideration in understanding the optative subjunctive. The present tense denotes that the wish is unfulfilled and could still happen. The imperfect tense also denotes a wish in the present, but stresses that it is unfulfilled. The pluperfect tense denotes a past wish that was never met.

| | | |
|---|---|---|
| Present | **(Utinam) veniat.** | *I wish that he would come.* |
| Imperfect | **(Utinam) venīret.** | *I wish that he were coming.* |
| Pluperfect | **(Utinam) vēnisset.** | *I wish that he had come.* |

Often, the word **utinam** introduces an optative subjunctive, but not always. The negative uses **nē**: **(Utinam) nē vēnisset.** *I wish that he hadn't come.*

<br>

**exercise     16-2**

*Translate these sentences into English.*

1. Utinam nē mihi īrātus essēs.

   _____

2. Utinam ad spectāculum ūnā adissēmus.

   _____

3. Utinam nē Marcum cum alterō invēnissem.

   _____

4. Utinam abeant atque ibi maneant.

   _____

5. Utinam frāter meus adesset.

   _____

## Subjunctive Clauses After Verbs of Fearing

Something unexpected happens in Latin clauses after verbs that denote fearing. Knowledge of hortatory and optative subjunctives, however, can dispel the confusion.

If an object of fear is a noun, an accusative direct object suffices.

Marcus arāneās timet.                    *Marcus is afraid of spiders.*

It is when the object of fear is an action that the unexpected happens: positive statements are introduced by **nē** and negative ones by **ut**!

| | |
|---|---|
| Marcus timet **nē** arāneae saliant. | *Marcus is afraid that the spiders **might** jump.* |
| Marcus timet **ut** arāneae effugiant. | *Marcus is afraid that the spiders **won't** run away.* |

or

| | |
|---|---|
| Marcus timet **nē** arāneae **nōn** effugiant. | *Marcus is afraid that the spiders **might not** run away.* |

The reason for this seemingly peculiar reversal of grammatical expectations is that to the ancient Latin speaker's mind, there were two events. The fearing was a fact (indicative). The action feared was expressed as a wish (subjunctive). In other words, after a verb of fearing comes a hortatory/optative clause.

| | |
|---|---|
| Marcus timet | **nē** arāneae saliant. |
| *Marcus is afraid.* | ***Don't** let the spiders jump!* |
| Marcus timet | **ut** arāneae effugiant. |
| *Marcus is afraid.* | ***Please** let the spiders run away!* |

## exercise    16-3

*Translate these sentences into English.*

1. Timet nē pecūniam suam nōn reddant.

   _____

2. Sollicitus sum ut mē intelligat.

   _____

3. Exercitus veritus est nē hostēs mediā nocte oppugnārent.

   _____

4. Metuimus nē lupus eōs mordēret.

   _____

5. Aenēās timēbat nē classis tempestāte dēlērētur.

   _____

## The Potential Subjunctive

Just as the optative subjunctive is purely original optative (wish), the potential subjunctive is purely original subjunctive (idea). It expresses an action as hypothetical without suggesting any desire.

| | |
|---|---|
| **Putēs** umbrās in domō esse. | *You'd **think** there were ghosts in the house.* |

Related to the potential subjunctive is a construction called the *relative clause of characteristic*, a type of relative clause that uses the subjunctive to describe a possible feature without claiming it as fact.

Sunt **quī** Propertium **mālint**.          *There are some people **who prefer** Propertius.*

For both of these constructions, the negative is **nōn**.

**exercise    16-4**

*Translate these sentences into English.*

1. Vir quem petēbam sīs. _____

2. Quis Marcum meum nōn amet? _____

3. Sonitus ille in culīnā mūs sit. _____

4. Forsitan mīrāminī quid faciant. _____

5. Illud haud sciam, Publī. _____

## The Deliberative Subjunctive

The deliberative subjunctive presents a question as an idea on the part of the speaker. No wish for anything more than an answer is expressed. Rather than the usual **nē**, the negative is **nōn**.

Et nunc quid faciam?          *So what do I do now?*

**exercise    16-5**

*Translate these sentences into English.*

1. Verbumne ullum quod dīcit crēdam? _____

2. Quid agerēmus perditī ut erāmus? _____

3. Quae cum ita sint, quō mē vertam? _____

4. Quid hāc rē facerent? _____

5. Appropinquemne ad eam annōn? _____

# *Cum* Clauses

The classical Latin word **cum** often causes confusion, because there are, in fact, two words that look and sound the same but that ultimately derive from two different words.

One **cum** is a preposition that takes a noun in the ablative, usually to express accompaniment or manner.

> **Cum fratre** in agrīs labōrābat.　　*He used to work in the fields **with his brother**.*

> **Magnā cum spē** in agrīs labōrābat.　　*He used to work in the fields **with great hope**.*

The other **cum** is a subordinating conjunction that in early Latin was spelled **quom**. This **cum** introduces a clause that provides background information for a main clause, much as an ablative absolute construction does.

> **Bellō confectō**, Rōmam rediit.　　*When/Since the war had been completed, he returned to Rome.*

> **Cum bellum confectum esset**, Rōmam rediit.　　*When/Since the war had been completed, he returned to Rome.*

The key to distinguishing the two words is simple: Is it followed by a noun in the ablative or does it introduce a clause?

The verb of a **cum** clause can be in either the indicative or subjunctive mood. When the verb is in the indicative mood, the sense is strictly *temporal*. It refers only to the time that the action of the main clause took place.

> **Cum bellum confectum erat**, Rōmam rediit.　　*When the war had been completed, he returned to Rome.*

When the verb is in the subjunctive mood, although it may translate in the same way, the emphasis is on the situation in which the action of the main clause takes place rather than merely the time. These **cum** clauses are referred to as *circumstantial*.

| | |
|---|---|
| **Cum bellum confectum esset**, Rōmam rediit. | ***When the war had been completed**, he returned to Rome.* |

Just as an ablative absolute or any participial phrase can, a **cum** clause can also suggest *cause*.

| | |
|---|---|
| **Cum bellum confectum esset**, Rōmam rediit. | ***Since the war had been completed**, he returned to Rome.* |

When the word **tamen** appears in the main clause, the sense of the **cum** clause is *concessive*.

| | |
|---|---|
| **Cum bellum confectum esset**, Rōmam **tamen** rediit. | ***Even though the war had been completed**, he returned to Rome (anyway).* |

It must be remembered that for an ancient Latin speaker, a **cum** clause was a **cum** clause. The terms *temporal, circumstantial, causal,* and *concessive* are how we modern English-speaking people describe the various ways we can view or translate **cum** clauses.

### exercise    17-1

*Translate these sentences into English, using circumstantial clauses.*

1. Cum in silvā ambulārēmus, perterritī erāmus.

   _____

2. Marcus, cum patrem videat, sollicitus fit.

   _____

3. Tē adiuvābō, cum mē petās.

   _____

4. Cum ā Graeciā regressī essent, multōs diēs Capuae quiescēbant.

   _____

5. Hostēs pācem petīvērunt, cum proelium pugnātum foret.

   _____

## exercise    17-2

*Translate these sentences into English, using causal clauses.*

1. Cum amīcus meus profectūrus esset, cōmissātiō habita est.

   _____

2. Cum rēgīna morerētur, deōs precāta est.

   _____

3. In viam effūgī cum aedificium ardēret.

   _____

4. Cum in silvā mediā nocte errārēmus, perterritī erāmus.

   _____

5. Cum mīles fābulam narrātūrus esset, omnēs conticuērunt.

   _____

## exercise    17-3

*Translate these sentences into English, using temporal, circumstantial, or concessive clauses as clues in the sentences themselves suggest.*

1. Cum superfuissent, tristēs tamen fuērunt.

   _____

2. Cum Augustus periit, tōta patria plōrāvit.

   _____

3. Bene dormīvimus cum tumultus in viā magnus foret.

   _____

4. Libenter matrem meam recipiam cum eam vidēbō.

   _____

5. Pompēius, cum prīmum in Aegyptum pervēnit, interfectus est.

   _____

6. Cum patrem verērētur, nōn tacēbat tamen Gāius.

   _____

7. Cum spectāculum confectum erat, nēmō plausit.

   _____

8. Rīdēbitis cum hunc iocum audīveritis.

   _____

9. Cum Hannibal moenia Rōmae conspexisset, reversus est.

   _____

10. Cum ad cōmissātiōnem pervēnimus, omnēs iam ēgressī erant.

    _____

# Unit 18

# Purpose Clauses and Indirect Commands

In English, we usually use an infinitive to express purpose, as in the sentence *We usually use an infinitive **to express purpose**.* Latin has several ways to express purpose, but an infinitive phrase is not one of them. In Latin, you can use the preposition **ad** with a gerund/gerundive in the accusative, a gerund/gerundive in the genitive with **causā** or **grātiā**, or a supine in the accusative (when the main verb is a verb of motion).

| | |
|---|---|
| In culīnam rediit **ad cēnam parandam**. | *He returned to the kitchen to prepare dinner.* |

In culīnam rediit **cēnae parandae causā**.
In culīnam rediit **cēnae parandae grātiā**.
In culīnam rediit **cēnam parātum**.

The most common way Latin expresses purpose, however, is in a separate clause with its verb in the subjunctive. This makes sense, since purpose is a wish or idea (subjunctive mood) rather than a fact (indicative mood). For example, in the sentence **Domum regressī sumus ut requiescerēmus.** *We went back home to rest.*, the action of going back home is expressed as a fact and so is in the indicative mood. The resting, however, is simply an idea and so is expressed in the subjunctive mood. The sentence doesn't assert that that ever actually happened.

## Adverbial Clauses of Purpose

As its name suggests, an adverbial clause of purpose shows the purpose of the verb of the main clause. It is introduced by the subordinating conjunction **ut**, and the verb is in the present subjunctive if the main verb is in the present, future, or future perfect tense; it is in the imperfect subjunctive if the main verb is in the imperfect, perfect, or pluperfect tense.

| | |
|---|---|
| In culīnam redit **ut** cēnam **paret**. | *He is returning to the kitchen **to prepare** dinner.* |
| In culīnam rediit **ut** cēnam **parāret**. | *He returned to the kitchen **to prepare** dinner.* |

If the idea is negative, the subordinating conjunction **nē** is used. Expressing negative purpose in English usually requires a construction other than an infinitive phrase.

| | |
|---|---|
| In culīnam rediit **nē** cēna **combūrerētur**. | *He returned to the kitchen **so that** dinner **wouldn't burn up**.* |

Sometimes, purpose clauses include a sense of ability and sound best when translated with *can* or *could*.

| | |
|---|---|
| In culīnam redit **ut** cēnam **paret**. | *He is returning to the kitchen **so he can prepare** dinner.* |

## exercise    18-1

*Translate these sentences into English.*

1. In forum descendit ut cibum emeret.

   _____

2. Fēminae fūgērunt nē caperentur.

   _____

3. Cum prīmum perveniāmus ut principem ipsum videāmus.

   _____

4. Aliī mīlitēs praemissī sunt ut pontem custōdīrent.

   _____

5. Pons dēfendēbātur nē hostēs flūmen transīrent.

   _____

6. Multī periērunt ut lībertātem nostram servārent.

   _____

7. Lucernās exstinguere dēbēs nē domus incendātur.

   _____

8. Domī manēbimus nē fūrēs aurum subdūcant.

   _____

9. Servus celerrimē cucurrit ut cum prīmum pervenīret.

_____

10. Pecūniam fers ut domum illam emāmus.

_____

## Relative Clauses of Purpose

Instead of using **ut** or **nē** to introduce a purpose clause, relative clauses of purpose use a _relative pronoun._ This type of purpose clause shows the purpose of the pronoun's antecedent rather than the purpose of the verb in the main clause.

| Coquum in culīnam mīsī **quī** cēnam **parāret.** | _I sent the cook to the kitchen **to prepare** dinner._ or |
|---|---|
| | _I sent the cook **who was (supposed) to prepare** dinner to the kitchen._ |

There is another type of clause that is introduced by a relative pronoun and uses a subjunctive verb, called a _relative clause of characteristic._ This type of clause refers to a quality or feature of the pronoun's antecedent.

| Quis est **quī** hoc **nesciat**? | _Who is there **who doesn't know** this?_ or |
|---|---|
| | _What kind of person is there **who doesn't know** this?_ |

**exercise     18-2**

_Translate these sentences into English._

1. Baculum petīvī quō lupum repellerem.

_____

2. Nuntius Rōmam missus est ā quō victōria nuntiārētur.

_____

3. Tibi necesse est amīcum invenīre quī fidēlis sit.

_____

4. Fossa circum castra fossa est quae hostēs arcēret.

_____

5. Hannibal elephantōs sēcum duxit ut Rōmānōs terrērent.

_____

## Indirect Commands

Indirect commands are similar in concept and identical in construction to adverbial clauses of purpose. They report what someone has advised, asked, or ordered someone else to do. In essence, they show the purpose of the command in the main clause. They are introduced by **ut** or **nē** and take a verb in the subjunctive.

<blockquote>

Mīlitibus imperāvit **ut** pontem **transīrent**.    *He ordered the soldiers **to cross** the bridge.*

</blockquote>

Here is a list of the most common verbs introducing an indirect command.

| | |
|---|---|
| **imperō, imperāre, imperāvī, imperātum** | *to order* (with dative) |
| **mandō, mandāre, mandāvī, mandātum** | *to order* (with dative) |
| **moneō, monēre, monuī, monitum** | *to warn* |
| **ōrō, ōrāre, ōrāvī, ōrātum** | *to beg (of someone)* (with the preposition **ā**) |
| **persuādeō, persuādēre, persuāsī, persuāsum** | *to persuade* (with dative) |
| **petō, petere, petiī/petīvī, petītum** | *to ask (of someone)* (with the preposition **ā**) |
| **quaerō, quaerere, quaesiī/quaesīvī, quaesītum** | *to ask (of someone)* (with the preposition **ā**) |
| **rogō, rogāre, rogāvī, rogātum** | *to ask* |

Note that a reflexive pronoun in an indirect command refers to the *subject* of the *main clause*.

<blockquote>

Marcō persuāsērunt ut **sēcum** redīret.    *They persuaded Marcus to return with **them**.*

</blockquote>

### exercise    18-3

*Translate these sentences into English.*

1. Sulla exercituī suō imperāvit ut Rōmam occupāret.

   _____

2. Multī Caesarem monuērunt nē domō eō diē relinqueret.

   _____

3. Ā comite meō petīvī ut mihi auxilium ferret.

   _____

4. Eī persuādēbimus ut dē hāc rē taceat.

   _____

5. Ā mē quaesīvistī ut omnia quam prīmum agerem.

   _____

6. Tē rogō nē ineptiās.

   _____

7. Ā dūce ōrābat nē illōs in pugnam mitteret.

_____

8. Ā mē quaerunt nē sē trādam.

_____

9. Eum rogābis ut tibi liceat.

_____

10. Imperātī sumus ut nāvēs custōdīrēmus.

_____

# Result Clauses

The tiny word **ut** and its subjunctive negative counterpart **nē**, when beginning a clause with a subjunctive verb, can show purpose or report an indirect command. Given that the subjunctive mood expresses ideas and wishes rather than facts, this makes sense. When **ut** appears with a verb in the indicative mood, which is not common, its sense is strictly temporal—which also makes sense, since what is being expressed is a simple fact. Result clauses, which largely report factual events, are where Latin surprises by using a subjunctive.

The grammatical term *result clause* refers to a clause that reports the consequences of another clause, as in the sentence *She was driving so fast that she lost control of the car.* In fact, the appearance of a *so* word in the main clause is a good sign that a result clause may follow.

The most common of these *so* words are the following.

| | |
|---|---|
| **adeō** | *to such an extent* |
| **ita** | *so, in such a way* |
| **sīc** | *so, in such a way* |
| **tālis, tāle** | *of such a kind* |
| **tam** | *so* |
| **tantus, tanta, tantum** | *so large, so great* |
| **tot** | *so many* |
| **totiens** | *so many times* |

Unlike other clauses with the subjunctive that are introduced by **ut**, result clauses do not use **nē** when the result is negative. Instead, other words are used, such as **nōn**, **nihil**, **nēmō**, or **numquam**.

| | |
|---|---|
| Tam celeriter cucurrit ut superāret. | *He ran so fast that he won.* |
| Tam ignāvus erat ut nihil faceret. | *He was so lazy that he did nothing.* |

Usually a *so* word alerts you to an oncoming result clause, but not always.

| | |
|---|---|
| Accidit ut omnia dēlēta essent. | *It turned out that everything had been destroyed.* |

At times, it can be difficult to tell whether a purpose or a result clause is being introduced. When a result clause is negative, some negative word other than **nē** appears. A *so* word is also a good indicator of a result clause. Apart from these clues, context must be your guide.

*Translate these sentences into English.*

1. Illa aestās tam calida erat ut plūrimī in urbe perīrent.

   _____

2. Ōrātiō Cicerōnis tālis erat ut vix intellegerem.

   _____

3. Sīc nostrī pugnāvērunt ut hostēs fugerent.

   _____

4. Accidet ut is numquam inveniātur.

   _____

5. Tot flōrēs sunt ut quōs legam nesciam.

   _____

6. Turba tanta erat ut Marcum invenīre nōn possēmus.

   _____

7. Eum dēsīderō ita ut dormīre nōn possim.

   _____

8. Quintus illud carmen totiens lēgit ut recitāre posset.

   _____

9. Claudia fābulās tālēs narrābat ut omnēs semper plōrārent.

   _____

10. Avus meus tam senex erat ut stāre vix posset.

   _____

# Indirect Questions; Sequence of Tenses

## Indirect Questions

Of all the forms of indirect discourse in Latin, the indirect question most closely resembles English in construction.

As is true for indirect statements and indirect commands, indirect questions depend on a main verb of saying, thinking, knowing, or perceiving. Like English, the Latin indirect question itself is a clause introduced by a question word. Unlike English, the Latin verb is in the subjunctive mood.

| Main verb of | saying<br>thinking<br>knowing<br>perceiving | Question<br>word | Clause with<br>subjunctive verb |
|---|---|---|---|
| **Nesciēbam** | **cūr** | | **mē relinquerēs.** |
| *I didn't know* | *why* | | *you were leaving me.* |

The most common question words are the following.

| | |
|---|---|
| **quis** | *who?* |
| **quid** | *what?* |
| **quī, quae, quod** | *which?* |
| **quot** | *how many?* |
| **quālis, quāle** | *what kind?* |
| **quantus, quanta, quantum** | *how great?* |
| **cūr** | *why?* |
| **num** | *whether* |
| **ubi** | *where? when?* |
| **quō** | *where to?* |
| **unde** | *where from?* |
| **quandō** | *when?* |
| **quōmodo** | *how?* |

# Sequence of Tenses

For an indirect question or any subordinate clause that requires a verb in the subjunctive mood (for example, purpose and result clauses, and clauses after verbs of fearing), the tense of the subjunctive verb depends on the tense of the verb in the main clause. If the main verb is in the present, future, or future perfect tense, the subjunctive verb is either present (if the action is at the same time as or after that of the main verb) or perfect (if the action has already been completed before that of the main verb). This is called *primary sequence*.

In *secondary sequence*, the main verb is in one of the past tenses (imperfect, perfect, or pluperfect). In this case, the subjunctive verb will be either imperfect (if the action is at the same time as or after that of the main verb) or pluperfect (if the action has already been completed before that of the main verb).

| | Main Verb | Subjunctive Verb | |
| --- | --- | --- | --- |
| | | **At the Same Time As or After** | **Before** |
| Primary sequence | Present<br>Future<br>Future Perfect | Present | Perfect |
| Secondary sequence | Imperfect<br>Perfect<br>Pluperfect | Imperfect | Pluperfect |

Occasionally, the sequencing of times (i.e., tenses) is quite clear in Latin, but virtually impossible to express in English. For instance, a present subjunctive after a future-tense main verb in Latin creates what is essentially a future-future reference. The best English can do in translation is to come close to the idea expressed in Latin. This isn't as confusing as it may seem. Here are some examples to illustrate the various translation permutations.

**Primary Sequence**

| | |
| --- | --- |
| Nesciō cūr mē relinquās. | *I don't know why you are leaving / will leave me.* |
| Nesciam cūr mē relinquās. | *I won't know why you will be leaving / will leave me.* |
| Nescīverō cūr mē relinquās. | *I won't have known why you will have been leaving me.* |
| Nesciō cūr mē relīqueris. | *I don't know why you left me.* |
| Nesciam cūr mē relīqueris. | *I won't know why you will have left me.* |
| Nescīverō cūr mē relīqueris. | *I won't have known why you will have left me.* |

**Secondary Sequence**

| | |
| --- | --- |
| Nesciēbam cūr mē relinquerēs. | *I didn't used to know why you were leaving / about to leave me.* |
| Nescīvī cūr mē relinquerēs. | *I didn't know why you were leaving / about to leave me.* |
| Nescīveram cūr mē relinquerēs. | *I hadn't known why you were leaving / about to leave me.* |
| Nesciēbam cūr mē relīquissēs. | *I didn't used to know why you had left me.* |
| Nescīvī cūr mē relīquissēs. | *I didn't know why you had left me.* |
| Nescīveram cūr mē relīquissēs. | *I hadn't known why you had left me.* |

| exercise | 20-1 |
|----------|------|

*Translate these sentences into English.*

1. Cūr istud fēcerīs numquam intellegam.

_____

2. Rogābant quō profectūrī essent.

_____

3. Mīrāris quis sit.

_____

4. Unde vēnissent audīvit.

_____

5. Mox explicābit cūr hīc manēre nōs oporteat.

_____

6. Dīc mihi num mentiātur annōn.

_____

7. Nesciēbant quālia tēla hostēs habērent.

_____

8. Mīrātī sumus quōmodo ā Galliā Rōmam iter tam celeriter fēcissent.

_____

9. Quanta victōria sit haud intellegitis.

_____

10. Nesciō quās epistulās lēgerit.

_____

11.  Negāsne quō abierit?

_____

12.  Mē docuistī quōmodo rēs gererentur.

_____

13.  Ā nōbīs quaerēbat quot forent.

_____

14.  Audīverant senātōrēs ubi castra Caesaris posita essent.

_____

15.  Quandō tū ventūrus essēs sensit soror mea.

_____

# Conditions

In grammar, the term *condition* refers to an if/then proposition: *If you touch the stove, then you are burned.* Conditions, however, are not as obvious as they seem. They fall into two groups, realistic and hypothetical.

Since Latin employs the indicative mood to treat an action as a fact and the subjunctive mood to treat an action as an idea or a wish, you can imagine how obvious and precise Latin is with regard to specific types of conditions.

In summary, the indicative mood governs conditions that are facts: *If you are touching the stove, then you are burned.* The subjunctive mood expresses conditions of a more musing variety: *If you were to touch the stove, you'd get burned.* Not saying that you did touch it or are touching it, but if you did, a burn would be the consequence. The most important thing to remember is that the indicative states facts, while the subjunctive states ideas.

The following chart gives the traditional names for each type of condition, along with examples in both Latin and English.

**Simple Fact Present: Present Indicative**
Sī hoc putās, doleō.                    *If you think this, I'm sad.*

**Simple Fact Past: Past Indicative**
Sī hoc putābās, dolēbam.                *If you were thinking this, I was sad.*

**Future More Vivid: Future Indicative**
Sī hoc putābis, dolēbō.                 *If you (will) think this, I'll be sad.*

**Future Less Vivid: Present Subjunctive**
Sī hoc putēs, doleam.                   *If you were to think this, I'd be sad.*

**Present Contrary to Fact: Imperfect Subjunctive**
Sī hoc putārēs, dolērem.                *If you thought this, I'd be sad.*

**Past Contrary to Fact: Pluperfect Subjunctive**
Sī hoc putāvissēs, doluissem.           *If you had thought this, I would have been sad.*

The *future less vivid* condition is traditionally taught as a should/would condition, which refers to a rather Victorian construction such as *Should you be wrong, I would be disappointed.* (As opposed to *If you're wrong, I'd be disappointed.*) As is often the case, this is simply a matter of breaking from the age-old Latin learning tradition to recognizing Latin as a language and bringing it into the English of the 21st century. In translating a *future less vivid* condition, it is best to think of it as a sort of "future contrary to fact," since it refers to something not predicted or expected to be true in the future.

**exercise 21-1**

*State which type of condition each of these Latin sentences reflects, then translate the sentence into English.*

EXAMPLE   Sī illum amīcum habēs, errās.   *__simple fact present__*
*__If you consider him a friend, you're wrong.__*

1. Sī canis latrat, perīculum est. _____

2. Sī canis latrāret, perīculum esset. _____

3. Sī canis latret, perīculum sit. _____

4. Nisi canēs latrant, tūtī sumus. _____

5. Nisi canēs latrābant, tūtī erāmus. _____

6. Sī frusta eius pullī comēdissēs, aeger fuissēs. _____

7. Sī frusta eius pullī comedēs, aeger eris. _____

8. Sī hoc scīret, stupērem. _____

9. Sī hoc sciat, stupeam. _____

_____

10. Sī ad spectāculum aderant, eōs nōn vīdimus. _____

_____

11. Citō fit sī deī volunt. _____

_____

12. Nisi castra mūniāmus, magnum sit perīculum. _____

_____

13. Nisi castra mūnīvissēmus, magnum fuisset perīculum. _____

_____

14. Sī mihi occurreret, omnia scīret. _____

_____

15. Sī mihi occurret, omnia sciet. _____

_____

# Review Exercises

These exercises reinforce everything you have learned about Latin verbs so far. The verb forms may come from any conjugation, any tense, any voice, and any mood. Irregular verbs may pop up anywhere as well; even though Latin has only a few irregular verbs, those few are very common. If you struggle with an exercise, review the relevant unit(s), and then try again!

### exercise 22-1

*Translate these verbs into English. (Some may be in the subjunctive mood. Since there is no way to translate Latin subjunctive mood forms out of context, for the purpose of this exercise, translate them as if they were in the indicative mood.)*

1. effugimus _____

2. occīsus essem _____

3. auxerimus _____

4. lavāte _____

5. reddit _____

6. vīsī sunt _____

7. advēneram _____

8. traxerint _____

9. poteris _____

10. pollicēbitur _____

11. ūsus sit _____

12. habitāta sunt _____

13. solvēbantur _____

14. constā _____

15. narrāverātis _____

16. erant _____

17. revertēbāminī _____

18. patēbō _____

19. descrīberent _____

20. meruit _____

**exercise    22-2**

*Translate these verbs and verb forms into Latin.*

1. I (*masc.*) had suffered _____

2. they were sailing _____

3. we will be joined _____

4. he doubts (*subjunctive*) _____

5. she has been betrayed _____

6. to be captured _____

7. it was broken (*subjunctive*) _____

8. they will have confessed _____

9. he opened _____

10. having been pretended (*masc. nom. sg.*) _____

11. be silent! (*sg.*) _____

12. we had harmed _____

13. it has been (*subjunctive*) _____

14. going to set free (*masc. nom. pl.*) _____

15. you (*pl.*) were being watched _____

16. they elected _____

17. to have pulled _____

18. he denies _____

19. it is being said _____

20. I will have hoped _____

**exercise 22-3**

*Change these verbs from singular to plural, keeping the same person, tense, voice, and mood. Then translate the new forms into English. (Some may be in the subjunctive mood. Since there is no way to translate Latin subjunctive mood forms out of context, for the purpose of this exercise, translate them as if they were in the indicative mood.)*

EXAMPLE    necābat    *necābant*    *they were killing*

1. flēbis _____ _____

2. optāverim _____ _____

3. intendit _____ _____

4. volāvistī _____ _____

5. necāvit _____ _____

6. nocuerat _____ _____

7. positus erō _____ _____

8. timuerat _____ _____

9. alor _____ _____

10. prohibeam _____ _____

11. explicābis _____ _____

12. sīvit _____ _____

13. respice _____ _____

14. vulnerāveram _____ _____

15. neglegēris _____ _____

16. admoneat    _____    _____

17. coquēbās    _____    _____

18. exercuerat    _____    _____

19. reperta sīs    _____    _____

20. orior    _____    _____

---

**exercise    22-4**

*Change these verbs from plural to singular, keeping the same person, tense, voice, and mood. Then translate the new forms into English. (Some may be in the subjunctive mood. Since there is no way to translate Latin subjunctive mood forms out of context, for the purpose of this exercise, translate them as if they were in the indicative mood.)*

EXAMPLE    complētis    ***complēs***    ***you fill***

1. finxerant    _____    _____

2. dōnārētis    _____    _____

3. caedēbāminī    _____    _____

4. laedētis    _____    _____

5. fracta essent    _____    _____

6. īrātī sunt    _____    _____

7. cōnābimur    _____    _____

8. iacēbant    _____    _____

9. intulistis    _____    _____

10. quiēverint    _____    _____

11. latrant    _____    _____

12. pariēbātis    _____    _____

13. cecidimus    _____    _____

14. facta sint    _____    _____

15. revocābāmus    _____    _____

16. venditis    _____    _____

17. imitārēmur  _____    _____

18. trāditī erimus  _____    _____

19. capiēbant  _____    _____

20. lēgimus  _____    _____

## exercise  22-5

*Change these verbs from active to passive, keeping the same person, number, tense, and mood. Then translate the new forms into English. (Some may be in the subjunctive mood. Since there is no way to translate Latin subjunctive mood forms out of context, for the purpose of this exercise, translate them as if they were in the indicative mood.)*

EXAMPLE    retinēret    *retinērētur*    *he was being held back*

1. pūniēbātis  _____    _____

2. aedificant  _____    _____

3. putem  _____    _____

4. līberāvimus  _____    _____

5. pepulerit  _____    _____

6. coēgistī  _____    _____

7. praemittēmus  _____    _____

8. fallimus  _____    _____

9. labōrent  _____    _____

10. vehēbātis  _____    _____

11. iubet  _____    _____

12. impōnerētis  _____    _____

13. tangēbat  _____    _____

14. perfēcistī  _____    _____

15. pugnāvērunt  _____    _____

16. exspectābās  _____    _____

17. instituī  _____    _____

18. amāverīs _____ _____

19. āmittam _____ _____

20. rogābimus _____ _____

## exercise  22-6

*Change these verbs from passive to active, keeping the same person, number, tense, and mood. Then translate the new forms into English. (Some may be in the subjunctive mood. Since there is no way to translate Latin subjunctive mood forms out of context, for the purpose of this exercise, translate them as if they were in the indicative mood.)*

  EXAMPLE   tectus est   *texit*                    *he covered*

1. doctus eris _____ _____

2. ornābar _____ _____

3. rumpēris _____ _____

4. exceptus eram _____ _____

5. vītātī sīmus _____ _____

6. agēmur _____ _____

7. dēfensus es _____ _____

8. cinctus essem _____ _____

9. mūtārēminī _____ _____

10. nōminātus eris _____ _____

11. raptī sumus _____ _____

12. terrēbantur _____ _____

13. statuēbāris _____ _____

14. dīcuntur _____ _____

15. habitus erō _____ _____

16. perterritus essem _____ _____

17. cupīta sīs _____ _____

18. mūnior _____ _____

19. portātus erit    _____      _____

20. comparātus eram    _____      _____

| exercise | 22-7 |
|---|---|

*For the following verbs, identify the verb form for each of the remaining tenses, keeping the same person, number, voice, and mood.*

1. <u>fīgit</u>    _____    _____

     *Present*        *Imperfect*        *Future*

   _____    _____    _____

     *Perfect*        *Pluperfect*        *Future perfect*

2. _____    <u>intrābantur</u>    _____

     *Present*        *Imperfect*        *Future*

   _____    _____    _____

     *Perfect*        *Pluperfect*        *Future perfect*

3. _____    _____    <u>nascēris</u>

     *Present*        *Imperfect*        *Future*

   _____    _____    _____

     *Perfect*        *Pluperfect*        *Future perfect*

4. _____    _____    _____

     *Present*        *Imperfect*        *Future*

   <u>conditī sīmus</u>    _____    _____

     *Perfect*        *Pluperfect*        *Future perfect*

5. _____    _____    _____

     *Present*        *Imperfect*        *Future*

   _____    <u>vēnerās</u>    _____

     *Perfect*        *Pluperfect*        *Future perfect*

6. _____    _____    _____

     *Present*        *Imperfect*        *Future*

   _____    _____    <u>prōdiderit</u>

     *Perfect*        *Pluperfect*        *Future perfect*

7. <u>pernoctat</u>    _____    _____

     *Present*        *Imperfect*        *Future*

   _____    _____    _____

     *Perfect*        *Pluperfect*        *Future perfect*

8. _____    mandābāmus    _____
   *Present*           *Imperfect*         *Future*

   _____    _____    _____
   *Perfect*           *Pluperfect*        *Future perfect*

9. _____    _____    erit _____
   *Present*           *Imperfect*         *Future*

   _____    _____    _____
   *Perfect*           *Pluperfect*        *Future perfect*

10. _____    _____    _____
    *Present*           *Imperfect*         *Future*

   ignōrāverītis _____    _____    _____
   *Perfect*           *Pluperfect*        *Future perfect*

## exercise    22-8

*Identify the form of each of these verbs by person, number, tense, voice, and mood. Then translate the verb into English. (Some may be in the subjunctive mood. Since there is no way to translate Latin subjunctive mood forms out of context, for the purpose of this exercise, translate them as if they were in the indicative mood.)*

EXAMPLE    sūmimus    <u>*1 pl. present active indicative*</u>    <u>**we are taking**</u>

1. servant            _____    _____

2. accessistis        _____    _____

3. suādeō             _____    _____

4. tenuerō            _____    _____

5. pandēbāmur         _____    _____

6. ēgressī erant      _____    _____

7. instruam           _____    _____

8. properāte          _____    _____

9. vetuerās           _____    _____

10. excēpit           _____    _____

11. superfuissem      _____    _____

12. precētur          _____    _____

13. monēbāminī     _____    _____

14. fugient     _____    _____

15. sonāverint     _____    _____

16. mōvī     _____    _____

17. lūderis     _____    _____

18. recitāverit     _____    _____

19. fundite     _____    _____

20. appellābātis     _____    _____

## exercise 22-9

*Form the five common infinitives for each of these verbs; you may skip the extremely rare future passive infinitive.*

1. nesciō

| _Present active_ | _Perfect active_ | _Future active_ | _Present passive_ | _Perfect passive_ |
|---|---|---|---|---|

2. nuntiō

| _Present active_ | _Perfect active_ | _Future active_ | _Present passive_ | _Perfect passive_ |
|---|---|---|---|---|

3. audiuvō

| _Present active_ | _Perfect active_ | _Future active_ | _Present passive_ | _Perfect passive_ |
|---|---|---|---|---|

4. dīvidō

| _Present active_ | _Perfect active_ | _Future active_ | _Present passive_ | _Perfect passive_ |
|---|---|---|---|---|

5. interficiō

| _Present active_ | _Perfect active_ | _Future active_ | _Present passive_ | _Perfect passive_ |
|---|---|---|---|---|

6. rīdeō

| _Present active_ | _Perfect active_ | _Future active_ | _Present passive_ | _Perfect passive_ |
|---|---|---|---|---|

7. scindō

| _Present active_ | _Perfect active_ | _Future active_ | _Present passive_ | _Perfect passive_ |
|---|---|---|---|---|

8. mittō

| _Present active_ | _Perfect active_ | _Future active_ | _Present passive_ | _Perfect passive_ |
|---|---|---|---|---|

9. noscō

| _Present active_ | _Perfect active_ | _Future active_ | _Present passive_ | _Perfect passive_ |
|---|---|---|---|---|

10. ēripiō

| _Present active_ | _Perfect active_ | _Future active_ | _Present passive_ | _Perfect passive_ |
|---|---|---|---|---|

11. occīdō

| Present active | Perfect active | Future active | Present passive | Perfect passive |
|---|---|---|---|---|

12. ferō

| Present active | Perfect active | Future active | Present passive | Perfect passive |
|---|---|---|---|---|

13. percutiō

| Present active | Perfect active | Future active | Present passive | Perfect passive |
|---|---|---|---|---|

14. transcrībō

| Present active | Perfect active | Future active | Present passive | Perfect passive |
|---|---|---|---|---|

15. verberō

| Present active | Perfect active | Future active | Present passive | Perfect passive |
|---|---|---|---|---|

16. gerō

| Present active | Perfect active | Future active | Present passive | Perfect passive |
|---|---|---|---|---|

17. dīligō

| Present active | Perfect active | Future active | Present passive | Perfect passive |
|---|---|---|---|---|

18. cūrō

| Present active | Perfect active | Future active | Present passive | Perfect passive |
|---|---|---|---|---|

19. petō

| Present active | Perfect active | Future active | Present passive | Perfect passive |
|---|---|---|---|---|

20. tollō

| Present active | Perfect active | Future active | Present passive | Perfect passive |
|---|---|---|---|---|

**exercise    22-10**

*Form the present active, perfect passive, and future active participles for each of these verbs.*

1. constituere

| Present active | Perfect passive | Future active |
|---|---|---|

2. creāre

| Present active | Perfect passive | Future active |
|---|---|---|

3. conspicere

| Present active | Perfect passive | Future active |
|---|---|---|

4. invidēre

| Present active | Perfect passive | Future active |
|---|---|---|

5. praebēre

| Present active | Perfect passive | Future active |
|---|---|---|

6. agitāre     _____     _____     _____
                     *Present active*       *Perfect passive*       *Future active*

7. nūbere     _____     _____     _____
                     *Present active*       *Perfect passive*       *Future active*

8. recipere     _____     _____     _____
                     *Present active*       *Perfect passive*       *Future active*

9. sūmere     _____     _____     _____
                     *Present active*       *Perfect passive*       *Future active*

10. tegere     _____     _____     _____
                      *Present active*       *Perfect passive*       *Future active*

11. tacēre     _____     _____     _____
                      *Present active*       *Perfect passive*       *Future active*

12. dūcere     _____     _____     _____
                      *Present active*       *Perfect passive*       *Future active*

13. intellegere     _____     _____     _____
                      *Present active*       *Perfect passive*       *Future active*

14. salūtāre     _____     _____     _____
                      *Present active*       *Perfect passive*       *Future active*

15. vexāre     _____     _____     _____
                      *Present active*       *Perfect passive*       *Future active*

16. gignere     _____     _____     _____
                      *Present active*       *Perfect passive*       *Future active*

17. accipere     _____     _____     _____
                      *Present active*       *Perfect passive*       *Future active*

18. sepelīre     _____     _____     _____
                      *Present active*       *Perfect passive*       *Future active*

19. onerāre     _____     _____     _____
                      *Present active*       *Perfect passive*       *Future active*

20. fodere     _____     _____     _____
                      *Present active*       *Perfect passive*       *Future active*

**exercise    22-11**

*Translate these sentences into English, rendering the participial phrases and ablative absolutes twice, according to the suggestions in parentheses.*

EXAMPLE    (temporal clause / causal clause) Caesare duce, senātus saepe conticuit.

*When Caesar was the ruler, the senate often fell silent.*

*Because Caesar was the ruler, the senate often fell silent.*

1.  (simple adjective / coordinate clause) Avēs canentēs in arbore gaudēbant.

    _____

    _____

2.  (temporal clause / causal clause) Labōre perfectō, nōs omnēs ad villam cucurrimus.

    _____

    _____

3.  (relative clause / temporal clause) Dē fābulā narrātā multum dīcēmus.

    _____

    _____

4.  (simple adjective / concessive clause) Terram alentem nēmō tamen colit.

    _____

    _____

5.  (coordinate clause / simple adjective) Turba premens pompam vidēre cōnātus est.

    _____

    _____

6.  (relative clause / causal clause) Marītus abitūram uxōrem nunc complectitur.

    _____

    _____

7.  (concessive clause / relative clause) Omnēs consiliō male ēventūrō crēdidērunt.

    _____

    _____

8. (simple adjective / relative clause) Ad āram dōnīs onerātam fīlius fīliaque adveniunt.

_____

_____

9. (temporal clause / causal clause) Tōtā Ītaliā superātā, imperium Rōmānum constitūtum est.

_____

_____

10. (coordinate clause / causal clause) Dux hostium verbīs mōtus exercitum suum revertere iussit.

_____

_____

**exercise   22-12**

_Choose the verbs in the list below that are likely to introduce indirect statements in Latin._

spargam    crēdēs    nōtum erat    dēlēvistī    lūsit    audīrētis    negāvit    essēs

dixerō    sollicitus sum    manent    scrībēbat    moriar    putāvimus    percussit

sciam    properāvī    imitor    vīderit    iacēbant    condiderit    narrābant

**exercise   22-13**

_Using the introductory phrase and the direct quotation, reword each of these sentences as an indirect statement in Latin. Be careful of verb tenses! Then translate the new sentence._

1. nuntiātum est / "Caligula ab urbe abest."

_____

_____

2. audīmus / "Exercitus crās oppugnābit."

_____

_____

3. Aenēās sensit / "Is nōbīs vēra dīcēbat."

_____

4. ille dīcit / "Omnibus necesse est iam fugere."

_____

_____

5. prōmīsī / "Numquam iterum errābō."

_____

_____

6. rēgīna crēdit / "Servī rēgis fidēlēs fuērunt."

_____

_____

7. dīc cīvibus / "Dux noster ā hostibus interfectus est."

_____

_____

8. saepe narrat ille / "Patriam meam amō."

_____

_____

9. quis nōn scit / "Hannibal cum elephantīs Alpēs transiit."

_____

_____

10. nunc confiteor / "Ego semper tē amābō."

_____

_____

**exercise    22-14**

_Label these verb forms as participles, gerunds, or gerundives. Identify all possible forms by gender, case, and number._
_Then translate the forms into English._

EXAMPLE  petentium

_participle_        _masc./fem./neut. gen. pl._

1. miscentēs  _____   _____

   _____

2. simulātibus  _____   _____

   _____

3. saliendās  _____   _____

   _____

4. ambulantis  _____   _____

   _____

5. cantōs  _____   _____

   _____

6. coniectūrī  _____   _____

   _____

7. vocātum  _____   _____

   _____

8. vigilandō  _____   _____

   _____

9. exstinguentium  _____   _____

   _____

10. addita  _____   _____

    _____

11. complētum  _____   _____

    _____

12. mīrantī  _____   _____

    _____

13. respondendōrum  _____   _____

    _____

14. mordentibus    _____    _____

_____

15. cautō    _____    _____

_____

16. locūtō    _____    _____

_____

17. memorātīs    _____    _____

_____

18. audiendī    _____    _____

_____

19. postulanda    _____    _____

_____

20. certantēs    _____    _____

_____

**exercise    22-15**

*All of these sentences contain a subjunctive verb. Identify which usage of the subjunctive each sentence shows, then translate accordingly into English.*

EXAMPLE    Cum Rōma valeat, valet populus Rōmānus.

*cum* clause

**When Rome is strong, the Roman people are strong.**

1. Accipiant pecūniam ā rēge datam. _____

_____

2. Agricola īrātus servīs imperāvit ut ad agrōs redeant. _____

_____

3. Tot mala Manliō accidēbant ut semper omnia timēret. _____

_____

4. Ut dominōs vītent, servī fugitūrī in nāvem ascendent. _____

_____

5. Cavē nē aedificium tuum ardeat. _____

_____

6. Plōrēmus omnēs, nam piscēs cecidērunt! _____

_____

7. Utinam Caecilia quam prīmum mē amet. _____

_____

8. Vulnera haec patiāmur, annōn? _____

_____

9. Hic homō nescit quī sint mōrēs maiorum. _____

_____

10. Cum fīnēs imperiī positī essent, plūs tamen dēsīderāvit princeps avārus. _____

_____

## exercise   22-16

*Readers sometimes confuse purpose clauses and result clauses. Identify which of the two clauses each of these sentences contains, then translate it into English.*

EXAMPLE  Tam multī sunt arborēs in silvā ut vidēre nēmō possit.

*result clause*

**There are so many trees in the forest that no one is able to see.**

1. Ōlim pater ad lūdum vēnit ut paedagōgō pecūniam daret. _____

_____

2. Avus meus ita dormit ut nōn plaustra in viā audīre possit. _____

_____

3. Mortem ita timuit mīlēs ut in proeliīs semper sē cēlāret. _____

_____

4.  Ut imperium habeat, quid nōn facit tyrannus? _____

_____

5.  Aedem hanc fēcī quam dī Rōmānī habitārent. _____

_____

6.  Fēminae ad theatrum adeunt ut videant et videantur. _____

_____

7.  Tālēs cēnās coquus coxit ut convīvae gaudērent. _____

_____

8.  Pullī tam territī sunt ut volāre incipiant. _____

_____

9.  Rēgīna aquam petiit ut lavārētur. _____

_____

10. Iūnōnī tam multa dōna tulistī ut dea tē faceret fēlīcem. _____

_____


**exercise    22-17**

*Each of these sentences contains a* cum *clause or an ablative absolute. Reword each sentence, changing the* cum *clause to an ablative absolute or the ablative absolute to a* cum *clause. Then translate the sentence into English.*

1.  Cum pompa perfecta esset, spectātōrēs tumultum fēcērunt.

_____

_____

2.  Equitibus laudātīs, poēta dē aliīs mīlitibus canēbat.

_____

_____

3.  Cum spēs āmissa sit, patria nostra tamen supererit.

_____

_____

4. Epistulā missā, nuntius tandem ad urbem suum revocātus est.

   _____

   _____

5. Cum ōrātiō scripta esset, Messalla dē librō novō cōgitāvit.

   _____

   _____

6. Aestāte redeunte, aprī et porcī in umbrā remanēbunt.

   _____

   _____

7. Cum verba haec audīverītis, spectātōrēs, plaudite.

   _____

   _____

8. Exercitū victō, vir mortem timens fugit.

   _____

   _____

9. Cum pax ante postulāta sit, populus Rōmānus tamen nunc bellum persequitur.

   _____

   _____

10. Sōle oriente, mala noctis iam nōn metuis.

    _____

    _____

### exercise  22-18

*Using the introductory phrase and the direct question, reword each of these sentences as an indirect question in Latin. Be careful of verb tenses! Then translate the new sentence.*

1. audīs / "Unde vēnit servus?"

   _____

   _____

2. potest cernere / "Quid mihi accidit?"

_____

_____

3. meministī / "Quō festīnās?"

_____

_____

4. nōn intellegēbam / "Cūr pecora rapuistī?"

_____

_____

5. quaerit / "Quandō expellētis matrem ex urbe?"

_____

_____

6. necesse est scīre / "Quis es?"

_____

_____

7. ille mīrātur / "Quid retinuērunt fūrēs?"

_____

_____

8. ignōrō / "Quī agricolae illōs fundōs magnōs colunt?"

_____

_____

9. ab amīcō petent / "Quōmodo cantant avēs tam multa carmina?"

_____

_____

10. nescimus / "Quāle consilium cēpistis?"

_____

_____

## exercise 22-19

*Supply the appropriate forms of the verbs in parentheses to create the type of condition listed, then translate the sentence. Note that some of the sentences require passive forms.*

1. (future less vivid) Sī tū _____ (rīdēre), ego tristis _____ (esse).

    _____

2. (simple fact past) Sī flōrēs _____ (morī), hortus _____ (neglegī).

    _____

3. (past contrary to fact) Sī tū labōrem _____ (perficere), nōs quiescere

    _____ (posse).

    _____

4. (present contrary to fact) Sī ego _____ (pugnāre), populus

    _____ (plaudere).

    _____

5. (future less vivid) Sī umbrae mē _____ (vexāre), vīnum illīs ego

    _____ (praebēre).

    _____

6. (future more vivid) Sī Caesar hostēs _____ (occīdere), urbs Rōma

    _____ (gaudēre).

    _____

7. (simple fact present) Sī nōs _____ (rogāre), ea _____ (respondēre).

    _____

8. (past contrary to fact) Sī consul madidus _____ (esse), metus nōs

    _____ (capere).

    _____

9. (present contrary to fact) Sī iānitor iānuam _____ (claudere), canis forīs

    _____ (relinquī).

    _____

10. (future less vivid) Sī vōs montem _____ (ascendere), tōtam terram

_____ (vidēre).

_____

*These sentences contain a mix of all the verb forms and verb constructions you have seen. Translate them into English.*

1. Agricola nesciit quis pecora ex agrīs cēpisset.

_____

2. Multī mihi dīcēbant sē piscēs in pavīmentō natantēs vīdisse, sed nōn persuāsus sum.

_____

3. Cum senātor ita imperāvisset, Cicerō Rōmā expulsus est et domum relīquit.

_____

4. Exercitum dūcat ē Graeciā atque ad Galliam.

_____

5. Cum plūrimīs nāvibus Graecī nāvigāverant ut moenia Trōiae oppugnārent.

_____

6. Princeps tam obēsus erat ut nulla cēna eī satis esset.

_____

7. In lapide scrībitur puellam flōrem familiae suae fuisse.

_____

8. Cum rīdeās, quid putem dē hōc vultū simulātō?

_____

9. Ego nōn vereor nē amīcī ōminibus mē fallant.

_____

10. Lupus statim ex silvīs ēgressus est ad lūnam aspiciendam.

_____

11. Aenēās ad Ītaliam iter fēcit ut urbem valitūram conderet.

_____

12. Puer plōrans omnibus narrāvit sē ā canibus morsum esse.

_____

13. Utinam iterum tē in Capuā complectar!

_____

14. Sī nōs hoc consilium consequāmur, omnia bene ēveniant.

_____

15. Ille flūmen celeriter transiit nandō.

_____

16. Senex nōs sīc hortātus est: "nostrōrum hostium urbs dēlenda est."

_____

17. Omnēs cōmissātōrēs scient tē multam aquam vīnō miscuisse.

_____

18. Sī exercitus in campō exercēret, vidērēs spectāculum mīrābile.

_____

19. Cum Augustus nōbīs imperat ut taceāmus, nōs omnēs conticescere decet.

_____

20. Domum aedificābam in quā familia mea vīveret.

_____

# Latin-English Glossary

In this glossary you will find all the Latin words that appear in this book. The English-Latin glossary that follows contains those words needed to complete the English to Latin exercises throughout the text. Here is a list of the abbreviations used both in the text and in these glossaries.

| | | | |
|---|---|---|---|
| **abl.** | ablative case | **m.** | masculine gender |
| **acc.** | accusative case | **masc.** | masculine gender |
| **c.** | common gender (masculine or feminine) | **n.** | neuter gender |
| | | **neut.** | neuter gender |
| **dat.** | dative case | **nom.** | nominative case |
| **f.** | feminine gender | **pl.** | plural |
| **fem.** | feminine gender | **prep.** | preposition |
| **gen.** | genitive case | **sg.** | singular |

## A

**ā, ab** (*prep. with abl.*) from, away from; (*with a passive verb and a people word*) by

**abeō, abīre, abiī/abīvī, abitum** to go away

**absum, abesse, āfuī, āfutūrus** to be away, be absent

**accēdō, accēdere, accessī, accessum** to approach, go near (*with* **ad** *or* **in** *and the acc.*)

**accidō, accidere, accidī** to fall down, ask for help; happen

**accipiō, accipere, accēpī, acceptum** to receive; welcome

**ad** (*prep. with acc.*) to, toward, at, near; (*with gerund/gerundive in the acc.*) in order to

**addō, addere, addidī, additum** to add, give to

**adeō, adīre, adiī, aditum** to go to, approach

**adhūc** still

**adiuvō, adiuvāre, adiūvī, adiūtum** to help

**admoneō, admonēre, admonuī, admonitum** to warn, advise

**adsum, adesse, adfuī, adfutūrus** to be present

**adveniō, advenīre, advēnī, adventum** to arrive

**aedēs, aedis** *f.* temple; *f.pl.* house

**aedificium, aedificiī** *n.* building

**aedificō, aedificāre, aedificāvī, aedificātum** to build

**aeger, aegra, aegrum** sick

**Aegyptus, Aegyptī** *f.* Egypt

**Aenēās, Aenēae** *m.* Aeneas

**aestās, aestātis** *f.* summer

**ager, agrī** *m.* field

**aggredior, aggredī, aggressus sum** to approach, attack

**agitō, agitāre, agitāvī, agitātum** to agitate, get (something) going; think about

**agō, agere, ēgī, actum** to do; drive, lead; be busy; spend

**agricola, agricolae** *m.* farmer

**alius, alia, aliud** some; other

**alō, alere, aluī, altum** to cherish, nourish

**Alpēs, Alpium** *f.pl.* the Alps

**alter, altera, alterum** the other

**ambulō, ambulāre, ambulāvī, ambulātum** to walk

**amīcus, amīcī** *m.* friend

**āmittō, āmittere, āmīsī, āmissum** to send away, let go, lose

**amō, amāre, amāvī, amātum** to like, love

**amor, amōris** *m.* love

**amplector, amplectī, amplexus sum** to embrace

**ancilla, ancillae** *f.* slave woman

**animus, animī,** *m.* mind, soul, spirit

 **in animō habēre,** to intend

**annōn** or not

**ante** (*prep. with acc./abl.*) before

**aper, aprī** *m.* boar

**aperiō, aperīre, aperuī, apertum** to open, uncover

**apis, apis** *f.* bee

**appāreō, appārēre, appāruī, appāritum** to appear

**appellō, appellāre, appellāvī, appellātum** to call (*usually by name*)

**appropinquō, appropinquāre, appropinquāvī** to approach

**aptus, apta, aptum** fit

**apud** (*prep. with acc.*) at the house of

**aqua, aquae** *f.* water

**aquaeductus, aquaeductūs** *m.* aqueduct

**āra, ārae** *f.* altar

**arānea, arāneae** *f.* spider

**arbitror, arbitrārī, arbitrātus sum** to think

**arbor, arboris** *f.* tree

**arceō, arcēre, arcuī** to keep (away) from, ward off, protect

**ardeō, ardēre, arsī, arsūrus** to burn, be on fire

**arēna, arēnae** *f.* sand, arena

**arma, armōrum** *n.pl.* arms, weapons

**armō, armāre, armāvī, armātum** to equip with weapons

**arō, arāre, arāvī, arātum** to plow

**arripiō, arripere, arripuī, arreptum** to grab

**ascendō, ascendere, ascendī, ascensum** to climb, go up

**aspiciō, aspicere, aspexī, aspectum** to look at

**atque** and

**attentus, attenta, attentum** at attention

**audeō, audēre, ausus sum** to dare

**audiō, audīre, audīvī/audiī, audītum** to hear, listen

**auferō, auferre, abstulī, ablātum** to carry away

**augeō, augēre, auxī, auctum** to increase, enlarge

**Augustus, Augustī** *m.* Augustus

**aurum, aurī** *n.* gold

**auxilium, auxiliī** *n.* help, assistance

**avis, avis** *f.* bird

**avus, avī** *m.* grandfather

## B

**baculum, baculī** *n.* stick

**bellum, bellī** *n.* war

**bene** well

**bibliothēca, bibliothēcae** *f.* library

**bibō, bibere, bibī, (pōtum)** to drink

**bona, bonōrum** *n.pl.* goods, possessions, things

**bonus, bona, bonum** good

**bōs, bovis** *c.* ox, cow

**bulla, bullae** *f.* pendant

## C

**cadō, cadere, cecidī, cāsum** to fall

**Caecilia, Caeciliae** *f.* Caecilia

**caecus, caeca, caecum** blind; unseen

**caedō, caedere, cecīdī, caesum** to cut, kill

**caelum, caelī** *n.* sky, heaven

**Caesar, Caesaris** *m.* Caesar

**calidus, calida, calidum** hot

**Caligula, Caligulae** *m.* Caligula

**campus, campī** *m.* field

**canis, canis** *c.* dog

**canō, canere, cecinī, cantum** to sing, play (an instrument)

**cantō, cantāre, cantāvī, cantātum** to sing, play (an instrument)

**capiō, capere, cēpī, captum** to take, catch

**captīvus, captīvī** *m.* prisoner

**Capua, Capuae** *f.* Capua

**careō, carēre, caruī, caritum** to lack, be without (*with an abl. object*)

**carmen, carminis** *n.* poem, song

**castra, castrōrum** *n.pl.* (military) camp

**catēna, catēnae** *f.* chain

**Catullus, Catullī** *m.* Catullus

**causā** (*with gerund/gerundive in the gen.*) in order to

**caveō, cavēre, cāvī, cautum** to beware, be on guard

**cēdō, cēdere, cessī, cessum** to go, withdraw, yield

**celebrō, celebrāre, celebrāvī, celebrātum** to visit often, make well known

**celeriter** quickly

**cēlō, cēlāre, cēlāvī, cēlātum** to hide

**cēna, cēnae** *f.* dinner

**cēnō, cēnāre, cēnāvī, cēnātum** to dine

**cernō, cernere, crēvī, crētum** to separate, distinguish, pick out; see

**certō, certāre, certāvī, certātum** to struggle, decide by contest

**cessō, cessāre, cessāvī, cessātum** to do nothing, slack off

**cibus, cibī** *m.* food

**Cicerō, Cicerōnis** *m.* Cicero

**cingō, cingere, cinxī, cinctum** to surround, wrap

**circum** (*prep. with acc.*) around

**cito** quickly

**cīvis, cīvis** *c.* citizen

**clāmō, clāmāre, clāmāvī, clāmātum** to shout

**clārē** brightly

**classis, classis** *f.* fleet

**Claudia, Claudiae** *f.* Claudia

**claudō, claudere, clausī, clausum** to close, conclude

**cōgitō, cōgitāre, cōgitāvī, cōgitātum** to think, ponder

**cognōscō, cognoscere, cognōvī, cognitum** to learn; (*in the perfect system*) to know

**cōgō, cōgere, coēgī, coactum** to compel, drive, force; gather

**colligō, colligere, collēgī, collectum** to gather, collect

**collis, collis** *m.* hill

**colō, colere, coluī, cultum** to pay attention to, nurture, tend, cultivate, grow

**combūrō, combūrere, combussī, combustum** to burn

**comedō, comesse/comedere, comēdī, comēsum/comestum** to eat up

**comes, comitis** *c.* companion, friend

**cōmissātiō, cōmissātiōnis** *f.* drinking party

**cōmissātor, cōmissātōris** *m.* partygoer

**committō, committere, commīsī, commissum** to connect, combine; entrust

**comparō, comparāre, comparāvī, comparātum** to prepare, buy, furnish

**complector, complectī, complexus sum** to hug, embrace

**compleō, complēre, complēvī, complētum** to fill

**condō, condere, condidī, conditum** to found, build; put in safe keeping, hide

**conficiō, conficere, confēcī, confectum** to finish

**confiteor, confitērī, confessus sum** to confess, admit

**coniciō, conicere, coniēcī, coniectum** to hurl, throw really hard

**cōnor, cōnārī, cōnātus sum** to try, attempt

**consequor, consequī, consecūtus sum** to follow, pursue; obtain

**consilium, consiliī** *n.* plan, advice

**consilium capere** to adopt a plan, devise a strategy

**conspiciō, conspicere, conspexī, conspectum** to catch sight of, spot

**constituō, constituere, constituī, constitūtum** to stand/set (something) up; decide

**constō, constāre, constitī, constātūrus** to stand together; stand still, stop

**construō, construere, construxī, constructum** to build, heap up

**consul, consulis** *m.* consul

**consulō, consulere, consuluī, consultum** to consult

**contemnō, contemnere, contempsī, contemptum** to despise

**contendō, contendere, contendī, contentum** to strain, hurry, fight

**conticescō, conticescere, conticuī** to fall silent

**contineō, continēre, continuī, contentum** to hold together, contain

**convīva, convīvae** *m.* party guest

**convocō, convocāre, convocāvī, convocātum** to call together

**coquō, coquere, coxī, coctum** to cook

**coquus, coquī** *m.* cook

**cōram** face to face, in person

**Cornēlia, Cornēliae** *f.* Cornelia

**corpus, corporis** *n.* body

**cottīdiē** every day

**crās** tomorrow

**crēdō, crēdere, crēdidī, crēditum** to trust, rely on, believe (*usually with dat.*)

**creō, creāre, creāvī, creātum** to create; elect

**crescō, crescere, crēvī, crētum** to grow

**cubiculum, cubiculī** *n.* bedroom

**cubitum īre** to go to bed

**culīna, culīnae** *f.* kitchen

**cum** (*conj.*) when, since, because, although

**cum** (*prep. with abl.*) with

**cum prīmum** as soon as

**cunctor, cunctārī, cunctātus sum** to hesitate, delay

**cupidus, cupida, cupidum** desirous

**cupiō, cupere, cupīvī, cupītum** to desire, long for

**cūr** why?

**Cūria, Cūriae** *f.* the Senate House

**cūrō, cūrāre, cūrāvī, cūrātum** to take care of

**currō, currere, cucurrī, cursum** to run

**custōdiō, custōdīre, custōdiī/custōdīvī, custōdītum** to guard

**custōs, custōdis** *c.* guard

**cymbala, cymbalōrum** *n.pl.* cymbals

**D**

**dē** (*prep. with abl.*) of, from, down from; concerning, about

**dēbeō, dēbēre, dēbuī, dēbitum** to owe; should, must

**decet, decēre, decuit** it is proper, it suits (*with an acc. object*)

**decimus, decima, decimum** tenth

**dēfendō, dēfendere, dēfendī, dēfensum** to defend, drive off

**dēleō, dēlēre, dēlēvī, dēlētum** to destroy

**dēmonstrō, dēmonstrāre, dēmonstrāvī, dēmonstrātum** to show

**descendō, descendere, descendī, descensum** to climb down

**describō, describere, descripsī, descriptum** to describe

**dēsīderō, dēsīderāre, dēsīderāvī, dēsīderātum** to long for; miss

**deus, deī** *m.* god

**dīcō, dīcere, dixī, dictum** to tell, say

**dictātor, dictātōris** *m.* dictator

**diēs, diēī** *m.* day

**dīligenter** carefully

**dīligō, dīligere, dīlexī, dīlectum** to love, esteem, pick out

**discēdō, discēdere, discessī, discessum** to leave, separate

**discipulus, discipulī** *m.* student

**discō, discere, didicī** to learn

**diutius** for too long (a time)

**dīves, dīvitis** *m.* a wealthy person

**dīvidō, dīvidere, dīvīsī, dīvīsum** to divide

**dō, dare, dedī, datum** to give

**doceō, docēre, docuī, doctum** to teach

**doleō, dolēre, doluī, dolitum** to feel pain; cause pain

**dolor, dolōris** *m.* pain, grief

**dominus, dominī** *m.* master

**domus, domūs/domī** *f.* house, home

**dōnō, dōnāre, dōnāvī, dōnātum** to give (as a gift)

**dōnum, dōnī** *n.* gift

**dormiō, dormīre, dormīvī, dormītum** to sleep

**dubitō, dubitāre, dubitāvī, dubitātum** to hesitate, doubt

**dūcō, dūcere, duxī, ductum** to take (someone) some place, draw, lead, bring

**dum** while

**dūrus, dūra, dūrum** tough, strong, hard

**dux, ducis** *c.* leader

**E**

**ē, ex** (*prep. with abl.*) out, out of, from

**edō, esse/edere, ēdī, ēsum** to eat

**effugiō, effugere, effūgī** to escape

**ego, meī** I

**ēgredior, ēgredī, ēgressus sum** to leave, go out

**elephantus, elephantī** *m.* elephant

**emō, emere, ēmī, emptum** to buy

**eō, īre, iī/īvī, itum** to go

**epistula, epistulae** *f.* letter

**eques, equitis** *m.* horseman

**equitēs, equitum** *m.pl.* cavalry

**equus, equī** *m.* horse

**ēripiō, ēripere, ēripuī, ēreptum** to grab, take out violently

**errō, errāre, errāvī, errātum** to wander; be wrong

**et** and, also; even

**et . . . et** both . . . and

**etiam** still, yet, even, also

**ēveniō, ēvenīre, ēvēnī, ēventum** to come out; result

**excipiō, excipere, excēpī, exceptum** to take out, take up, catch, receive

**exeō, exīre, exiī/exīvī, exitum** to go out, end

**exerceō, exercēre, exercuī, exercitum** to make strong, train; harass

**exercitus, exercitūs** *m.* army

**existimō, existimāre, existimāvī, existimātum** to think, judge, evaluate

**expellō, expellere, expulī, expulsum** to drive

**experior, experīrī, expertus sum** to try, test, prove

**explicō, explicāre, explicāvī, explicātum** to explain

**exspectō, exspectāre, exspectāvī, exspectātum** to wait for

**exstinguō, exstinguere, exstinxī, exstinctum** to put out (*a fire*)

**exuō, exuere, exuī, exūtum** to strip

**F**

**fābula, fābulae** *f.* story

**faciō, facere, fēcī, factum** to make, do

**factum, factī** *n.* deed

**fallō, fallere, fefellī, falsum** to deceive

**familia, familiae** *f.* household

**fātum, fātī** *n.* fate

**fēlēs, fēlis** *f.* cat

**fēlix, fēlīcis** fruitful, happy, lucky

**fēmina, fēminae** *f.* woman

**fenestra, fenestrae** *f.* window

**ferō, ferre, tulī, lātum** to bring, carry, bear

**festīnō, festīnāre, festīnāvī, festīnātum** to rush, hurry

**fidēlis, fidēle** faithful

**fīdō, fīdere, fīsus sum** to trust

**fīgō, fīgere, fixī, fixum** to fasten, affix

**fīlia, fīliae** *f.* daughter

**fīlius, fīliī** *m.* son

**fingō, fingere, finxī, fictum** to shape, form

**fīniō, fīnīre, fīnīvī, fīnītum** to finish

**fīnis, fīnis** *m.* end, limit, boundary

**fīō, fīerī, factus sum** to be, be made, be done, become; happen

**fleō, flēre, flēvī, flētum** to weep

**flōs, flōris** *m.* flower

**flūmen, flūminis** *n.* river

**fluō, fluere, fluxī, fluxum** to flow

**fodiō, fodere, fōdī, fossum** to dig

**forīs** outside

**forsitan** maybe

**fortasse** maybe

**fortis, forte** brave, strong

**forum, forī** *n.* marketplace, forum

**fossa, fossae** *f.* ditch

**frangō, frangere, frēgī, fractum** to break

**frāter, fratris** *m.* brother

**frūmentum, frūmentī** *n.* grain

**fruor, fruī, fructus sum** to enjoy (*usually with abl.*)

**frustum, frustī** *n.* a scrap

**fugiō, fugere, fūgī, fugitūrus** to run away, flee

**fulgor, fulgōris** *m.* lightning bolt

**fundō, fundere, fūdī, fūsum** to pour

**fundus, fundī** *m.* farm

**fungor, fungī, functus sum** to perform (*usually with abl.*)

**fūr, fūris** *c.* thief

## G

**Gāius, Gāiī** *m.* Gaius

**Gallī, Gallōrum** *m.pl.* Gauls

**Gallia, Galliae** *f.* Gaul

**Gallicus, Gallica, Gallicum** Gallic

**gaudeō, gaudēre, gāvīsus sum** to rejoice, be happy

**geminus, gemina, geminum** twin

**genus, generis** *n.* kind, manner, way

**Germānī, Germānōrum** *m.pl.* Germans

**gerō, gerere, gessī, gestum** to carry, wage, accomplish; wear

**gignō, gignere, genuī, genitum** to give birth; cause

**gladiātor, gladiātōris** *m.* gladiator

**gladius, gladiī** *m.* sword

**Graecia, Graeciae** *f.* Greece

**Graecus, Graeca, Graecum** Greek

**grātiā** (*with gerund/gerundive in the gen.*) for the sake of, in order to

## H

**habeō, habēre, habuī, habitum** to have, hold; consider, regard

**habitō, habitāre, habitāvī, habitātum** to live, dwell, inhabit

**Hannibal, Hannibalis** *m.* Hannibal

**haud** not

**heri** yesterday

**hīc** here

**hilaris, hilare** happy, cheerful, fun

**hodiē** today

**homō, hominis** *m.* person

**hōra, hōrae** *f.* hour, time

**horreō, horrēre, horruī** to bristle, have one's hair stand on end

**hortor, hortārī, hortātus sum** to encourage, urge

**hortus, hortī** *m.* garden

**hostēs, hostium** *c.pl.* the enemy

**hostis, hostis** *c.* an enemy

**hūc** to this place

**hūmānus, hūmāna, hūmānum** human

## I

**iaceō, iacēre, iacuī, iacitum** to recline, lie

**iaciō, iacere, iēcī, iactum** to throw

**iam** now, already, at this point in time

**iamdūdum** for a while now

**iānitor, iānitōris** *m.* doorkeeper

**iānua, iānuae** *f.* door

**ibi** there

**idōneus, idōnea, idōneum** suitable, appropriate

**ientāculum, ientāculī** *n.* breakfast

**ignāvus, ignāva, ignāvum** lazy

**ignis, ignis** *m.* fire

**ignōrō, ignōrāre, ignōrāvī, ignōrātum** not to know

**ille, ille, illud** that; he, she, it

**imber, imbris** *m.* rain

**imitor, imitārī, imitātus sum** to copy, imitate

**imperium, imperiī** *n.* command, power

**imperō, imperāre, imperāvī, imperātum** to order (*with dat.*)

**impius, impia, impium** unfaithful

**impleō, implēre, implēvī, implētum** to fill up

**impōnō, impōnere, imposuī, impositum** to put on

**in** (*prep. with acc.*) into, in, to; (*prep. with abl.*) in, on

**incendō, incendere, incendī, incensum** to set on fire

**incipiō, incipere, incēpī, inceptum** to begin

**incognitus, incognita, incognitum** unknown

**indicō, indicāre, indicāvī, indicātum** to make known, betray

**induō, induere, induī, indūtum** to put on, dress

**ineptiō, ineptīre** to act foolish

**infans, infantis** *c.* baby

**inferō, inferre, intulī, illātum** to bring in

**ingredior, ingredī, ingressus sum** to step in, enter; begin

**instituō, instituere, instituī, institūtum** to set up, instruct; decide

**instruō, instruere, instruxī, instructum** to build; equip

**intellegō, intellegere, intellexī, intellectum** to understand, be aware of, appreciate

**intendō, intendere, intendī, intentum** to stretch; intend, aim at

**inter** (*prep. with acc.*) between, among

**interficiō, interficere, interfēcī, interfectum** to kill

**intrō, intrāre, intrāvī, intrātum** to enter

**inveniō, invenīre, invēnī, inventum** to come upon, find

**invideō, invidēre, invīdī, invīsum** to cast the evil eye; envy (*with dat.*)

**iocus, iocī** *m.* joke

**īrascor, īrascī, īrātus sum** to become angry

**is, ea, id** this, that; he, she, it

**iste, ista, istud** that (one) near you

**ita** so, in such a way

**Ītalia, Ītaliae** *f.* Italy

**iter, itineris** *n.* journey, trip

**iterum** again

**iubeō, iubēre, iussī, iussum** to order

**iūdicō, iūdicāre, iūdicāvī, iūdicātum** to judge

**Iūlia, Iūliae** *f.* Julia

**iungō, iungere, iunxī, iunctum** to join, connect

**Iūnō, Iūnōnis** *f.* Juno

**iūrō, iurāre, iurāvī, iurātum** to swear

**iuvat, iuvāre, iūvit** it pleases

**iuvenis** young

**iuventus, iuventūtis** *f.* youth

**iuvō, iuvāre, iūvī, iūtum** to help, please

## L

**lābor, lābī, lapsus sum** to slip

**labor, labōris** *m.* work, suffering

**labōrō, labōrāre, labōrāvī, labōrātum** to work, suffer

**laedō, laedere, laesī, laesum** to hurt, harm

**lapis, lapidis** *m.* stone

**larva, larvae** *f.* ghost, skeleton

**lateō, latēre, latuī** to lie hidden

**Latium, Latiī** *n.* Latium

**latrō, latrāre, latrāvī, latrātum** to bark

**laudō, laudāre, laudāvī, laudātum** to praise

**lavō, lavāre, lāvī, lautum/lavātum/lōtum** to wash

**lectus, lectī** *m.* bed, dining couch

**legō, legere, lēgī, lectum** to choose, pick, gather; read

**libenter** gladly

**liber, librī** *m.* book

**līberī, līberōrum** *m.pl.* children

**līberō, līberāre, līberāvī, līberātum** to set free

**lībertās, lībertātis** *f.* freedom

**libet, libēre, libuit / libitum est** it is pleasing (*with a dat. object*)

**licet, licēre, licuit / licitum est** it is allowed (*with a dat. object*)

**lingua Latīna, linguae Latīnae** *f.* the Latin language

**longē** far

**loquor, loquī, locūtus sum** to talk, speak

**lūceō, lūcēre, luxī** to shine

**lucerna, lucernae** *f.* lamp

**Lūcius, Lūciī** *m.* Lucius

**lūdō, lūdere, lūsī, lūsum** to play; deceive

**lūdus, lūdī** *m.* game; school

**lūna, lūnae** *f.* moon

**lupus, lupī** *m.* wolf

**lutus, lutī** *m.* mud

**lux, lūcis** *f.* light

# M

**madidus, madida, madidum** wet; drunk

**magistrātus, magistrātūs** *m.* magistrate, elected official

**magnus, magna, magnum** great; loud

**maiorēs, maiorum** *m.pl.* ancestors

**male** badly

**mālō, malle, māluī** to want more, prefer

**mālum, mālī** *n.* apple

**malus, mala, malum** bad, evil

**mandō, mandāre, mandāvī, mandātum** to entrust, order

**māne** in the morning

**maneō, manēre, mansī, mansum** to stay

**Manlius, Manliī** *m.* Manlius

**manus, manūs** *f.* hand

**Marcus, Marcī** *m.* Marcus

**mare, maris** *n.* sea

**marītus, marītī** *m.* husband

**māter, matris** *f.* mother

**mēcum** with me

**medius, media, medium** the middle of

**meminī, meminisse** to remember, be mindful (*with a gen. object*)

**memorō, memorāre, memorāvī, memorātum** to remind, mention

**mensa, mensae** *f.* table

**mentior, mentīrī, mentītus sum** to lie, deceive

**mereō, merēre, meruī, meritum** to deserve, earn

**Messalla, Messallae** *m.* Messalla

**metuō, metuere, metuī, metūtum** to fear, be afraid

**metus, metūs** *m.* fear

**meus, mea, meum** my

**mīles, mīlitis** *m.* soldier

**mīlia, mīlium** thousands

**mīrābilis, mīrābile** amazing, wonderful

**mīror, mīrārī, mīrātus sum** to marvel at, wonder, be amazed

**misceō, miscēre, miscuī, mixtum** to mix

**mittō, mittere, mīsī, missum** to send, release, throw to make (something) go away under its own power

**modo** only, just

**moenia, moenium** *n.pl.* walls

**molestus, molesta, molestum** bothersome, annoying

**moneō, monēre, monuī, monitum** to warn, advise

**mons, montis** *m.* mountain

**monstrō, monstrāre, monstrāvī, monstrātum** to show

**mordeō, mordēre, momordī, morsum** to bite

**morior, morī, mortuus sum** (*future participle* **moritūrus**) to die

**moror, morārī, morātus sum** to hesitate, delay, kill time

**mors, mortis** *f.* death

**mortuus, mortua, mortuum** dead

**mōs, mōris** *m.* custom, way

**moveō, movēre, mōvī, mōtum** to move

**mulceō, mulcēre, mulsī, mulsum** to soothe, stroke

**multus, multa, multum** much, many

**mūniō, mūnīre, mūnīvī, mūnītum** to fortify

**mūs, mūris** *m.* mouse

**mūtō, mūtāre, mūtāvī, mūtātum** to change, move

# N

**narrō, narrāre, narrāvī, narrātum** to tell (in story form)

**nascor, nascī, nātus sum** to be born

**nauta, nautae** *m.* sailor

**nāvigō, nāvigāre, nāvigāvī, nāvigātum** to sail

**nāvis, nāvis** *f.* ship

**nē** (*negative adverb/conjunction*)

**-ne** (*interrogative enclitic*)

**nec . . . nec** neither . . . nor

**necesse est** it is necessary (*with a dat. object*)

**necō, necāre, necāvī, necātum** to kill

**nefastus, nefasta, nefastum** unlucky, unholy

**neglegō, neglegere, neglexī, neglectum** to neglect

**negō, negāre, negāvī, negātum** to deny, say no

**nēmō, nēminis** *m.* no one

**nēquissimus, nēquissima, nēquissimum** utterly worthless

**nesciō, nescīre, nescīvī, nescītum** not to know

**nihil** nothing

**nimis** very much, too much

**nisi** if not, unless, except

**nō, nāre, nāvī** to swim

**noceō, nocēre, nocuī, nocitum** to harm, be harmful (*with dat.*)

**nōlō, nolle, nōluī** not to want, be unwilling

**nōmen, nōminis** *n.* name

**nōminō, nōmināre, nōmināvī, nōminātum** to name, mention

**nōn** not

**nōn sōlum . . . sed etiam** not only . . . but also

**nōs, nostrī** we

**noscō, noscere, nōvī, nōtum** to learn; (*in the perfect system*) to know, recognize

**noster, nostra, nostrum** our

**nōtitia, nōtitiae** *f.* knowledge, fame, news

**nōtus, nōta, nōtum** known, famous

**nox, noctis** *f.* night

**nūbēs, nūbis** *f.* cloud

**nūbō, nūbere, nupsī, nuptum** to marry

**nullus, nulla, nullum** no, none

**num** (*introduces a question that expects a negative answer*)

**num** whether

**numquam** never

**nunc** now

**nuntiō, nuntiāre, nuntiāvī, nuntiātum** to announce

**nuntius, nuntiī** *m.* messenger

## O

**obeō, obīre, obiī/obīvī, obitum** to meet; die

**obēsus, obēsa, obēsum** fat

**oblīviscor, oblīviscī, oblītus sum** to forget (*with gen.*)

**occidō, occidere, occidī, occāsum** to fall down, set

**occīdō, occīdere, occīdī, occīsum** to kill

**occupō, occupāre, occupāvī, occupātum** to seize

**occurrō, occurrere, occurrī, occursum** to meet, run into (*with dat.*)

**ōdī, ōdisse, ōsum** to hate

**ōlim** someday

**ōmen, ōminis** *n.* omen

**omnēs, omnium** everyone

**omnia, omnium** everything

**omnis, omne** each, every, all

**onerō, onerāre, onerāvī, onerātum** to load

**onus, oneris** *n.* load, burden

**oportet, oportēre, oportuit** one should (*with an acc. object*)

**oppidum, oppidī** *n.* town

**oppugnō, oppugnāre, oppugnāvī, oppugnātum** to attack

**optimus, optima, optimum** excellent, outstanding, amazing, best

**optō, optāre, optāvī, optātum** to choose

**opus est** there is need (*with a dat. object*)

**opus, operis** *n.* a work

**ōrātiō, ōrātiōnis** *f.* speech

**orior, orīrī, ortus sum** to rise

**ornātus, ornāta, ornātum** decorated

**ornō, ornāre, ornāvī, ornātum** to decorate

**ōrō, ōrāre, ōrāvī, ōrātum** to beg, ask, speak, pray

**os, ossis** *n.* bone

**ostendō, ostendere, ostendī, ostentum** to show

**ōvum, ōvī** *n.* egg

## P

**paedagōgus, paedagōgī** *m.* tutor, (male) nanny

**pandō, pandere, pandī, pansum/passum** to open up, stretch

**pānis, pānis** *m.* bread

**parcō, parcere, pepercī/parsī, parsūrus** to spare, be sparing (*with dat.*)

**pāreō, pārēre, pāruī, pāritum** to be obedient, obey (*with dat.*)

**pariēs, parietis** *m.* wall

**pariō, parere, peperī, partum** to give birth (to); produce

**parō, parāre, parāvī, parātum** to get ready, prepare; obtain

**pateō, patēre, patuī** to lie open, lie exposed

**pater, patris** *m.* father

**patior, patī, passus sum** to suffer, experience, put up with

**patria, patriae** *f.* country

**paucī, paucae, pauca** few

**pavīmentum, pavīmentī** *n.* floor

**pax, pācis** *f.* peace

**pecūnia, pecūniae** *f.* money

**pecus, pecoris** *n.* flock, herd, sheep

**pellō, pellere, pepulī, pulsum** to push, drive

**pendō, pendere, pependī, pensum** to hang; weigh; pay

**per** (*prep. with acc.*) through

**percutiō, percutere, percussī, percussum** to hit, strike

**perdō, perdere, perdidī, perditum** to lose, squander, destroy, waste

**pereō, perīre, periī/perīvī, peritum** to die; go through; be lost

**perficiō, perficere, perfēcī, perfectum** to complete

**pergō, pergere, perrexī, perrectum** to continue

**perīculum, perīculī** *n.* danger

**perītus, perīta, perītum** skilled

**permittō, permittere, permīsī, permissum** to allow, send through, throw

**pernoctō, pernoctāre, pernoctāvī, pernoctātum** to spend the night

**persequor, persequī, persecūtus sum** to chase, follow closely

**persuādeō, persuādēre, persuāsī, persuāsum** to persuade (*with dat.*)

**perterreō, perterrēre, perterruī, perterritum** to frighten

**perveniō, pervenīre, pervēnī, perventum** to arrive

**petō, petere, petiī/petīvī, petītum** to look for, ask (of someone, *with the preposition* ā); head for, attack

**pila, pilae** *f.* ball

**pinguis, pingue** fat; rich

**piscis, piscis** *m.* fish

**placeō, placēre, placuī, placitum** to please (*with dat.*)

**placet, placēre, placuit** it is pleasing (*with a dat. object*)

**plaudō, plaudere, plausī, plausum** to applaud

**plaustrum, plaustrī** *n.* cart, wagon

**plebs, plēbis** *f.* the plebeians, the common people

**plōrō, plōrāre, plōrāvī, plōrātum** to weep, mourn (for)

**plūrimus, plūrima, plūrimum** very much, very many

**plūs, plūris** more

**poēta, poētae** *m.* poet

**polliceor, pollicērī, pollicitus sum** to promise

**pompa, pompae** *f.* parade

**Pompēius, Pompēiī** *m.* Pompey

**pōnō, pōnere, posuī, positum** to put, lay, set down

**pons, pontis** *m.* bridge

**populus, populī** *m.* people

**porcus, porcī** *m.* pig, hog

**porta, portae** *f.* gate

**Porta Capēna, Portae Capēnae** *f.* the Porta Capena, the Capena Gate

**portō, portāre, portāvī, portātum** to carry, bring

**possum, posse, potuī** to be able

**post** (*prep. with acc.*) after, behind

**posteritās, posteritātis** *f.* posterity

**postulō, postulāre, postulāvī, postulātum** to demand

**potior, potīrī, potītus sum** to acquire

**praebeō, praebēre, praebuī, praebitum** to offer

**praemittō, praemittere, praemīsī, praemissum** to send ahead

**praesum, praeesse, praefuī, praefutūrus** to be in charge, be in front

**precor, precārī, precātus sum** to pray

**premō, premere, pressī, pressum** to press, push

**prīmā lūce** at dawn

**princeps, principis** *m.* emperor

**priusquam** before

**procul** far off

**prōdō, prōdere, prōdidī, prōditum** to betray, hand over

**proelium, proeliī** *n.* battle

**proficiscor, proficiscī, profectus sum** to set out, leave

**prōgredior, prōgredī, prōgressus sum** to go forward, advance

**prohibeō, prohibēre, prohibuī, prohibitum** to hold back, prohibit, forbid

**prōmittō, prōmittere, prōmīsī, prōmissum** to promise; send ahead

**properō, properāre, properāvī, properātum** to hurry

**Propertius, Propertiī** *m.* Propertius

**propter** (*prep. with acc.*) on account of

**prōsum, prōdesse, prōfuī, prōfutūrus** to profit, be useful

**Publius, Publiī** *m.* Publius

**puella, puellae** *f.* girl

**puer, puerī** *m.* boy, child

**pugna, pugnae** *f.* fight, battle

**pugnō, pugnāre, pugnāvī, pugnātum** to fight

**pulcher, pulchra, pulchrum** pretty, handsome

**pullus, pullī** *m.* chicken

**pūniō, pūnīre, pūnīvī/pūniī, pūnītum** to punish

**purgō, purgāre, purgāvī, purgātum** to clean

**putō, putāre, putāvī, putātum** to think, value

## Q

**quaerō, quaerere, quaesiī/quaesīvī, quaesītum** to look for, ask (of someone, *with the preposition* ā)

**quālis, quāle** what kind?

**quam prīmum** as soon as possible

**quandō** when?

**quantus, quanta, quantum** how great?

**-que** (*enclitic*) and

**queror, querī, questus sum** to complain (about)

**quī, quae, quod** what, which, that; which?

**quīdam, quaedam, quoddam** a certain (person/thing)

**quiescō, quiescere, quiēvī, quiētum** to rest

**quis, quid** who?, what?

**quō** where to?

**quōmodo** how?

**quot** how many?

## R

**rapiō, rapere, rapuī, raptum** to take (forcefully)

**recipiō, recipere, recēpī, receptum** to accept, take back

**recitō, recitāre, recitāvī, recitātum** to recite

**reddō, reddere, reddidī, redditum** to give back, surrender; repeat

**redeō, redīre, rediī, reditum** to go back, return

**rēgia, rēgiae** *f.* palace

**rēgīna, rēgīnae** *f.* queen

**regnō, regnāre, regnāvī, regnātum** to rule

**regō, regere, rexī, rectum** to rule, guide

**regredior, regredī, regressus sum** to go back

**relinquō, relinquere, relīquī, relictum** to abandon, leave

**reor, rērī, ratus sum** to think

**repellō, repellere, reppulī, repulsum** to drive away

**reperiō, reperīre, repperī, repertum** to find

**requīrō, requīrere, requīsiī/requīsīvī, requīsītum** to demand, ask; miss

**rēs, reī** *f.* thing

**respiciō, respicere, respexī, respectum** to look back

**respondeō, respondēre, respondī, responsum** to answer, correspond (*usually with dat.*)

**responsum, responsī** *n.* answer

**retineō, retinēre, retinuī, retentum** to hold back, keep

**revertō, revertere, revertī, reversum** to turn back

**revocō, revocāre, revocāvī, revocātum** to call back

**rex, rēgis** *m.* king

**rīdeō, rīdēre, rīsī, rīsum** to laugh, smile

**rīma, rīmae** *f.* a crack, chink

**rogō, rogāre, rogāvī, rogātum** to ask

**Rōma, Rōmae** *f.* Rome

**Rōmānus, Rōmāna, Rōmānum** Roman

**Rōmulus, Rōmulī** *m.* Romulus

**rumpō, rumpere, rūpī, ruptum** to break, burst

# S

**saepe** often

**sagitta, sagittae** *f.* arrow

**saliō, salīre, saluī, saltum** to dance, jump

**salūs, salūtis** *f.* health

**salūtō, salūtāre, salūtāvī, salūtātum** to greet

**sānus, sāna, sānum** sound, healthy, sane

**satis** enough

**saxum, saxī** *n.* rock

**scelestus, scelesta, scelestum** evil, wicked

**scindō, scindere, scidī, scissum** to cut

**sciō, scīre, scīvī, scītum** to know

**Scīpiō, Scīpiōnis** *m.* Scipio

**scrībō, scrībere, scripsī, scriptum** to write, draw

**secundus, secunda, secundum** second

**sedeō, sedēre, sēdī, sessum** to sit, stay put

**semper** always

**senātor, senātōris** *m.* senator

**senex, senis** *m.* old man; *adj.* old

**sententia, sententiae** *f.* opinion

**sentiō, sentīre, sensī, sensum** to perceive, experience, realize

**sepeliō, sepelīre, sepeliī/sepelīvī, sepultum** to bury

**sequor, sequī, secūtus sum** to follow

**serviō, servīre, servīvī, servītum** to be a slave, serve (*with dat.*)

**servō, servāre, servāvī, servātum** to preserve

**servus, servī** *m.* slave

**sī** if

**sīc** so, in such a way

**signum, signī** *n.* signal

**silva, silvae** *f.* forest

**simulō, simulāre, simulāvī, simulātum** to pretend

**sinō, sinere, sīvī, situm** to let, allow

**socius, sociī** *m.* ally

**sōl, sōlis** *m.* sun

**soleō, solēre, solitus sum** to be accustomed to, usually (do something)

**sollicitus, sollicita, sollicitum** worried, nervous, anxious

**sōlum** only

**sōlus, sōla, sōlum** only, alone

**solvō, solvere, solvī, solūtum** to loosen, untie; pay

**sonitus, sonitūs** *m.* sound

**sonō, sonāre, sonuī, sonitum** to make a sound

**soror, sorōris** *f.* sister

**spargō, spargere, sparsī, sparsum** to scatter, sprinkle

**spectāculum, spectāculī** *n.* a show

**spectātor, spectātōris** *m.* spectator

**spectō, spectāre, spectāvī, spectātum** to look at, watch

**spēlunca, spēluncae** *f.* cave

**spernō, spernere, sprēvī, sprētum** to reject, scorn

**spērō, spērāre, spērāvī, spērātum** to expect, hope

**spēs, speī** *f.* hope

**spīrō, spīrāre, spīrāvī, spīrātum** to breathe

**statim** immediately

**statuō, statuere, statuī, statūtum** to set up; stop; decide

**stella, stellae** *f.* star

**sternō, sternere, strāvī, strātum** to spread, stretch

**stō, stāre, stetī, statum** to stand, stay

**studeō, studēre, studuī** to be eager (for), be busy with (*usually with dat.*)

**stultus, stulta, stultum** foolish, silly

**stupeō, stupēre, stupuī** to be surprised, amazed

**suādeō, suādēre, suāsī, suāsum** to advise

**sub** (*prep. with acc./abl.*) under

**subdūcō, subdūcere, subduxī, subductum** to raise; steal

**subsum, subesse** to be under, be nearby

**Sulla, Sullae** *m.* Sulla

**sum, esse, fuī, futūrus** to be, exist

**sūmō, sūmere, sumpsī, sumptum** to take, assume

**superō, superāre, superāvī, superātum** to overcome, conquer, win

**supersum, superesse, superfuī, superfutūrus** to survive, be left over

**surgō, surgere, surrexī, surrectum** to rise

**suscipiō, suscipere, suscēpī, susceptum** to undertake; accept

**sustineō, sustinēre, sustinuī** to support, uphold

**suus, sua, suum** his, her, its, their (own)

# T

**taceō, tacēre, tacuī, tacitum** to be quiet

**tālis, tāle** of such a kind

**tam** so

**tamen** nevertheless

**Tanaquil, Tanaquīlis** *f.* Tanaquil

**tandem** finally, at last

**tangō, tangere, tetigī, tactum** to touch

**tantum** only

**tantus, tanta, tantum** so large, so great

**tēcum** with you

**tegō, tegere, texī, tectum** to cover

**tēlum, tēlī** *n.* weapon

**tempestās, tempestātis** *f.* storm

**templum, templī** *n.* temple

**temptō, temptāre, temptāvī, temptātum** to try, test

**tendō, tendere, tetendī, tentum/tensum** to stretch; try

**tenebrae, tenebrārum** *f.pl.* darkness, shadows

**teneō, tenēre, tenuī, tentum** to hold, have

**terra, terrae** *f.* earth, land

**terreō, terrēre, terruī, territum** to scare

**theatrum, theatrī** *n.* theater

**Tiberius, Tiberiī** *m.* Tiberius

**Tibullus, Tibullī** *m.* Tibullus

**timeō, timēre, timuī** to be afraid of, fear

**toga, togae** *f.* toga

**tollō, tollere, sustulī, sublātum** to raise; carry away; destroy

**tot** so many

**totiens** so many times

**tōtus, tōta, tōtum** whole, entire

**trādō, trādere, trādidī, trāditum** to hand over, surrender

**trahō, trahere, traxī, tractum** to pull, drag

**trans** (*prep. with acc.*) across

**transcrībō, transcrībere, transcripsī, transcriptum** to translate

**transeō, transīre, transīvī/transiī, transitum** to cross, go across

**trīclīnium, trīclīniī** *n.* dining room

**Trimalchiō, Trimalchiōnis** *m.* Trimalchio

**tristis, triste** sad

**Trōia, Trōiae** *f.* Troy

**Trōiānus, Trōiāna, Trōiānum** Trojan

**tū, tuī** you (*singular*)

**tueor, tuērī, tūtus/tuitus sum** to watch, protect

**tum** then

**tumultus, tumultūs** *m.* noise

**turba, turbae** *f.* crowd, gang

**turris, turris** *f.* tower

**tuus, tua, tuum** your (*singular*)

**tyrannus, tyrannī** *m.* tyrant

**U**

**ubi** when, where

**ulciscor, ulciscī, ultus sum** to avenge

**ullus, ulla, ullum** any

**umbra, umbrae** *f.* shadow; ghost

**umquam** ever

**ūnā** together

**unde** where from?

**urbs, urbis** *f.* city

**urna, urnae** *f.* jug

**utinam** (*reinforces wishes*)

**ūtor, ūtī, ūsus sum** to use; to benefit oneself (*with abl. of means*)

**ūva, ūvae** *f.* grape

**uxor, uxōris** *f.* wife

**V**

**valdē** very

**valeō, valēre, valuī, valitūrus** to be strong

**vehō, vehere, vexī, vectum** to carry; (*in the middle voice with abl.*) to ride

**vendō, vendere, vendidī, venditum** to sell

**veniō, venīre, vēnī, ventum** to come

**vēnor, vēnārī, vēnātus sum** to hunt, go hunting

**verberō, verberāre, verberāvī, verberātum** to beat

**verbum, verbī** *n.* word

**vereor, verērī, veritus sum** to be afraid

**versus, versūs** *m.* verse, poetry

**vertō, vertere, vertī, versum** to turn

**vērus, vēra, vērum** true, real

**Vespāsiānus, Vespāsiānī** *m.* Vespasian

**vester, vestra, vestrum** your (*plural*)

**vetō, vetāre, vetuī, vetitum** to deny, say no

**vexō, vexāre, vexāvī, vexātum** to annoy

**via, viae** *f.* road, street

**Via Appia, Viae Appiae** *f.* the Via Appia, the Appian Way

**victōria, victōriae** *f.* victory

**videō, vidēre, vīdī, vīsum** to see; (*passive voice*) to seem, be seen

**vigilō, vigilāre, vigilāvī, vigilātum** to be awake, watch

**villa, villae** *f.* farmhouse, farm

**vincō, vincere, vīcī, victum** to conquer

**vinculum, vinculī** *n.* chain, fetter

**vīnum, vīnī** *n.* wine

**vir, virī** *m.* a man

**virga, virgae** *f.* a crop, switch

**vīta, vītae** *f.* life

**vītō, vītāre, vītāvī, vītātum** to avoid

**vix** barely, hardly

**vocō, vocāre, vocāvī, vocātum** to call, summon

**volō, velle, voluī** to want, be willing

**volō, volāre, volāvī, volātum** to fly

**vōs, vestrī** you (*plural*)

**vulnerō, vulnerāre, vulnerāvī, vulnerātum** to wound

**vulnus, vulneris** *n.* wound

**vultus, vultūs** *m.* face

# English-Latin Glossary

This glossary contains only those words used in the English-to-Latin exercises in this book; it is not a reverse version of the Latin-to-English glossary. Unless otherwise noted, all words in this glossary are verbs.

**A**

**abandon** relinquō

**accept** recipiō

**allow** permittō, sinō

**announce** nuntiō

**answer** respondeō

**approach** adeō

**arm** armō

**arrive** perveniō

**attack** aggredior

**avenge** ulciscor

**B**

**be** sum

**be a slave** serviō

**be able** possum

**be accustomed to** soleō

**be eager** studeō

**be happy** gaudeō

**be in charge** praesum

**be made** fīō

**be on fire** ardeō

**be open** pateō

**be present** adsum

**be quiet** taceō

**be strong** valeō

**be under** subsum

**be unwilling** nōlō

**be willing** volō

**become** fīō

**beg** ōrō

**begin** incipiō

**betray** prōdō

**break** rumpō

**bring** ferō

**bristle** horreō

**bury** sepeliō

**C**

**call** vocō

**call back** revocō

**can** possum

**capture** capiō

**carry** ferō, portō, vehō

**carry away** auferō

**catch** capiō

**change** mūtō

**choose** legō, optō

**climb down** descendō

**close** claudō

**come** veniō

**compel** cōgō

**complain** queror

**complete** cōnficiō

**confess** cōnfiteor

**consider** habeō

**copy** imitor

**cover** tegō

**cut** scindō

**D**

**dare** audeō

**decorate** ornō

**delay** moror

**demand** postulō
**deny** negō, vetō
**deserve** mereō
**destroy** dēleō, perdō
**die** morior, obeō, pereō
**divide** dīvidō
**do nothing** cessō
**doubt** dubitō
**drag** trahō
**dress** induō
**drink** bibō

**E**
**elect** creō
**embrace** amplector, complector
**encourage** hortor
**enjoy** fruor
**enter** intrō
**escape** effugiō

**F**
**fear** metuō, timeō, vereor
**feel** sentiō
**fight** pugnō
**fill** compleō
**fill up** impleō
**find** inveniō, reperiō
**finish** fīniō
**follow** sequor
**force** cōgō
**fortify** mūniō
**friend** amīcus

**G**
**girl** puella
**give** dō
**give back** reddō
**go** eō
**go away** abeō
**grab** arripiō, ēripiō
**grow** crescō
**guard** custōdiō

**H**
**hand over** trādō
**hang** pendō
**happen** fīō
**harm** laedō
**have** habeō
**hear** audiō
**help** adiuvō
**hesitate** dubitō
**hold** habeō
**hope** spērō

**I**
**increase** augeō
**into** *prep.* in (*with the acc.*)

**J**
**join** iungō

**K**
**kill** interficiō, necō, occīdō
**know** sciō

**L**
**laugh** rīdeō
**lead** dūcō
**lie** mentior
**lie hidden** lateō
**lift** tollō
**live** vīvō
**look back** respiciō
**look for** petō
**loosen** solvō
**lose** āmittō, perdō
**love** amō, dīligō

**M**
**make a sound** sonō
**make known** indicō
**marvel at** mīror
**meet** obeō
**mix** misceō
**move** moveō

**N**

**name** nōminō
**never** numquam
**not know** nesciō
**not want** nōlō
**nourish** alō

**O**

**obey** pāreō
**offer** praebeō
**open** aperiō
**order** imperō, iubeō
**overcome** superō
**owe** dēbeō

**P**

**pay** solvō
**perceive** sentiō
**perform** fungor
**persuade** persuādeō
**play** lūdō
**praise** laudō
**pray** ōrō, precor
**prefer** mālō
**prepare** parō
**pretend** simulō
**profit** prōsum
**pull** trahō
**push** premō, pellō
**put on** impōnō

**R**

**raise** tollō
**read** legō
**recline** iaceō
**rejoice** gaudeō
**remain** maneō
**rest** quiescō
**result** ēveniō
**return** redeō
**rise** orior

**run** currō
**run away** fugiō

**S**

**sail** nāvigō
**say** dīcō
**sea** mare
**see** videō
**sell** vendō
**send** mittō
**serve** serviō
**set free** līberō
**set out** proficiscor
**shape** fungor
**ship** *noun* nāvis
**show** monstrō, ostendō
**sing** canō, cantō
**sit** sedeō
**sleep** dormiō
**slip** lābor
**spare** parcō
**stand** stō
**step in** ingredior
**stone** *noun* lapis
**stretch** tendō
**strike** percutiō
**student** discipulus
**suffer** patior
**support** sustineō
**surround** cingō

**T**

**take** capiō, sūmō
**take back** recipiō
**take by force** rapiō
**take care of** cūrō
**take out** excipiō
**teach** doceō
**test** temptō
**think** putō
**throw** iaciō
**touch** tangō

**trust** fīdō
**turn** vertō
**turn back** revertō

**U**
**understand** intellegō
**use** ūtor

**V**
**visit often** celebrō

**W**
**wander** errō
**want** volō
**want more** mālō
**warn** moneō
**wash** lavō
**watch** spectō
**work** labōrō
**write** scrībō

# Answer Key

## Unit 2

**2-1**

1. I think
2. they give
3. you are washing
4. we tell (in story form)
5. you ask
6. they name
7. he stands
8. we are waiting
9. I am singing
10. you are changing
11. you are decorating
12. they are taking caring of
13. I live
14. we are calling back
15. he does nothing

**2-2**

1. labōrās
2. necant
3. laudō
4. datis
5. labōrat
6. labōrāmus
7. cantant
8. ornās
9. spērō
10. portat
11. dubitāmus
12. errātis
13. sonō
14. parat
15. vocās

**2-3**

1. The slave helps his master.
2. Marcus loves his friends.
3. I am preparing dinner.
4. Birds are flying in the sky.
5. The master frees the slave woman.

**2-4**

1. purgat / The slave woman is cleaning the dining room.
2. ambulāmus / We are walking home.
3. portās / You are carrying water.
4. simulant / Boys often pretend.
5. vocat / The mother is calling the girl.

**2-5**

1. I see
2. they have
3. you lack
4. we are reclining
5. he deserves
6. you are offering
7. they are holding together
8. I am staying
9. we dare
10. he laughs
11. you are destroying
12. you do move
13. we owe
14. he is training
15. you are mixing

**2-6**

1. ardēs
2. habent
3. patet
4. moneō
5. docēmus
6. rīdētis
7. vidēs
8. praebent
9. habeō
10. iubet
11. sedēmus
12. monētis
13. dēlent
14. iubēs
15. augeō

**2-7**

1. Marcus is moving the table.
2. You are often quiet.
3. They deserve chains.
4. I teach boys.
5. You have an awesome army.

**2-8**

1. sedent / They are sitting under a tree.
2. timet / The boy is afraid of his sisters.
3. student / The students are eager for work.
4. habet / The senator has a letter.
5. caveō / I now beware of the dog.

**2-9**

1. he is setting (something) up
2. we are saying
3. they are reading
4. I am sending
5. you are living
6. you are falling
7. they are turning
8. he learns
9. you are lifting
10. we grow
11. I esteem
12. they are compelling
13. you are giving birth
14. you are running
15. I am reading

**2-10**

1. legit
2. tollō
3. dīcunt
4. mittitis
5. currimus
6. scribis
7. vendunt
8. trahō
9. ostendit
10. dīcimus
11. permittitis
12. scindis
13. dūcunt
14. premit
15. solvō

**2-11**

1. The girl is climbing the mountain.
2. I am writing a book.
3. The boys are playing with a ball.
4. I am untying the dog from its chain.
5. The tutor is gathering the boys/children.

**2-12**

1. describit / Marcus describes the spiders.
2. vehunt / The oxen are carrying the loads to the town with carts.
3. metuit / My mother is afraid of mice.
4. canō / I sing about arms and a man.
5. accēdunt / The enemy is not approaching the city.

**2-13**
1. they are accepting
2. you are throwing really hard
3. I am making
4. we are undertaking
5. you are looking at
6. I am looking back
7. he is receiving
8. they desire
9. he is hitting
10. you are giving birth

**2-14**
1. conficimus
2. rapit
3. excipiō
4. iacis
5. fugis
6. interficit
7. effugiunt
8. ēripit
9. incipiunt
10. capiō

**2-15**
1. We are taking back our gifts.
2. The gladiator is grabbing the sword from the other one.
3. Birds lay eggs.
4. Old men look back at their youth.
5. At the theater we often look at the spectators.

**2-16**
1. cupit / A wealthy person always desires more money.
2. conficiunt / After many hours the soldiers are finishing the battle.
3. percutit / Lightning is striking the tower.
4. interficiunt / The Greeks are killing the Trojan prisoners.
5. faciunt / The slaves are doing many things in the fields.

**2-17**
1. he is opening
2. he knows
3. you are hearing
4. they are guarding
5. they are finding

**2-18**
1. servīs
2. mūniō
3. venītis
4. nescīs
5. pervenit
6. sepelīs
7. inveniunt
8. scītis
9. ēvenit
10. serviunt

**2-19**
1. We are finishing our game now.
2. Everything is turning out well.
3. I am finding few true friends.
4. We are arriving at the drinking party with a crowd of partygoers.
5. You are burying your brother on the Via Appia.

**2-20**
1. servīs / You are still a slave to Messalla.
2. mūnit / Caesar is fortifying the camp quickly.
3. sentiō / I feel your pain.
4. reperīmus / We find a skeleton in the cave.
5. custōdiunt / What guards are guarding the guards?

**2-21**

1. third / they are straining
2. second / you are teaching
3. third / I esteem
4. third / they are cutting
5. first / we are awake
6. second / we are persuading
7. third **-iō** / I welcome
8. first / he is fighting
9. first / you are fighting
10. first / they are calling
11. third / he believes
12. first / I am praising
13. third **-iō** / we are undertaking
14. third / you are falling
15. third / we are consulting
16. third **-iō** / they are killing
17. first / they stand together
18. third / they despise
19. first / he is singing
20. first / I swear

# Unit 3

**3-1**

1. you were completing
2. you were owing
3. I was putting
4. I was holding back
5. we were telling
6. we were being
7. you were betraying
8. they were lying
9. you were harming
10. they were wandering

**3-2**

1. nuntiābātis
2. tegēbant
3. parcēbāmus
4. vetābam
5. quiescēbant
6. superābātis
7. excipiēbās
8. claudēbat
9. erat
10. trahēbāmus
11. legēbās
12. mūtābam
13. studēbant
14. vīvēbant
15. valēbās
16. implēbat
17. erās
18. cessābat
19. serviēbat
20. revertēbam

**3-3**

1. I was losing everything.
2. He was offering many things to him.
3. I was freeing the slaves.
4. They slept for the whole night.
5. They were finishing the war.

**3-4**

1. sedēbāmus / We were sitting in the senate.
2. erātis / You used to be friends.
3. descendēbam / I was coming down from the mountain.
4. audiēbant / The boys used to hear many stories.
5. revocābat / The mother was calling back her children.

# Unit 4

**4-1**

1. he will be awake
2. I will persuade
3. we will fight
4. you will call
5. they will answer
6. he will stand
7. you will owe
8. we will help
9. I will call
10. they will hold back

**4-2**

1. indicābimus
2. iacēbunt
3. nuntiābit
4. intrābit
5. audēbitis
6. nāvigābō
7. superābis
8. mūtābunt
9. studēbimus
10. valēbō

**4-3**
1. You will be praising the gods.
2. The citizens will elect the magistrates.
3. A fire will destroy everything.
4. I will tell a story about a woman.
5. You will be lying on the bed.

**4-4**
1. vocābit / Marcus will call his son.
2. monēbimus / We will warn the army tomorrow.
3. cessābis / You will be doing nothing after the war.
4. manēbunt / They will remain under the stars.
5. cantābō / I will sing only to my friends.

**4-5**
1. I will love
2. you will cut
3. we will compel
4. they will welcome
5. you will undertake
6. you will fall
7. I will consult
8. he will find
9. we will put
10. you will finish

**4-6**
1. sinet
2. trādet
3. capient
4. traham
5. perdēs
6. laedētis
7. cōgent
8. audiet
9. sciam
10. respiciēs

**4-7**
1. We will withdraw from the fight.
2. You will hand the prisoners over to the Romans.
3. They will take my things (goods).
4. You will send the cavalry across the Alps.
5. Tiberius will throw stones into the sea.

**4-8**
1. fīniet / He will finish.
2. colligent / They will gather the grapes.
3. tangēmus / We will touch the boundary.
4. custōdiet / The slave will guard the door.
5. vertam / I will turn (myself) toward you.

**4-9**
1. labōrābis / you will work
2. tenēbimus / we will hold
3. iacēbitis / you will recline
4. laedet / he will hurt
5. veniam / I will come
6. studēbit / he will be eager
7. vocābimus / we will call
8. capient / they will take
9. vidēbis / you will see
10. rogābō / I will ask
11. tenēbit / he will hold
12. pōnent / they will put
13. fīniēs / you will finish
14. mittētis / you will send
15. timēbimus / we will fear

## Unit 5

**5-1**
1. you loved
2. he placed
3. they lived
4. you took
5. I denied
6. he sat
7. we gave
8. you sought
9. they sang
10. he played
11. you knew
12. they slept
13. he climbed
14. we tested
15. you learned

**5-2**

1. pepulistī
2. quiēvit
3. lēgērunt
4. mūtāvistī
5. implēvit
6. perdidērunt
7. praebuistī
8. līberāvī
9. vexistis
10. trādidērunt
11. pāruī
12. celebrāvimus
13. sēdistis
14. descendit
15. revertimus

**5-3**

1. He saw the fire.
2. You destroyed the flowers.
3. We did lie hidden among the trees.
4. I offered my hand to you.
5. Hannibal deceived the Romans.
6. A brave soldier will not run away from a battle.
7. You threw the stones into the sea.
8. I scared your mother yesterday.
9. Books train the mind.
10. Caesar waged war against very many people.

**5-4**

1. fluxit / it flowed
2. sparsī / I sprinkled
3. terruimus / we scared
4. promīsistis / you promised
5. mōvistī / you moved
6. addidērunt / they added
7. recurristis / you ran back
8. creāvit / he created
9. dīvīsimus / we divided
10. tacuērunt / they were quiet
11. accessistis / you approached
12. habitāvit / he inhabited
13. ostendī / I showed
14. pandērunt / they opened up
15. recēpistis / you accepted
16. occurristī / you met
17. sonuimus / we made a sound
18. genuī / I gave birth
19. requīsīvit / he demanded
20. ēvēnērunt / they came out

**5-5**

1. syllabic augment
2. aorist
3. temporal augment
4. syllabic augment
5. aorist
6. temporal augment
7. reduplication
8. aorist
9. syllabic augment
10. temporal augment

# Unit 6

**6-1**

1. they had waited
2. he had stretched
3. you had hurried
4. I had desired
5. he had touched
6. they had equipped
7. you had committed
8. I had worked
9. we had known
10. she had given birth

**6-2**

1. manserant
2. necāverātis
3. intellexerās
4. postulāverant
5. optāverat
6. biberātis
7. āmīserās
8. imposuerāmus
9. errāveram
10. relīquerātis

**6-3**

1. The dogs had warned the household before the guests arrived.
2. I had covered the dead bodies that night.
3. You had set up an altar in the garden.
4. I had taught the students the Greek language.
5. We had already poured wine for the guests before the slaves brought in the dinner.

**6-4**

1. arripuerās / You had grabbed the pendant from my son.
2. percusserant / They had struck the cymbals.
3. duxerāmus / We had taken the guests to the door.
4. simulāverat / Caligula had pretended to be a god.
5. verteram / I had turned my face toward the speaker.

**6-5**

1. you will have struggled
2. we will have come
3. he will have believed
4. we will have thought
5. they will have looked at
6. you will have decorated
7. we will have been on guard
8. you will have laughed
9. we will have died
10. I will have ordered

**6-6**

1. rūperit
2. sumpseris
3. prōdiderint
4. manserit
5. lāveris
6. miscueritis
7. cinxerint
8. habuerit
9. induerō
10. nōmināverint

**6-7**

1. You will have mentioned a certain story about the Gallic War.
2. You will have burned the temple.
3. Juno will have warned Manlius before the Gauls attack the Romans.
4. I will have found my friend before he leaves the city.
5. The emperor will have built many temples.

**6-8**

1. ēmerō / I will have bought fish at the market.
2. neglexerit / Caesar will not have neglected the common people.
3. laudāverimus / We will not have praised the gods enough.
4. metuerit / The mother will have feared her own daughter.
5. duxerit / Pompey will have led the army.

# Unit 7

**7-1**

1. we were being judged
2. you are advised
3. I was being carried
4. they are owed
5. he is hidden
6. we will be moved
7. I am soothed
8. he is held
9. you will be asked
10. they were being cared for
11. it was being increased
12. we will be warned
13. you used to be loved
14. you will be awaited
15. I will be killed

**7-2**

1. monēbor
2. putāris
3. iubeor
4. lavābuntur
5. docēbimur
6. pugnābātur
7. laudāmur
8. parābāminī
9. dēbeor
10. temptāberis
11. nuntiābitur
12. complentur
13. rīdēberis
14. sustinēbāmur
15. habēbātur

**7-3**

1. Soror ā fratre vexātur. / The sister is being bothered by her brother.
2. Oppidum ā mīlitibus oppugnābitur. / The town will be attacked by the soldiers.
3. Ego sagittā vulnerābor. / I will be wounded by an arrow.
4. Nōs metū numquam superābāmur. / We were never overcome by fear.
5. Lībertās ā servīs dēsīderātur. / Freedom is longed for by slaves.

**7-4**

1. Id factum Caesarem movēbit. / This deed will move Caesar.
2. Consul signum dabat. / The consul was giving the signal.
3. Puella omnia narrābit. / The girl will tell everything.
4. Quis Germānōs superābat? / Who was conquering the Germans?
5. Iūnō Aenēan longē Latiō arcēbat. / Juno kept Aeneas far from Latium.

**7-5**

1. dubitāris / You are doubted.
2. tenentur / The dogs are being held.
3. videor / I seem. / I am seen.
4. spectāminī / You are being watched.
5. regnāmur / We are ruled.

**7-6**

1. dēlēbāmur / We were being destroyed.
2. tenēbantur / The soldiers were being held.
3. laudābāminī / You used to be praised.
4. vītābātur / Lucius used to be avoided.
5. monēbāris / You were being warned.

**7-7**

1. dēmonstrābuntur / The dangers will be shown.
2. docēbor / I will be taught.
3. vulnerābimur / We will be wounded.
4. habēberis / You will be considered.
5. superābitur / The queen will be conquered.

**7-8**

1. he is conquered
2. I will be loved
3. you used to be consulted
4. we will be despised
5. they used to be ruled
6. you are being taken
7. it will be done
8. they are found
9. it was being covered
10. they are being put
11. you will be dragged
12. I was riding
13. I am being deceived
14. they will be fortified
15. it used to be known

**7-9**

1. iaciēminī
2. creābar
3. consulēbar
4. reciperis
5. tangitur
6. percutitur
7. tollēmur
8. alēbātur
9. custōdiēbantur
10. iungiminī
11. vertar
12. inveniris
13. solvētur
14. relinquēris
15. petuntur

**7-10**

1. Ā quō exercitus ad montem dūcētur? / By whom will the army be led to the mountain?
2. Omnēs ā Marcō terrēbantur. / Everyone used to be frightened by Marcus.
3. In hortō tuō multī et pulchrī flōrēs ā mē semper inveniuntur. / In your garden many beautiful flowers are always found by me.
4. Sub pavīmentō pecunia ā tē reperītur. / The money is found by you under the floor.
5. Bellum in Gallōs ā Caesare gerēbātur. / War against the Gauls was being waged by Caesar.

**7-11**

1. Crās nōs Rōmam petēmus. / We will head for Rome tomorrow.
2. Tū mē numquam trādēbās. / You never betrayed me.
3. Virga equōs celerius agit. / A crop drives horses more quickly.
4. Nūbēs terram tegēbant. / Clouds were covering the land.
5. Ego lupum ē fundō expellō. / I am driving the wolf from the farm.

**7-12**
1. perficitur / The work is being completed.
2. dēfendimur / We are defended.
3. mittiminī / You are being sent.
4. caperis / You are being taken.
5. aperiuntur / The gates are being opened.

**7-13**
1. dīligēbar / I used to be loved.
2. colēbātur / The field was being cultivated.
3. pūniēbantur / The boys were being punished.
4. audiēbātur / A sound kept being heard.
5. āmittēbāris / You were lost.

**7-14**
1. claudētur / The door will be closed.
2. iaciētur / The rock will be thrown.
3. audientur / My opinions will be heard.
4. occīdēris / You will be killed.
5. dūcar / I will be led.

**7-15**
1. she had been taught
2. they were waited for
3. it will have been demanded
4. I was carried
5. we had been desired
6. he had been touched
7. they will have been armed
8. they had been entrusted
9. I will have been killed
10. you were understood
11. it was asked
12. you will have been chosen
13. they had been lost
14. we will have been abandoned
15. they were grabbed
16. they had been struck
17. I was shown
18. you were raised
19. she had been turned
20. I was guarded

**7-16**
1. captus eram
2. inventa est
3. aperta sunt
4. dubitātus erit
5. sensum erat
6. cūrātī sunt
7. auctum est
8. redditī erāmus
9. spectātī estis
10. pulsus es
11. armātus erō
12. relictae sunt
13. ductus erās
14. dīvīsī erātis
15. respectī erimus

**7-17**
1. Castra nostra ab hostibus nōn capta sunt. / Our camp was not taken by the enemy.
2. Senātōrēs ā principe convocātī erant. / The senators had been called together by the emperor.
3. Cēna in mensās ā servīs imposita erit. / The dinner will have been put on the tables by the slaves.
4. Ignis imbre exstinctus est. / The fire was put out by the rain.
5. Epistulae Rōmam ā nuntiīs portātae sunt. / The letters were carried to Rome by the messengers.

**7-18**
1. Amīcus mīlitem vulnerātum in campō relīquerat. / His friend had left the wounded soldier on the field.
2. Rōmulus Rōmam condidit. / Romulus founded Rome.
3. Ōmina mē monuerint. / Omens will have warned me.
4. Larva puellās perterruerat. / A ghost had frightened the girls.
5. Nōs sociōs servāvimus. / We saved our allies.

**7-19**
1. audītus es / You were heard.
2. emptum est / The grain was bought.
3. sitī sumus / We were allowed.
4. revocātī estis / You were called back.
5. petītus sum / I was looked for.

**7-20**
1. consultus erat / Publius had been consulted.
2. falsī erāmus / We had been deceived.
3. cūrātus erās / You had been cared for.
4. aedificāta erant / Temples had been built.
5. sepulta erat / Caecilia had been buried.

**7-21**
1. vītātum erit / The danger will have been avoided.
2. victī erimus / We will have been conquered.
3. sprētus eris / You will have been rejected.
4. collectī erunt / The flowers will have been gathered.
5. parāta erunt / Everything will have been prepared.

# Unit 8

**8-1**
1. he acquires
2. we will try
3. they thought
4. I used to encourage
5. you had been accustomed to
6. he will become angry
7. you will have dared
8. I am thinking
9. they will test
10. we had marveled at
11. you will leave
12. you were hesitating
13. she rejoiced
14. we were dying
15. I will suffer
16. you will watch
17. they had prayed
18. he was following
19. I am promising
20. they will be afraid

**8-2**
1. fungitur
2. morātī erunt
3. solēbātis
4. mentītī erant
5. ulciscimur
6. fīdet
7. lapsus sum
8. aggressī erant
9. imitābiminī
10. gāvīsus erit
11. ūtar
12. querēmur
13. mīror
14. ortum est
15. complectī erunt
16. audēbō
17. ingressī erātis
18. confitēbimur
19. sequar
20. fruuntur

**8-3**
1. Did you trust me?
2. Publius will have acquired many things.
3. I am leaving without you.
4. We had pursued the enemy.
5. You will protect your house.

**8-4**
1. experīmur / We try to be good.
2. hortāris / You are urging my son.
3. precāminī / You are praying to the gods.
4. cōnor / I am trying to gather the grapes.
5. imitantur / The students are imitating Cicero today.

**8-5**
1. persecūtus est / That man chased me for three years.
2. ūsī sumus / We used the money well.
3. gāvīsus sum / I was happy to see you.
4. ēgressus es / When I entered, you left.
5. lapsa est / She slipped on the wet floor.

**8-6**
1. mentiētur / The slave will lie about Marcus.
2. loquēminī / You will speak without fear.
3. gaudēbis / You will rejoice after the victory.
4. nascētur / Maybe my son will be born tomorrow.
5. sequentur / The dogs will follow me home.

**8-7**
1. complectēbātur / Marcus was embracing his mother.
2. imitābar / I used to imitate Cicero.
3. patiēbantur / The citizens were never able to put up with this.
4. querēbātur / The Roman people were complaining to the senators.
5. morābāminī / You were hesitating to leave the forum.

# Unit 9

**9-1**
1. put!
2. tell!
3. try!
4. take!
5. enter!
6. push!
7. announce!
8. cover!
9. deny!
10. spare!

**9-2**
1. excipe!
2. claudite!
3. dūc!
4. perdite!
5. ferte!
6. sedē!
7. precāminī!
8. audīte!
9. lūde!
10. canite!

**9-3**
1. Boy, listen to your mother!
2. Kill the enemy!
3. Slave, bury this body now!
4. Seize that man!
5. Fear an evil tyrant!

**9-4**
1. Dēlēte nāvēs!
2. Numquam respice, amīce!
3. Iace lapidēs in mare!
4. Discipulī, tacēte!
5. Gaudēte, puellae!

# Unit 10

**10-1**
1. we were
2. they are
3. I will be in charge
4. he will have been
5. you are
6. I am away
7. we were present
8. be!
9. he will be
10. they had been

**10-2**
1. I am
2. you were
3. he was
4. he is
5. they are profiting
6. I am surviving
7. you were
8. we were in charge
9. I was
10. they are away

**10-3**

1. estis
2. erāmus
3. fuerat
4. es
5. sunt
6. prōsum
7. adfuī
8. eritis
9. suberātis
10. erit

**10-4**

1. sit
2. essem
3. superessētis
4. esset
5. adsīs
6. prōdesset
7. essent
8. praesint
9. sītis
10. subessēmus

**10-5**

1. Marcus is stupid.
2. While I am present, everyone stands at attention.
3. Your sons are at home.
4. When you were there, I was away.
5. The lucky soldiers will survive.
6. This bread is excellent.
7. Someday we will be famous.
8. Many lands used to be unknown.
9. I will always be here for you.
10. At this moment, Caesar is away from Rome.

**10-6**

1. sum / I am a good man.
2. erunt / They will be in the Senate House.
3. fuit / Augustus was here.
4. est / That girl is bad.
5. erāmus / We used to be in danger.
6. fuerātis / You had been foolish.
7. fuit / Scipio was a great leader.
8. es / You are so handsome to me.
9. suberat / My friend was often under that tree.
10. aderimus / We will be at home.

**10-7**

1. we are able
2. he used to be able
3. they were able
4. you will be able
5. we will have been able
6. I will be able
7. they will be able
8. you used to be able
9. I was able
10. he is able

**10-8**

1. we are able
2. you used to be able
3. he had been able
4. I used to be able
5. you used to be able
6. they used to be able
7. you are able
8. we had been able
9. they are able
10. you will have been able

**10-9**

1. poterit
2. potes
3. poterātis
4. potuit
5. possumus
6. poterunt
7. potuerimus
8. poterat
9. potuerō
10. possunt

**10-10**

1. potuissem
2. possit
3. possītis
4. potuerint
5. possim
6. possint
7. possēs
8. possīmus
9. possīs
10. potuissētis

**10-11**
1. Our enemies will be able to destroy the city.
2. You are always able to think well.
3. My son cannot see.
4. You, soldiers, will be able to kill the evil men.
5. He was not able to walk in the gardens today.

**10-12**
1. poteris / You will be able to go into the palace.
2. poterat / Vespasian was able to finish many buildings.
3. possumus / We are able to undertake the work.
4. potuit / He was able to give the book to me.
5. possunt / The prisoners cannot escape from the chains.

**10-13**
1. we want
2. you will want
3. I wanted
4. they were wanting
5. you will be willing
6. you will have wanted
7. we wanted
8. they are willing
9. you want
10. I had wanted

**10-14**
1. he wants
2. I was wanting
3. you were wanting
4. we want
5. you want
6. you are willing
7. they were willing
8. you were willing
9. he was wanting
10. I am willing

**10-15**
1. volunt
2. voluerat
3. volam
4. volēbāmus
5. volētis
6. voluistī
7. volent
8. vīs
9. volō
10. voluimus

**10-16**
1. velim
2. vellent
3. velīs
4. vellētis
5. velīmus
6. velit
7. velint
8. vellēs
9. vellet
10. vellem

**10-17**
1. The leader wants to sail now.
2. I will want to grow my flowers.
3. I wanted to sell my house then.
4. The guests want dinner to be prepared now.
5. The doorkeeper was willing to close the door.

**10-18**
1. volēbam / I was willing to tell those things about our household.
2. volunt / Everyone wants to live longer.
3. volent / The boy and girl will want to sit under the tree.
4. voluit / Caesar wanted to give orders to the soldiers.
5. vult / The master wants to set his (own) slaves free.

**10-19**
1. he does not want
2. they will not want
3. he will not have wanted
4. you are not willing
5. I was not willing
6. we did not want
7. you will not want
8. I am not willing
9. you do not want
10. they had not been willing

**10-20**
1. you do not want
2. I was not willing
3. you are not willing
4. they were not wanting
5. we are not willing
6. they had not wanted
7. I do not want
8. we were not wanting
9. you used to be unwilling
10. you were not willing

**10-21**
1. nōlet
2. nōn vīs
3. nōlēbāmus
4. nōluerātis
5. nōlunt
6. nōluerimus
7. nōn vult
8. nōlent
9. nōn vultis
10. nōlētis

**10-22**
1. nōlīs
2. nollent
3. nōlīmus
4. nōlueris
5. nōlit
6. nollēmus
7. nōlim
8. nollet
9. nollētis
10. nōluissem

**10-23**
1. Marcus does not want to sleep.
2. I did not want to listen to the speaker.
3. The army will not want to go up the mountain.
4. Do you not want to read the letter?
5. The boys don't want to play with the ball.

**10-24**
1. nōlō / I do not want you to be killed.
2. nōluit / He did not want to bury the body.
3. nōlētis / Will you not want to go to Rome as soon as possible?
4. nōn vult / She does not want you to fear dogs.
5. nōlunt / The brave sailors do not want to flee from the battle.

**10-25**
1. you prefer
2. he will prefer
3. we used to prefer
4. they prefer
5. you will prefer
6. he preferred
7. they will prefer
8. I will prefer
9. we prefer
10. you had preferred

**10-26**
1. you prefer
2. they used to prefer
3. I prefer
4. we used to prefer
5. he used to prefer
6. you prefer
7. you have preferred
8. they prefer
9. he prefers
10. we had preferred

**10-27**
1. mālent
2. mālam
3. māvult
4. mālō
5. māluimus
6. mālēs
7. māluī
8. mālēbant
9. mālet
10. māluerāmus

**10-28**
1. mālīs
2. mālim
3. mallet
4. mālint
5. mallētis
6. mālit
7. māluissent
8. mālīmus
9. māluerint
10. mallēs

**10-29**
1. I prefer to read that.
2. Cornelia will prefer to be married to a good man.
3. Trimalchio prefers this wine over that one.
4. Did you prefer not to know about your friends?
5. These guys used to prefer to work than to do nothing.

**10-30**
1. mālam / I will prefer to stay than to leave.
2. māluit / Aeneas preferred to sail to Italy.
3. mālunt / Evil men prefer to hate than to love.
4. mālēbat / He used to prefer to stay at home.
5. māluistī / Why did you prefer to forget me?

**10-31**
1. they go
2. you will go
3. you are going
4. you were going away
5. we are going
6. he returns
7. I will go out
8. we were going
9. you went to
10. they went
11. they were dying
12. we had gone
13. I am going
14. you will have approached
15. he is going

**10-32**
1. you are going
2. I am going out
3. you were going
4. he is returning
5. we are dying
6. I was going
7. you are going away
8. they are dying
9. we used to go
10. I was approaching
11. they are going
12. he was returning
13. I am dying
14. they are going away
15. you were going

**10-33**
1. ībat
2. redībam
3. eunt
4. adītis
5. īs
6. perīvit
7. abīmus
8. ībunt
9. obībō
10. adierimus

**10-34**
1. eat
2. īrem
3. exeātis
4. īrēs
5. redeāmus
6. abeam
7. eant
8. perīrēmus
9. eātis
10. obeam

**10-35**
1. The soldiers are now returning to Rome.
2. Caesar went to Gaul.
3. I am going into battle with you!
4. Die!
5. They were going away from the city.

**10-36**
1. it / The mouse is going under the table.
2. adībunt / The old men will approach the forum with me tomorrow.
3. redībātis / Were you returning to the camp with us?
4. rediistī / When did you return home?
5. it / The farmer is going into the field with the slaves.

**10-37**
1. they are carrying
2. he is being carried
3. I will bring
4. you used to bear
5. you were being carried
6. I will be carried
7. to carry
8. they will bring
9. you are carrying
10. I was being carried

**10-38**
1. you are carrying
2. they were bringing
3. I am being carried
4. you are bringing
5. he was carrying
6. you are being carried
7. I was bearing
8. he is carrying
9. you were being carried
10. you are being carried

**10-39**
1. fert
2. ferētis
3. tulistis
4. ferētur
5. feror
6. ferentur
7. ferrī
8. fertis
9. ferēmur
10. feruntur

**10-40**
1. ferāris
2. ferrent
3. ferāmus
4. ferrētis
5. ferās
6. ferrētur
7. ferāminī
8. ferrer
9. ferret
10. ferrēmus

**10-41**
1. The farmer is bringing apples.
2. We will carry your books home.
3. The soldiers are being carried by the ships.
4. This girl was carrying a flower.
5. The food will be brought by me.

**10-42**
1. ferēbāmus / We were carrying his bones.
2. ferō / I am carrying the stones out of the field.
3. ferētur / The table will be carried by us.
4. tulit / The army brought excellent weapons.
5. lāta est / The water was carried to the city by aqueducts.

**10-43**
1. it is made
2. we will become
3. you are becoming
4. I will become
5. they were becoming

**10-44**
1. we are becoming
2. I was becoming
3. it is being made
4. they were being made
5. you are becoming

**10-45**
1. fit
2. fīet
3. fīēbant
4. fīēbās
5. fīō

**10-46**
1. fierem
2. fīat
3. factī sīmus
4. fīant
5. fieret

**10-47**
1. This is being done by that guy.
2. The boy will be made happy by the dog.
3. Are you becoming blind?
4. The fools will become more sane.
5. The pig was becoming fat.

**10-48**
1. factus est / Caesar became dictator.
2. fit / My son is becoming a man today.
3. fīent / All these things will soon become better.
4. fīēbam / I became sad.
5. factus erat / The way of the ancestors had become our way.

# Unit 11

**11-1**
1. augentēs / increasing
2. lābentia / slipping
3. habitantem / living
4. iacientī / throwing
5. exuentēs / stripping
6. nōlentī / not wanting
7. perveniens / arriving
8. ulciscentēs / avenging
9. moventium / moving
10. tacentibus / being quiet

**11-2**
1. masc./fem./neut. dat./abl. pl. / running
2. masc./fem./neut. nom. sg. / neut. acc. sg. / following
3. masc./fem./neut. dat./abl. sg. / creating
4. masc./fem./neut. dat./abl. pl. / nourishing
5. masc./fem. nom./acc. pl. / hurling
6. masc./fem./neut. nom. sg. / neut. acc. sg. / confessing
7. neut. nom./acc. pl. / feeling
8. masc./fem./neut. gen. sg. / being born
9. masc./fem./neut. gen. pl. / not wanting
10. masc./fem. acc. sg. / laughing

**11-3**
1. coactum / (having been) forced
2. doctīs / (having been) taught
3. dīlectārum / (having been) loved
4. iussa / (having been) ordered
5. persuāsīs / (having been) persuaded
6. crēditum / (having been) believed
7. laudātum / (having been) praised
8. scissae / (having been) cut
9. inceptae / (having been) begun
10. iūta / (having been) helped

**11-4**
1. masc./fem./neut. dat./abl. pl. / (having been) done
2. masc. nom. sg. / having followed
3. neut. nom. sg. / masc./neut. acc. sg. / (having been) elected
4. fem. nom. sg. / neut. nom./acc. pl. / (having been) ruled
5. masc./neut. dat./abl. sg. / (having been) given
6. masc. nom. sg. / (having been) owed
7. fem. gen./dat. sg. / fem. nom. pl. / (having been) put
8. masc./fem./neut. dat./abl. pl. / (having been) covered
9. masc./neut. gen. pl. / (having been) dragged
10. fem. acc. sg. / (having been) closed

**11-5**

1. lectūrī / about to choose
2. ūsūrae / about to use
3. habitūram / about to live
4. iactūrō / about to throw
5. clausūrī / about to close

6. vetitūrō / about to forbid
7. mīrātūram / about to wonder
8. parsūrōs / about to spare
9. mōtūrōrum / about to move
10. emptūrīs / about to buy

**11-6**

1. masc./fem./neut. dat./abl. pl. / about to find
2. neut. nom. sg. / masc./neut. acc. sg. / about to fly
3. fem. nom. sg. / neut. nom./acc. pl. / about to create
4. fem. gen. pl. / about to look for
5. masc. nom. sg. / about to give
6. fem. acc. sg. / about to put
7. masc./neut. dat./abl. sg. / about to hear
8. fem. gen./dat. sg. / fem. nom. pl. / about to close
9. masc./neut. gen. pl. / about to urge
10. fem. abl. sg. / about to make

**11-7**

1. [Hostēs fugientēs] / They chased the fleeing enemy.
2. [Rēgīna moriens] / The dying queen prayed to the gods.
3. [dūcem interfectum] / Everyone mourned for the slain leader.
4. [pecūniā āmissā] / We said nothing about the lost money.
5. [cēnam bene parātam] / The guests praised the well-prepared dinner.

**11-8**

1. [Rēgīna moritūra] / The queen, who was about to die, prayed to the gods.
2. [dūcem interfectum] / Everyone mourned for the leader who had been killed.
3. [pecūniā āmissā] / We said nothing about the money that had been lost.
4. [cēnam bene parātam] / The guests praised the dinner, which had been well prepared.
5. [aedificiō ardentī] / I barely escaped from the building that was burning.

**11-9**

1. [Rēgīna moritūra] / Since the queen was about to die, she prayed to the gods.
2. [dūcem interfectum] / Everyone mourned the leader because he had been killed.
3. [pecūniā āmissā] / We said nothing about the money because it had been lost.
4. [cēnam bene parātam] / The guests praised the dinner since it had been well prepared.
5. [aedificiō ardentī] / I barely escaped from the building because it was burning.

**11-10**

1. [Hostēs fugientēs] / They chased the enemy as it was fleeing.
2. [dūcem moritūrum] / Everyone wept for the leader when he was about to die.
3. [pecūniā āmissā] / We said nothing about the money after it had been lost.
4. [cēnam bene parātam] / The guests kept praising the dinner after it had been well prepared.
5. [aedificiō ardentī] / I barely escaped from the building as it was burning.

**11-11**

1. [pecūniā āmissā] / The money was lost, and we said nothing about it.
2. [dūcem interfectum] / The leader was killed, and everyone mourned for him.
3. [aedificiō ardentī] / The building was burning, and I barely escaped from it.
4. [cēnam bene parātam] / The dinner had been well prepared, and the guests kept praising it.
5. [Comitem tuum moritūrum] / Your friend was about to die, and you left him in the field.

**11-12**

1. [Mīles mortem metuens] / Even though the soldier was fearing death, he rushed into battle anyway.
2. [pecūniā inventā] / The money had been found, but we said nothing about it.
3. [cēnam male parātam] / Although the dinner had been poorly prepared, the guests kept praising it anyway.
4. [aedificium ardens] / I ran quickly into the building, even though it was burning.
5. [Comitem tuum moritūrum] / Although your friend was about to die, you left him in the field.

**11-13**

1. Since Troy had been destroyed, the Greeks left.
2. Marcus and Publius put on their togas, because the emperor was calling the senators back to the Senate House.
3. Since Aeneas was about to tell about Troy, everyone fell silent.
4. The gladiator entered the arena, because he had devised a strategy.
5. The crowd will cheer, since the signal will have been given.

**11-14**

1. After Troy had been destroyed, the Greeks left.
2. Marcus and Publius put on their togas when the emperor was calling the senators back to the Senate House.
3. Everyone fell silent when Aeneas was about to tell about Troy.
4. The gladiator entered the arena after he had devised a strategy.
5. Once the signal has been given, the crowd will cheer.

**11-15**

1. Troy was destroyed, and the Greeks left.
2. The emperor was calling the senators back to the Senate House, and Marcus and Publius put on their togas.
3. Aeneas was about to tell about Troy, and everyone fell silent.
4. The gladiator devised a strategy and entered the arena.
5. The signal will be given, and the crowd will cheer.

**11-16**

1. Although it is an unlucky day, we will go to the forum anyway.
2. The Greeks stayed, even though Troy had been destroyed.
3. Aeneas was going to tell about Troy, but everyone went to bed anyway.
4. Although he hadn't devised a strategy, the gladiator entered the arena.
5. The signal will be given, but no one will cheer.

# Unit 12

**12-1**

1. of putting
2. to/for telling
3. to go selling
4. of sailing
5. by hearing
6. to rest
7. to/for finding
8. to overcome
9. to/for reading
10. of changing

**12-2**

1. pendendī
2. crescendī
3. pellendī
4. inveniendī
5. cessandī
6. perdendī
7. praebendī
8. līberandī
9. dormiendī
10. fīniendī

**12-3**

1. He is going into the bedroom in order to sleep.
2. He is coming today to fight.
3. That king was not fit for reigning.
4. The soldiers are not desirous of dying.
5. I am returning to Rome to live.
6. Cicero was skilled at speaking.
7. I promise to talk about working.
8. We came here to listen.
9. We learn to teach by teaching.
10. Breakfast is not suitable for eating without wine.

**12-4**

1. They had arrived at the forum to elect magistrates.
2. I am leaving in order to scare people.
3. Publius will work to have money.
4. We are staying here to kill the enemy.
5. He struck the boar to kill it.
6. Are you hurrying to put on your togas?
7. Caesar announced the names of the soldiers to praise them.
8. I hurried to warn them about the omens.
9. He pretends to be stupid to fool people.
10. Slaves will be called to copy the books.

**12-5**

1. In the morning, the carts will have to be loaded.
2. You need to send your unfaithful friends away.
3. We all need to seek health.
4. Babies must be nourished.
5. We had to defend the camp.

**12-6**

1. He fled to hide himself in the crowd.
2. Everything in the parade had been amazing to watch.
3. That guy used to be fun to know.
4. Who will come here to ask?
5. I went to the library to read.

# Unit 13

**13-1**

1. to be filled up
2. to have brought together
3. to be about to call back
4. to have promised
5. to allow
6. to have obeyed
7. to be finished
8. to be a slave
9. to have been turned back
10. to be about to be built

**13-2**

1. līberārī
2. merēre
3. āmīsisse
4. malle
5. apertum īrī
6. trādī
7. hortārī
8. amplectī
9. audītus esse
10. aggressūrus esse

**13-3**

1. That day, you decided to stay at home.
2. We intended to set out today.
3. Julia does not wish to return to Rome.
4. That night, I was able to see thousands of stars.
5. We should leave while we can.

**13-4**

1. There was need to build a large fleet.
2. It doesn't suit you to act foolish like that.
3. You should spend the night at my house.
4. In the summer, they used to like to leave the city.
5. It will be necessary to fortify the town immediately.

**13-5**

1. subjective / Is it allowed for me to ask?
2. subjective / I will enjoy sleeping soon.
3. objective / Father forbade you to go into that forest.
4. complementary / At the tenth hour, they decided to pitch camp.
5. complementary / They were not able to arrive before the second hour.
6. complementary / I cannot live either without you or with you.
7. complementary / I prefer to spend my life with you.
8. objective / The leader ordered the cavalrymen to hold their horses.
9. complementary / Then the moon seemed to shine more brightly.
10. complementary / I hesitate to believe that creep.

# Unit 14

**14-1**

1. I hope that the slave women are cleaning the dining room carefully.
2. He denies that Marcus is making a trip to Rome.
3. Who is teaching you to read Latin?
4. You see that my buddy is sitting in the garden.
5. Do you know that the daughter is being called home by her mother?
6. They hear that he is no longer in the city.
7. I know that you are often quiet and say nothing.
8. We think that the consul is wrong.
9. I believe that flowers are being picked for me.
10. He denies that he is afraid of the dogs.

**14-2**

1. I thought that he was being helped.
2. Why did you announce that we were no longer friends?
3. He wrote me that the slaves were taking care of the farm.
4. The senators will deny that they are wrong.
5. He had felt that danger was hidden not far away.
6. We hope that the enemy are not able to approach the city.
7. They used to think that I was stupid.
8. He understands that all of us are staying here.
9. He was saying that two dogs used to sleep in bed with him.
10. We heard that your mother was afraid of mice.

**14-3**

1. You don't know that they have received our gifts.
2. They were saying that the gladiator had lost his sword in the middle of the fight.
3. I learned that Julia had given birth to twin sons.
4. It will be said that he lived well.
5. We understood that the matter had not been decided.
6. They believe that Publius followed his friends to the theater.
7. He wrote that the soldiers had finished that battle in only two hours.
8. They will say that they had barely had enough money.
9. You saw that the tower had been struck by lightning.
10. I feel that I have not been understood.

**14-4**

1. They didn't know you would be here.
2. You will see that all the slaves will be working in the fields for the entire night.
3. I hope that we will finish our game.
4. We thought that you were going to bury your brother on the Via Appia.
5. They hoped that Caesar would pitch camp very quickly.

**14-5**
1. I understood that I had few true friends.
2. You knew that he would be Messalla's slave for a long time now.
3. He wrote that he felt our pain.
4. We hear that the guards were guarded by no one.
5. You had seen that we were walking home.
6. You won't know that they have already left.
7. Tanaquil kept denying over and over that the king was dying.
8. I thought that the father was going to punish the boys on account of the squandered money.
9. Tell what happened to you as a young man.
10. He taught him that birds usually fly, not swim.

# Unit 15

**15-1**
1. you are working
2. they are begging
3. I am being called
4. it is being changed
5. it is making a sound
6. we are elected
7. you are showing
8. they are giving
9. I am doing nothing
10. they are being named

**15-2**
1. negētis
2. dubitent
3. adiuver
4. putēs
5. simulēmus
6. līberentur
7. imperet
8. celebrēs
9. precēminī
10. revocentur

**15-3**
1. you are being warned
2. it is allowed
3. they are being filled up
4. we are eager
5. I am held
6. you are staying
7. he deserves
8. you have
9. he is owed
10. I dare

**15-4**
1. habeāmur
2. studeam
3. valeās
4. persuadeātur
5. augeant
6. sustineāminī
7. sustineātis
8. horreant
9. respondeāmus
10. docear

**15-5**
1. I am neglecting
2. he is setting up
3. you are being nourished
4. we are leaving
5. he is shaping
6. they are being broken
7. he is betraying
8. you are surrounding
9. we are dressing
10. I am joined

**15-6**
1. trahar
2. metuant
3. pendātur
4. proficiscāmur
5. fungāris
6. sinat
7. tendant
8. crescātis
9. dīligam
10. dūcāmur

**15-7**
1. I am dying
2. he is leaving
3. we are looking back
4. you are taking
5. they desire

**15-8**
1. iaciar
2. effugiās
3. recipiant
4. interficiātur
5. patiāmur

**15-9**
1. we are finishing
2. you are coming
3. it is rising
4. it turns out
5. I am acquiring

**15-10**
1. custōdiāmur
2. sentiāminī
3. sepeliant
4. aperiātur
5. reperiar

**15-11**
1. I used to eat
2. we were weeping
3. you kept meeting
4. you used to be received
5. I was being surrounded
6. you were
7. he used to walk
8. he was being hurled
9. they were stretching
10. they were being looked back at

**15-12**
1. stārēs
2. peterer
3. dēbērentur
4. arriperētis
5. adessētis *or* adforētis
6. cōgerētur
7. effugerent
8. mūnīrēmus
9. auferrētur
10. valērem

**15-13**
1. you have brought
2. I have taken
3. he has founded
4. they have dressed
5. you have worked

**15-14**
1. mōverim
2. ōrāverīs
3. vocāverītis
4. latuerīmus
5. mūtāverit

**15-15**
1. they have been elected
2. I have been warned
3. she has used
4. we have followed
5. they have been changed

**15-16**
1. clausum sit
2. monstrātus sit
3. veritus sim
4. data sint
5. iactus sīs

**15-17**
1. they had been willing
2. he had found
3. I had feared
4. they had done nothing
5. you had destroyed

**15-18**
1. nōminavissem
2. fīnīvissēmus
3. pervēnissētis
4. scīvissent
5. sumpsisset

**15-19**
1. you had been called back
2. I had been taught
3. they had been doubted
4. we had been angry
5. he had been struck

**15-20**
1. scissus essem/forem
2. mortuī essent/forent
3. implētum esset/foret
4. āmissus essēs/forēs
5. secūtī essēmus/forēmus

# Unit 16

**16-1**
1. That slave shouldn't have been bought.
2. Let him tell me in person.
3. We should have hurried, since the gates were closing.
4. Let me teach you about the birds and the bees.
5. Don't let the dogs stay outside for too long.
6. Let's take the money and run.
7. He should have been here already.
8. Don't let me see you with that man again.
9. We should never have trusted you.
10. Let him set out at dawn.

**16-2**
1. I wish that you weren't angry at me.
2. I wish that we had gone to the show together.
3. I wish that I hadn't found Marcus with the other guy.
4. I wish that they would go away and stay there.
5. I wish that my brother were here.

**16-3**
1. He is afraid that they won't give him his money back.
2. I am worried that he doesn't understand me.
3. The army was afraid that the enemy might attack in the middle of the night.
4. We were frightened that the wolf would bite them.
5. Aeneas was afraid that the fleet would be destroyed by the storm.

**16-4**
1. You might be the man for whom I was looking.
2. Who wouldn't love my Marcus?
3. That noise in the kitchen might be a mouse.
4. Perhaps you are wondering what they are doing.
5. I wouldn't know that, Publius.

**16-5**
1. Should I believe a word he says?
2. What could we do lost as we were?
3. Since things are like this, where can I turn?
4. What could they do in this situation?
5. Should I approach her or not?

# Unit 17

**17-1**
1. When we were walking in the forest, we were very scared.
2. Marcus becomes nervous when he sees his father.
3. I will help you when you ask me.
4. When they had returned from Greece, they rested for many days in Capua.
5. The enemy sued for peace when the battle had been fought.

**17-2**
1. Since my friend was about to set out, a party was held.
2. Since the queen was dying, she prayed to the gods.
3. I fled into the street because the building was on fire.
4. Because we were wandering in the forest in the middle of the night, we were very scared.
5. Since the soldier was about to tell the story, everyone fell silent.

**17-3**
1. Although they survived, they were sad.
2. When Augustus died, the entire country mourned.
3. We slept well, even though the noise in the street was loud.
4. When I see my mother, I will greet her gladly.
5. Pompey was killed as soon as he arrived in Egypt.
6. Even though Gaius feared his father, he did not keep quiet.
7. When the show was finished, no one applauded.
8. You will laugh when you hear this joke.
9. When Hannibal caught sight of the walls of Rome, he turned back.
10. When we arrived at the party, everyone had already left.

# Unit 18

**18-1**
1. He went down into the forum to buy food.
2. The women fled so they wouldn't be captured.
3. Let's arrive as soon as possible so we can see the emperor himself.
4. Other soldiers were sent ahead to guard the bridge.
5. The bridge was being defended so that the enemy wouldn't cross the river.
6. Many have died in order to preserve our freedom.
7. You should put out the lamps so the house isn't set on fire.
8. We will stay at home so that robbers won't steal the gold.
9. The slave ran very quickly so he could arrive as soon as possible.
10. You are bringing the money so we can buy that house.

**18-2**
1. I looked for a stick with which I could drive the wolf away.
2. A messenger was sent to Rome by whom the victory would be reported.
3. You need to find a friend who is faithful.
4. A ditch was dug around the camp to keep the enemy away.
5. Hannibal took elephants with him in order to frighten the Romans.

**18-3**

1. Sulla ordered his army to seize Rome.
2. Many people warned Caesar not to leave the house that day.
3. I asked my friend to help me.
4. We will persuade him to be quiet about this matter.
5. You asked me to do everything as soon as possible.
6. I am asking you not to act foolish.
7. He begged the leader not to send those men into battle.
8. They are asking me not to betray them.
9. You will ask him that you be allowed.
10. We were ordered to guard the ships.

## Unit 19

**19-1**

1. That summer was so hot that many people in the city perished.
2. Cicero's speech was such that I could barely understand.
3. Our men fought in such a way that the enemy fled.
4. It will turn out that he will never be found.
5. There are so many flowers that I don't know which to choose.
6. The crowd was so large that we couldn't find Marcus.
7. I miss him such that I can't sleep.
8. Quintus read that poem so many times that he was able to recite it.
9. Claudia told such stories that everyone always cried.
10. My grandfather was so old that he could barely stand.

## Unit 20

**20-1**

1. I will never understand why you did that.
2. They were asking where they were setting out for.
3. You wonder who he is.
4. He heard where they had come from.
5. He will soon explain why we should stay here.
6. Tell me whether he is lying or not.
7. They didn't know what kind of weapons the enemy had.
8. We wondered how they had traveled from Gaul to Rome so quickly.
9. You don't understand how great a victory it is.
10. I don't know which letters he has read.
11. Do you deny where he has gone to?
12. You taught me how things are accomplished.
13. He was asking us how many there were.
14. The senators had heard where Caesar's camp had been pitched.
15. My sister knew when you were going to come.

## Unit 21

**21-1**

1. simple fact present / If the dog is barking, there is danger.
2. present contrary to fact / If the dog were barking, there would be danger.
3. future less vivid / If the dog were to bark, there would be danger.
4. simple fact present / If the dogs aren't barking, we are safe.
5. simple fact past / If the dogs weren't barking, we were safe.
6. past contrary to fact / If you had eaten scraps of that chicken, you would have been sick.
7. future more vivid / If you eat scraps of that chicken, you will be sick.
8. present contrary to fact / If he knew this, I'd be shocked.
9. future less vivid / If he were to know this, I'd be shocked.
10. simple fact past / If they were at the show, we didn't see them.
11. simple fact present / It happens quickly if the gods are willing.
12. future less vivid / If we weren't to fortify the camp, the danger would be great.
13. past contrary to fact / If we hadn't fortified the camp, the danger would have been great.
14. present contrary to fact / If he ran into me, he would know everything.
15. future more vivid / If he runs into me, he'll know everything.

# Unit 22

**22-1**

1. we are escaping
2. I had been killed (*subjunctive*)
3. we will have increased
4. wash!
5. he is returning
6. they seemed / they were seen
7. I had arrived
8. they will have pulled / they pulled (*subjunctive*)
9. you will be able
10. he will promise
11. he used (*subjunctive*)
12. they were inhabited
13. they were being loosened
14. stand still!
15. you had told
16. they were
17. you were being turned back
18. I will lie exposed
19. they were describing (*subjunctive*)
20. he deserved

**22-2**

1. passus eram
2. nāvigābant
3. iungēmur
4. dubitet
5. prōdita est
6. capī
7. ruptum sit
8. confessī erunt
9. aperuit
10. simulātus
11. tacē!
12. laeserāmus
13. fuerit
14. līberātūrī
15. spectābāminī
16. creāvērunt
17. traxisse
18. negat / vetat
19. dīcitur
20. spērāverō

**22-3**

1. flēbitis / you will weep
2. optāverīmus / we chose (*subjunctive*)
3. intendunt / he stretches / intendērunt / they stretched
4. volāvistis / you flew
5. necāvērunt / they killed
6. nocuerant / they had harmed
7. positī erimus / we will have been put
8. timuerant / they had feared
9. alimur / we are cherished
10. prohibeāmus / we prohibit (*subjunctive*)
11. explicābitis / you will explain
12. sīvērunt / they allowed
13. respicite / look back!
14. vulnerāverāmus / we had wounded
15. neglegēminī / you will be neglected
16. admoneant / they warn (*subjunctive*)

17. coquēbātis / you were cooking
18. exercuerant / they had trained
19. repertae sītis / you were found (*subjunctive*)
20. orimur / we rise

**22-4**

1. finxerat / he had shaped
2. dōnārēs / you were giving (*subjunctive*)
3. caedēbāris / you were being cut
4. laedēs / you will harm
5. fractum esset / it was broken (*subjunctive*)
6. īrātus est / he became angry
7. cōnābor / I will try
8. iacēbat / he was lying
9. intulistī / you brought in
10. quiēverit / he will have rested / he rested (*subjunctive*)
11. latrat / he barks
12. pariēbās / you were giving birth
13. cecidī / I fell
14. factum sit / it was done (*subjunctive*)
15. revocābam / I was calling back
16. vendis / you are selling
17. imitārer / I was imitating (*subjunctive*)
18. trāditus erō / I will have been handed over
19. capiēbat / he was catching
20. lēgī / I read

**22-5**

1. pūniēbāminī / you were being punished
2. aedificantur / they are being built
3. puter / I was being thought
4. līberātī sumus / we were freed
5. pulsus erit / he will have been driven / pulsus sit / he was driven (*subjunctive*)
6. coactus es / you were forced
7. praemittēmur / we will be sent ahead
8. fallimur / we are being deceived
9. labōrentur / they are worked (*subjunctive*)
10. vehēbāminī / you were being carried
11. iubētur / he is being ordered
12. impōnerēminī / you were being put on
13. tangēbātur / he was being touched
14. perfectus es / you are completed
15. pugnātī sunt / they were fought
16. exspectābāris / you were being waited for
17. institūtus sum / I was set up
18. amātus sīs / you were loved (*subjunctive*)
19. āmittar / I will be lost
20. rogābimur / we will be asked

**22-6**

1. docueris / you will have taught
2. ornābam / I was decorating
3. rumpēs / you will break
4. excēperam / I had received
5. vītāverīmus / we avoided (*subjunctive*)
6. agēmus / we will do
7. dēfendistī / you defended
8. cinxissem / I had surrounded (*subjunctive*)
9. mūtārētis / you were changing (*subjunctive*)
10. nōmināveris / you will have named
11. rapuimus / we took

12. terrēbant / they were scaring
13. statuēbās / you were setting up
14. dīcunt / they say
15. habitāverō / I will have inhabited
16. perterruissem / I had frightened (*subjunctive*)
17. cupīverīs / you desired (*subjunctive*)
18. muniō / I fortify
19. portāverit / he will have carried
20. compārāveram / I had prepared

**22-7**

1. fīgit / fīgēbat / fīget / fixit / fixerat / fixerit
2. intrantur / intrābantur / intrābuntur / intrātī sunt / intrātī erant / intrātī erunt
3. nasceris / nascēbāris / nascēris / nātus es / nātus erās / nātus eris
4. condāmur / conderēmur / (*no future subjunctive*) / conditī sīmus / conditī essēmus / (*no future perfect subjunctive*)
5. venīs / veniēbās / veniēs / vēnistī / vēnerās / vēneris
6. prōdit / prōdēbat / prōdet / prōdidit / prōdiderat / prōdiderit
7. pernoctat / pernoctābat / pernoctābit / pernoctāvit / pernoctāverat / pernoctāverit
8. mandāmus / mandābāmus / mandābimus / mandāvimus / mandāverāmus / mandāverimus
9. est / erat / erit / fuit / fuerat / fuerit
10. ignōrētis / ignōrārētis / (*no future subjunctive*) / ignōrāverītis / ignōrāvissētis / (*no future perfect subjunctive*)

**22-8**

1. 3 pl. present active indicative / they preserve
2. 2 pl. perfect active indicative / you approached
3. 1 sg. present active indicative / I advise
4. 1 sg. future perfect active indicative / I will have held
5. 1 pl. imperfect passive indicative / we were being revealed
6. 3 pl. pluperfect deponent indicative / they had left
7. 1 sg. future active indicative / I will build / 1 sg. present active subjunctive / I build
8. 2 pl. present active imperative / hurry!
9. 2 sg. pluperfect active indicative / you had denied
10. 3 sg. perfect active indicative / he received
11. 1 sg. pluperfect active subjunctive / I had survived
12. 3 sg. present deponent subjunctive / he prays
13. 2 pl. imperfect passive indicative / you were being warned
14. 3 pl. future active indicative / they will flee
15. 3 pl. future perfect active indicative / they will have made a sound / 3 pl. perfect active subjunctive / they made a sound
16. 1 sg. perfect active indicative / I moved
17. 2 sg. present passive indicative / you are being deceived
18. 3 sg. future perfect active indicative / he will have recited / 3 sg. perfect active subjunctive / he recited
19. 2 pl. present active imperative / pour!
20. 2 pl. imperfect active indicative / you were calling

**22-9**

1. nescīre / nescīrī / nescīvisse / nescītum esse / nescītūrum esse
2. nuntiāre / nuntiārī / nuntiāvisse / nuntiātum esse / nuntiātūrum esse
3. adiuvāre / adiuvārī / adiūvisse / adiūtum esse / adiūtūrum esse
4. dīvidere / dīvidī / dīvīsisse / dīvīsum esse / dīvīsūrum esse
5. interficere / interficī / interfēcisse / interfectum esse / interfectūrum esse
6. rīdēre / rīdērī / rīsisse / rīsum esse / rīsūrum esse
7. scindere / scindī / scidisse / scissum esse / scissūrum esse
8. mittere / mittī / mīsisse / missum esse / missūrum esse
9. noscere / noscī / nōvisse / nōtum esse / nōtūrum esse
10. ēripere / ēripī / ēripuisse / ēreptum esse / ēreptūrum esse
11. occīdere / occīdī / occīdisse / occīsum esse / occīsūrum esse
12. ferre / ferrī / tulisse / lātum esse / lātūrum esse

13. percutere / percutī / percussisse / percussum esse / percussūrum esse
14. transcrībere / transcrībī / transcripsisse / transcriptum esse / transcriptūrum esse
15. verberāre / verberārī / verberāvisse / verberātum esse / verberātūrum esse
16. gerere / gerī / gessisse / gestum esse / gestūrum esse
17. dīligere / dīligī / dīlexisse / dīlectum esse / dīlectūrum esse
18. cūrāre / cūrārī / cūrāvisse / cūrātum esse / cūrātūrum esse
19. petere / petī / petīvisse / petītum esse / petītūrum esse
20. tollere / tollī / sustulisse / sublātum esse / sublātūrum esse

**22-10**

1. constituens / constitūtus -a -um / constitūtūrus -a -um
2. creans / creātus -a -um / creātūrus -a -um
3. conspiciens / conspectus -a -um / conspectūrus -a -um
4. invidens / invīsus -a -um / invīsūrus -a -um
5. praebens / praebitus -a -um / praebitūrus -a -um
6. agitans / agitātus -a -um / agitātūrus -a -um
7. nūbens / nupta / nuptūra
8. recipiens / receptus -a -um / receptūrus -a -um
9. sūmens / sumptus -a -um / sumptūrus -a -um
10. tegens / tectus -a -um / tectūrus -a -um
11. tacens / tacitus -a -um / tacitūrus -a -um
12. dūcens / ductus -a -um / ductūrus -a -um
13. intellegens / intellectus -a -um / intellectūrus -a -um
14. salūtans / salūtātus -a -um / salūtātūrus -a -um
15. vexans / vexātus -a -um / vexātūrus -a -um
16. gignens / genitus -a -um / genitūrus -a -um
17. accipiens / acceptus -a -um / acceptūrus -a -um
18. sepeliens / sepultus -a -um / sepultūrus -a -um
19. onerans / onerātus -a -um / onerātūrus -a -um
20. fodiens / fossus -a -um / fossūrus -a -um

**22-11**

1. The singing birds were rejoicing in the tree. / The birds were singing and rejoicing in the tree.
2. When the work was completed, we all ran to the villa. / Because the work was completed, we all ran to the villa.
3. We will say a lot about the story that has been told. / We will say a lot about the story when it has been told.
4. No one, however, tends to the nourishing land. / Although the land is nourishing, still no one tends to it.
5. The crowd pressed and tried to see the parade. / The pressing crowd tried to see the parade.
6. The husband is now hugging the wife, who is about to leave. / The husband is now hugging the wife because she is about to leave.
7. Everybody believed in the plan even though it was going to come out badly. / Everybody believed in the plan that was going to come out badly.
8. The son and daughter are coming to the altar loaded with gifts. / The son and daughter are coming to the altar, which is loaded with gifts.
9. When all Italy had been conquered, Roman power was set up. / Because all Italy had been conquered, Roman power was set up.
10. The leader was moved by the enemies' words and ordered his army to turn back. / Because the leader was moved by the enemies' words, he ordered his army to turn back.

**22-12**

crēdēs / nōtum erat / audīrētis / negāvit / dixerō / scrībēbat / putāvimus / sciam / vīderit / narrābant

**22-13**

1. Nuntiātum est Caligulam ab urbe abesse. / It was announced that Caligula was away from the city.
2. Audīmus exercitum crās oppugnātūrum esse. / We hear that the army is going to attack tomorrow.
3. Aenēās sensit eum nōbīs vēra dixisse. / Aeneas perceived that he had told us the truth.
4. Ille dīcit omnibus necesse esse iam fugere. / He says that it is necessary for everyone to run away now.
5. Prōmīsī numquam iterum errātūrum esse. / I promised that I would not be wrong again.
6. Rēgīna crēdit servōs rēgis fidēlēs fuisse. / The queen trusts that the king's slaves were faithful.

7. Dīc cīvibus ducem nostrum ā hostibus interfectum esse. / Tell the citizens that our leader has been killed by the enemies.
8. Saepe narrat ille sē patriam suam amāre. / He often tells that he loves his country.
9. Quis nōn scit Hannibalem cum elephantīs Alpēs transisse? / Who doesn't know that Hannibal crossed the Alps with elephants?
10. Nunc confiteor mē semper tē amātūrum esse. / Now I admit that I will always love you.

**22-14**

1. participle / masc./fem. nom./acc. pl. / mixing
2. participle / masc./fem./neut. dat./abl. pl. / pretended
3. gerundive / fem. acc. pl. / about to be mounted
4. participle / masc./fem. / neut. gen. sg. / walking
5. participle / masc. acc. pl. / sung
6. participle / masc. nom. pl. / masc. / neut. gen. sg. / about to hurl
7. participle / masc. acc. sg. / neut. nom. / acc. sg. / called
8. gerund / neut. dat./abl. sg. / watching / gerundive / masc./neut. dat./abl. sg. / about to be watched
9. participle / masc./fem./neut. gen. pl. / putting out
10. participle / fem. nom. sg. / neut. nom./acc. pl. / added
11. participle / masc. acc. sg. / neut. nom./acc. sg. / filled
12. participle / masc./fem./neut. dat./abl. sg. / marveling at
13. gerundive / masc./neut. gen. pl. / about to be answered
14. participle / masc./fem./neut. dat./abl. pl. / biting
15. participle / masc./neut. dat./abl. sg. / guarded against
16. participle / masc./neut. dat./abl. sg. / spoken
17. participle / masc./fem./neut. dat./abl. pl. / mentioned
18. gerund / neut. gen. sg. / listening / gerundive / masc./neut. gen. sg. / masc. nom. pl. / about to be heard
19. gerundive / fem. nom. sg. / neut. nom./acc. pl. / about to be demanded
20. participle / masc./fem. nom./acc. pl. / struggling

**22-15**

1. jussive / Let them accept the money given by the king.
2. indirect command / The angry farmer ordered the slaves to return to the fields.
3. result clause / So many bad things were happening to Manlius that he always feared everything.
4. purpose clause / In order to avoid their masters, the slaves who are intending to flee will climb into the ship.
5. subjunctive clause after verb of fearing / Beware lest your building burn.
6. hortatory / Let us all weep, for the fish have died!
7. optative / I wish that Caecilia would love me as soon as possible.
8. deliberative question / Should we put up with these wounds or not?
9. indirect question / This man doesn't know what the ways of our ancestors are.
10. *cum* clause / Although the limits of power had been set down, the greedy emperor still longed for more.

**22-16**

1. purpose / Once the father went to the school to give the tutor money.
2. result / My grandfather is sleeping in such a way that he can't hear the carts in the road.
3. result / The soldier was so afraid of death that he always hid himself in battles.
4. purpose / In order to have power, what doesn't a tyrant do?
5. purpose / I made this temple so that the Roman gods could inhabit it.
6. purpose / The women go to the theater in order to see and to be seen.
7. result / The cook cooked meals of such a kind that the party guests rejoiced.
8. result / The chickens were so terrified that they began to fly.
9. purpose / The queen asked for water so that she could bathe.
10. result / You have brought so many gifts to Juno that the goddess is making you lucky.

**22-17**

1. Pompā perfectā / Because the parade had been completed, the spectators made a noise.
2. Cum equitēs laudātī essent / Since the cavalry had been praised, the poet was singing about other soldiers.
3. Spē āmissā / Although hope was lost, our country will still survive.

4. Cum epistula missa esset / When the letter had been sent, the messenger was finally recalled to his own city.
5. Ōrātiōne scriptā / After the speech had been written, Messalla thought about a new book.
6. Cum aestās redeat / Since summer is returning, the boars and the pigs will remain in the shade.
7. Hīs verbīs audītīs / When you have heard these words, spectators, applaud.
8. Cum exercitus victus sit / Since the army has been conquered, the man who fears death is fleeing.
9. Pāce ante postulātā / Although peace was demanded before, the Roman people now are pursuing war.
10. Cum sōl oriātur / When the sun is rising, you don't fear the evils of the night.

**22-18**

1. Audīs unde vēnerit servus. / You hear where the slave came from.
2. Potest cernere quid mihi accidat. / He is able to see what is happening to me.
3. Meministī quō festīnārēs. / You remembered where you were hurrying.
4. Nōn intellegēbam cūr pecora rapuissēs. / I didn't understand why you had stolen the herds.
5. Quaerit quandō expellātis matrem ex urbe. / He is asking when you will drive your mother out of the city.
6. Necesse est scīre quis sīs. / It is necessary to know who you are.
7. Ille mīrātur quid retinuerint fūrēs. / He wonders what the thieves kept.
8. Ignōrō quī agricolae illōs fundōs magnōs colant. / I don't know which farmers tend those large farms.
9. Ab amīcō petent quōmodo cantent avēs tam multa carmina. / They will ask their friend how the birds sing so many songs.
10. Nescimus quāle consilium cēperītis. / We don't know what kind of plan you adopted.

**22-19**

1. rīdeās / sim / If you laughed, I'd be sad.
2. mortuī sunt / neglectus est / If the flowers died, the garden was neglected.
3. perfēcissēs / potuissēmus / If you had completed the work, we would have been able to rest.
4. pugnārem / plauderet / If I were fighting, the people would be applauding.
5. vexent / praebeam / If the shades should annoy me, I would offer them wine.
6. occīdet / gaudēbit / If Caesar kills the enemies, the city of Rome will rejoice.
7. rogāmus / respondet / If we ask, she answers.
8. fuisset / cēpisset / If the consul had been drunk, fear would have taken us.
9. clauderet / relinquerētur / If the doorman were closing the door, the dog would be left outside.
10. ascendātis / videātis / If you climbed the mountain, you would see the whole land.

**22-20**

1. The farmer did not know who had taken the flocks from the fields.
2. Many men were saying to me that they saw fish swimming in the floor, but I was not persuaded.
3. After the senator had ordered it so, Cicero was driven out of Rome and abandoned his house.
4. Let him lead the army out of Greece and toward Gaul.
5. The Greeks had sailed with very many ships in order to attack the walls of Troy.
6. The emperor was so fat that no dinner was enough for him.
7. It is written on a stone that the girl was the flower of her family.
8. When you smile, what should I think about this pretended face?
9. I do not fear that my friends will deceive me with omens.
10. The wolf immediately walked out of the forests to look at the moon.
11. Aeneas made a journey to Italy so that he could found a city that would thrive.
12. The crying boy told everyone that he had been bitten by dogs.
13. I wish that I could embrace you again in Capua!
14. If we followed this plan, everything would come out well.
15. He crossed the river quickly by swimming.
16. The old man urged us in such a way: "Our enemies' city must be destroyed."
17. All the partygoers will know that you mixed a lot of water with the wine.
18. If the army were training on the field, you would be seeing a marvelous show.
19. When Augustus orders us to be silent, it is proper for us all to fall silent.
20. I was building a home so that my family could live in it.

# About the Author

**Dr. Richard E. Prior (1962-2010)** was chair of the Department of Classics at Furman University (Greenville, SC) from 2009 until his death; he was a professor there beginning in 1994. He was the author of many well-received books on Latin, including *Latin Demystified, Latin Verb Drills, Practice Makes Perfect: Latin Verb Tenses,* and *501 Latin Verbs*, a classic reference embraced by Latin students all over. Prior was fluent in Latin, Greek, French, Spanish, German, and Italian, and he often appeared as a commentator for programs that aired on the cable television networks The History Channel and The National Geographic Channel.